LATHE-WORK: A PRACTICAL TREATISE ON THE TOOLS, APPLIANCES, AND PROCESSES EMPLOYED IN THE ART OF TURNING

Published @ 2017 Trieste Publishing Pty Ltd

ISBN 9780649625703

Lathe-Work: A Practical Treatise on the Tools, Appliances, and Processes Employed in the Art of Turning by Paul N. Hasluck

Edited by Trieste Publishing Pty Ltd.
Cover @ 2017

www.triestepublishing.com

PAUL N. HASLUCK

LATHE-WORK: A PRACTICAL TREATISE ON THE TOOLS, APPLIANCES, AND PROCESSES EMPLOYED IN THE ART OF TURNING

Trieste

LATHE-WORK.

LATHE-WORK

A PRACTICAL TREATISE

ON

THE TOOLS, APPLIANCES, AND PROCESSES EMPLOYED IN

THE ART OF TURNING

INCLUDING

HAND-TURNING, BORING AND DRILLING, THE USE OF SLIDE-
RESTS AND OVERHEAD GEAR, SCREW-CUTTING BY HAND
AND SELF-ACTING MOTION, WHEEL-CUTTING,
ETC., ETC.

BY

PAUL N. HASLUCK

With Numerous Illustrations Drawn by the Author

LONDON

CROSBY LOCKWOOD AND CO.

7, STATIONERS' HALL COURT, LUDGATE HILL

1881

PREFACE.

WHEN first I occupied myself in mechanical manipulations and lathe-work engrossed my attention, the want of a handy guide-book, treating the subject in a practical manner, was greatly felt. Though much has been done since then towards placing technical education within the reach of all, yet I recently found, in my official capacity as editor of a journal largely devoted to mechanics, that beginners at the lathe still continue to seek such a book, and I have therefore prepared the following pages.

In the form of desultory articles, written by me, much of the information has already appeared in various technical papers. The whole has been re-written for publication in book form, and it has been my endeavour to bring within the available space the information most useful to the beginner at lathe-work.

Though I make no claim to special literary merit, yet I believe that the instructions are made clear without verbiage; and as I write from personal experience, the book may be accepted as trustworthy and practical by those who study its contents.

The illustrations have been engraved from my own drawings, and show, at a glance, constructive details that could not be explained in letterpress. The drawings are from the objects they represent, and will convey much useful information, and working drawings of the full size can be made from the woodcuts; the measurements can be filled in from the text.

P. N. HASLUCK.

LONDON, *February*, 1881.

CONTENTS.

CHAPTER I.

THE ART OF TURNING.

CHAPTER II.

THE FOOT LATHE DESCRIBED.

CHAPTER III.

HAND TURNING.

CHAPTER IV.

SCREW-CUTTING BY HAND.

CHAPTER V.

BORING AND DRILLING.

CHAPTER VI.

MOUNTING WORK FOR TURNING.

CHAPTER VII.

FITTING CHUCKS TO THE LATHE-NOSE.

CHAPTER VIII.

VARIOUS USEFUL CHUCKS DESCRIBED.

CHAPTER IX.

SLIDE-RESTS.

CHAPTER X.

SLIDE-REST TOOLS.

CHAPTER XI.

SLIDE-REST CUTTER-BARS.

CHAPTER XII.

OVERHEAD GEARING.

CHAPTER XIII.

DIVIDING APPARATUS.

CHAPTER XIV.

THE DRILLING SPINDLE.

CHAPTER XV.

VERTICAL CUTTER-FRAME.

CHAPTER XVI.

SCREW-CUTTING BY SELF-ACTING MOTION.

LIST OF ILLUSTRATIONS.

LATHE-WORK.

CHAPTER I

THE ART OF TURNING.

Its importance and antiquity—Primitive methods of turning—The potter's wheel—Early forms of the lathe—Its development— Lathes on standards—Fly-wheels—Literature of the art— Modern lathes.

OF all the mechanical arts none can claim a more important place than that of turning, and the practice of this branch of mechanical manipulation is capable of developing the highest skill and intelligence of the artificer. The lathe, which has been dubbed the father of mechanism, has claimed the close attention of statesmen and philosophers ; even monarchs have sought recreation in the practice of turning. Skilled artisans, who depend largely on the lathe for the production of their work, enjoy to an extent a superior position in their sphere of life, whether they be engaged in fashioning the rough wares made on the potter's wheel, or the highest and most refined specimens of turnery, which are probably to be found in the

B

finest grades of chronometric art. We disregard
those extraordinary productions of skill and taste
which come from the hands of the amateur turner,
who uses for the production of a fragile gewgaw
tools and appliances that only affluence can afford.

The date of the origin of turning is lost in antiquity. Probably long before historians began to write,
the lathe—in a primitive form—was known and used,
the potter's wheel being, perhaps, the primogenitor.
The savage's process of kindling fire by twirling a
stick against another piece of wood gives the
motion now used for the alternating drill, and for
small lathes driven with a drill bow; how this
motion developed into the continuous one of the
potter's wheel we can but surmise.   The symmetrical cylinder is to be found throughout nature,
and art in its desire to reproduce the admirable
form has developed the turning lathe.

The Bible affords a distinct reference to the
potter's wheel; we read that about five hundred
years before the Christian era Jeremiah went down
to the potter's house, " and behold he was doing a
work on the wheel, making a vessel of clay with
his hands." The use of the lathe, however, dates
long prior to this, and the manufacture of pottery
ware is frequently spoken of in sacred history.
Amongst the relics of antiquity unearthed from the
buried Egyptian cities are numerous specimens
bearing unmistakable evidence of having been
wrought in the lathe.

The lathe used by the Orientals for generations

consisted of two short posts driven into the ground; a nail driven through each formed the centres on which the work revolved, actuated by a drill-bow. The work was thus only a few inches from the ground, and the operator in his accustomary position—squatting on the ground—was able to use his toes in assisting the application of the tools. The Orientals use the toes as deftly as they do the fingers in many of their handicrafts. At the Paris Exhibition of 1867 a group of aborigines were working in this manner with the lathe just described, displaying considerable skill in using these primitive appliances, and producing work of intricate and elaborate patterns, chiefly ornamental.

Lathes of this primitive form it would appear are employed at the present time by the native turners of India. The skill of the Hindoos in the mechanical arts and in the delicate fashioning of ivory and metal is universally appreciated, and that they should succeed so well with such rude tools is a proof of their natural aptitude. The turner of India carries on his vocation in the style of our itinerant tinker; he carries all his tools, lathe included, about with him, and when he gets a job establishes himself near the door of his employer's house. Assisted by his boy, the turner fixes up his lathe, consisting of two posts driven into the ground, as described previously. The work is mounted between the centres, a rope is passed twice round it, and the boy, by pulling each end of the rope alternately, gives motion to the work, the workman guiding the edge of his tool with his toes only, the handle being held by the hands at some distance from the work, both man and boy invariably squatting on the ground, as is the national custom.

Many nations in all parts of the globe employ a lathe somewhat resembling, but still an improvement on, the one just mentioned. This lathe has a frame so that it is complete in itself, yet it has to be fixed to the ground for use; it consists of two cross pieces held together by a tie-bar on which they slide, and may be wedged as required. The cross pieces have iron spikes fitted to them to form centres, the work is put between these, and they are fixed by wedging on the tie-bar. The lathe is laid on the ground and secured by means of a few spikes, a straight bar of wood is laid across the cross pieces as near as convenient to the work, and forms a rest for the turning tools. This form of lathe is still largely used in Spain, Egypt, and other places; the pattern can be traced back to the Moors, who introduced the lathe to Spain. The Spaniards in migrating took with them the lathe and the art of turning, and thus in those parts of the American continent that Spain has populated the lathe is found made as last described.

The continuous motion of the fly-wheel, which had been employed by the potter from the earliest times, was not used in the lathes of the ancients, who only had the alternating revolutionary motion derived from the bow. When introduced into the workshops of the Western nations, the lathe was modified to suit their customs, and whilst the Orientals kept their turning appliances low, to suit their habitual squatting position, Europeans mounted the same contrivance on a framework to bring it to a convenient height to work at when standing. This altered arrangement allowed the bow worked by hand to be replaced by a flexible pole fixed overhead, from which a cord descended, and after passing round the work it joined a treadle, which was worked by the foot; then both hands were at liberty to manipulate the tools.

A picture published in a German book in the year 1568 shows a turner working a sphere in a lathe; a quantity of turned objects are lying on the bench and about the workshop. This illustration seems to be the first record of the lathe mounted on standards, and we see by it that the pole lathe was in use at that date. In books of about the same period different kinds of lathes are mentioned, but the cord up to this time appears to have been used round the work itself, which always had to run between centres. It is difficult to decide precisely when the independent mandrel came into use.

The first book devoted to the art of the turner was published at Lyons in 1701 ; it was written by Plumier, and probably did much for the art by placing before its votaries a record of the condition that it was then in. That there was a demand for this ponderous book appears evident from the fact of a second edition having been published in Paris forty-eight years afterwards ; in the interim nothing was done to enrich the literature of the turner.

Bergeron's valuable book, consisting of three volumes lavishly illustrated, and containing a vast deal of information, valuable even at the present day, was next published in 1792, nearly a century after Plumier's first edition. Bergeron himself was a manufacturer of lathes and other tools used by turners, and probably in writing his book he was partially influenced by commercial considerations outside of the book itself. However, some of the information there given is equally applicable to tools now used in some cases in improved forms. The improvements made in many appliances connected with turnery since Bergeron's time, however, place his book at a disadvantage, some of the arrangements admirably sketched by him being now obsolete. Soon after this other Frenchmen wrote books on turning, the most notable being those of MM. Pauline Desormeaux and Dessables.

Holtzapffel's treatise on mechanical manipulation, which was intended to be comprised in six volumes, the first of which appeared in 1847, is the most important work on the lathe in the English language, and its value is universally acknowledged. Three volumes only were published during the lifetime of the author, and it was thought that the remaining three would never be issued. The fourth volume has, however, recently appeared as a posthumous work, and the other two may yet see light. The price of this work places it beyond the reach of the majority of mechanics, a circumstance much to be regretted.

The modern lathe in its various forms, from the tiny tool used by the watchmaker, worked with a slip of whalebone for a bow and a horsehair for a cord, on which he fashions with a graver pivots of correct proportion and precise form on axes that are themselves sometimes less than one-hundredth of an inch in diameter and weigh but a grain, to the leviathan machine, itself weighing sometimes upwards of 60 tons, and large enough to take in work of 20 to 30 feet in diameter, and double that length, is, therefore, the result of continuous improvements, from at least the time of Jeremiah, nearly 2,500 years ago.

The employment of cast iron as a constructive material for lathes at once gave a great impetus to machinery of all kinds. The planing machine used for iron, itself an outgrowth of the lathe, did for flat surfaces what had already been done on cylindrical work, and it is to the judicious use of the lathe and the application of its modified functions that the present degree of accuracy has been attained in the manufacture of every grade of machinery.

CHAPTER II.

THE FOOT LATHE DESCRIBED.

Its various forms and sizes—Watchmaker's lathes—Bench lathes—Iron beds of various forms—Back-gearing—Slow motion—Screw-cutting motion—The lathe best suited for general purposes—The framework, bed, and fly-wheel—Mandrel headstock—Back-centre headstock—The hand-rest and collar-plate—Testing a lathe.

THE foot lathe is the tool to which we confine ourselves throughout this treatise, as it is by far the most generally adopted, though in factories where heavy work is done and steam power available the foot lathe generally is superseded by a similar tool driven by steam. The ordinary form of foot lathe is too well known to need minute description. Speaking roughly, it may be said to consist of a bed, supported at a convenient distance from the ground, carrying the headstocks. Beneath the bed a fly-wheel is fixed to revolve freely, and to the cranked axis of this wheel a treadle is attached. The motive power consists of the muscular force of the leg applied to the treadle each time that this falls on the revolution of the fly-wheel, the weight of this wheel being sufficient to cause it to revolve by its own momentum during the time when power cannot be applied through the treadle. A band from the fly-wheel to the mandrel conveys the motion, and in this simple contrivance are the elements of a foot lathe.

The size of a lathe is described by the height of its centres—that is, the distance from the centre of the mandrel to the top of the bed. In other words, the height of centre is just half the diameter of the largest circle that will revolve in the lathe, thus the face-plate is usually a safe guide to the size of a lathe. The length of bed has much to do with the bulk, and to a certain extent with the capabilities of a lathe; for, though increasing the length of bed does not increase the capacity of a given lathe so far as diameter is concerned, yet the length of work which may be wrought on it is increased usually by about the amount of the added length. The length of bed decides the length of material that can be turned, whilst the height of centre governs the diameter; thus, a lathe on which discs of 40 inches diameter can be turned with ease is often incapable of receiving a cylinder of even 6 inches in length, and the lathes used for turning shafting, perhaps 40 feet long, are commonly not more than 6 inch centre.

Lathes over 6 inch centre are seldom driven by foot power, the exertion being too great for one man who has also to manipulate the tools. From a commercial point of view it is found to be more economical to employ steam power rather than an assistant to help tread the lathe. This latter expedient is a common practice in small

workshops where mechanical power is not available. The heavier lathes of 6 inch centre are also
generally driven by steam, but some very light
ones used by wood turners are driven by the foot,
even though they are 7 or 8 inch centre. The
hand-driven fly-wheel is generally used as the
source of motion by those wood turners who do
not employ steam power.

The smallest lathe is that used by watchmakers;
motion is given to the work by means of a bow, the
lathe is held in the jaws of the bench vice when in
use. The clockmakers' throw is rather larger; it is
driven by a hand-wheel, and has always dead
centres; a small pulley on the left headstock, having
a projecting pin to catch the tail of a carrier, being
used to drive the work. The smallest of foot
lathes has generally a bar-bed, of triangular section, and may be from 2 to 3 inch centre, and is in
general arrangement similar to the throw, except
that it has a revolving mandrel driven by a foot-
wheel, and consequently some modifications are
essential.

Bench lathe, or table lathe, is the name given to
all those which, complete in themselves, fix on any
bench that may be convenient. Lathes up to 4 inch
centre having beds up to 3 feet in length are
usually mounted on small standards about 3 or
4 inches high, and by these they may be screwed
down to any bench. The fly-wheel for driving these
lathes will have to be fixed beneath quite inde-
pendently of the lathe bed and headstocks. Beds

of any sectional shape may be used for bench
lathes, but the triangular bar is most in favour
for small ones and is a most suitable form of
bed. The triangle is placed with one angle uppermost, the two upper sides are wrought quite
true and straight, the whole of the headstocks and
fittings are adjusted to these sides, the lower face
being that on which all the clamping screws take
their bearings.   Small screw-cutting lathes have
sometimes a triangular bed cast with a groove
along the lower surface, in which the leading screw
lies protected from any falling dust and shavings
made in turning. A peculiarity about triangular
bar lathes is that the mandrel headstock is invariably made of two distinct pieces, one taking the
tail-pin and the other the collar, each fixed inde-
pendently on the bed.   Though able to withstand
considerable downward pressure, the triangular
bar cannot resist torsion so well as the usual form
of bed.

Lathes of 4 inch centre and upwards have generally a cast-iron bed, the top surface of which is
planed to take the headstocks, &c.   The most
usual forms of fitting are the V and flat and the
double flat.   In the former the V-shaped bearer is
the surface which guides the movable fittings when
shifted along the bed, and in the latter the continuity of the line of centres is insured by having
parallel tenons on the bottom of each piece, fitting
without shake along the inner edges of the bed.
Occasionally the outer edges are planed true ; the

side shake of the headstocks, &c., is prevented by strips screwed to their base and fitting the outer edges of the bed. This latter plan may offer some advantage in being easier to fit, but is not nearly so accurate as that of fitting the tenon to the inner sides. Some beds have a break or gap near the fast headstock, allowing large discs to be turned, but this is not desirable for ordinary use. The beds of lathes of this size are usually bolted to iron standards which carry the centre points on which the crank revolves, and also those on which the treadle oscillates. To prevent spreading at the base a stretcher-bar connects the standards at the back; and in some cases the front feet are similarly braced by means of a flat bar of iron lying close to the ground so as to be out of the way of the feet and the foot-board of the treadle.

Back gear is an arrangement of wheel-work by which a very slow motion is imparted to the mandrel; it usually consists of a wheel and pinion on the mandrel and a wheel and pinion on a shaft revolving parallel with the mandrel. Instead of fixing the pulley on the mandrel it is allowed to run loose with its front edge close to a toothed wheel which is keyed to the mandrel; a nut prevents the pulley getting away from this wheel. A pinion is fixed to the small end of the pulley on the mandrel, gearing into a wheel fixed to an axis, which also carries a pinion gearing into the wheel fixed to the mandrel. Thus on turning the pulley motion is conveyed to the mandrel through the wheel-work, and by this means the speed is usually reduced to one-ninth; nine revolutions of the pulley produce but one turn of the mandrel. For ordinary purposes the back shaft is thrown out of gear; the pulley is then attached to the wheel, keyed to the mandrel, by means of a sliding bolt.

The illustration, Fig. 1, shows a horizontal section of a back-geared headstock. The mandrel runs in double bearings, and its tail-end is prolonged to form a stud, on which change-wheels for screw-cutting purposes are placed. Referring to the mandrel, and commencing at the right-hand end, first comes the nose, on which chucks are screwed, immediately behind it the shoulder, and then a conical part, forming the front bearing. Against a shoulder the wheel keyed to the mandrel is shown; the pulley and pinion solid with it revolving loose, except when attached to the wheel by the bolt arrangement. Behind the pulley is a nut, shown in section, and a washer, made of hard steel, fitted tightly to the mandrel. This washer, bearing against the collar in the casting, takes the back thrust in boring and such operations. That part of the mandrel passing through the collar is coned to form the back bearing; a washer comes next this, being secured by a nut, as shown. The end-shake of the mandrel is regulated by the adjustment of the nuts on each side of the back collar. The stud forming the tail-end has a key fixed to it, shown white in the illustration.

The back spindle is a plain steel arbor carrying

a wheel and pinion securely fixed together, and
tight on the spindle. In the position shown in
Fig. 1 the wheel and pinion are out of gear with
those on the mandrel. A peg put into the hole in
the casting (see left-hand end) prevents the back

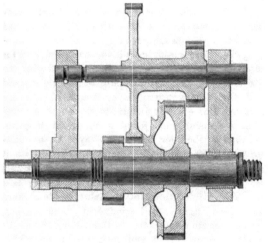

Fig. 1.—Plan Section of Back-gear, Double Bearing, Screw-cutting Mandrel
Headstock.

spindle shifting and getting into gear. When it
is desired to put the wheels in gear the peg is
withdrawn, the spindle moved towards the left
till the right side groove is under the hole. The
peg is then replaced to keep the spindle in its new
position. The mandrel-wheel and pulley are at

the same time disconnected to allow the gearing to act.

Though back-gearing is undoubtedly a very valuable auxiliary to a lathe on which much heavy metal turning is done, yet for most purposes an arrangement of slow-motion bands will suffice. By this means the constant noise and jarring accompanying the use of wheel-gearing is done away with. Much smoother work is produced by having a strong gut band from a small pulley on the crank shaft to a large one on the mandrel. When these two pulleys are of equal size it is possible to turn up a cast-iron face-plate of the full diameter that the lathe will take, and by putting a pulley of half the diameter on the crank-shaft such a job could be accomplished with tolerable ease. Such heavy work is, however, usually done by steam-power, and all the power that can be judiciously got out of a foot lathe is usually obtainable with simple slow-motion bands.

The slide-rest is an attachment of so much importance that an entire chapter is devoted to the description of its varieties and merits. The chief object of this—all that need here be mentioned— is to form a perfectly rigid tool-holder, which, holding the tool mechanically, does not allow the inequalities of the work to exert so much influence as is unavoidable in hand turning; moreover, guiding the tool mechanically, it does so with a precision unattainable in hand-work.

Screw-cutting lathes are those which, by an

arrangement of wheels receiving motion from the mandrel and conveying it to the leading screw, move the slide-rest along the lathe bed at a uniform rate, so that a tool fixed in the rest will cut a regular spiral on the surface of a cylinder revolving between the centres. By arranging the wheels which transmit the motion from the mandrel to the screw in relative proportions, the rate or pitch of the thread cut on the work may be coarse or fine to any degree within the compass of the wheels available; these are called change-wheels, twenty-two usually constituting the set.

The leading screw itself revolves, in bearings attached to the bed, sometimes inside but generally on the near side of the bed; the end towards the mandrel projects and is made to take the change-wheels. A slotted arm called the wheel-plate, swinging round the screw, carries one or more studs on which the change-wheels also fit, the piece of mandrel projecting at the tail-end being similarly shaped; and thus a wheel on the leading screw, another on the stud, and another on the mandrel make a combination producing an effect proportionate to their relative diameters. The slide-rest is fitted with a clutch gearing into the leading screw and forming a nut, which may be detached instantly. A screw-cutting lathe not only enables one to cut threads of any rate and diameter perfectly true, but it is also available for working as a self-acting machine when turning cylinders, the rate of screw then being cut amounting to nothing more than a regular feed.

It is unnecessary, in this treatise, to speak of the more uncommon modifications of lathes, which fit them for special purposes and are not of general interest. The next consideration will be, What is a suitable lathe for general use?

Probably the requirements of each individual reader will have certain peculiarities which it is quite impossible to take into consideration when treating of the subject in a general manner. For small work in metal a heavy 4-inch centre lathe will be useful, whilst for working in wood a light 6-inch would be more appropriate. Brass work requires quick speeds, which are best maintained with a light lathe; but heavy iron and steel work is wrought at a slow speed on a heavy substantial tool. The exertion required to drive a 6-inch lathe will be much more than that necessary for a smaller lathe of similar calibre, and thus it is but a waste of energy to employ a lathe unnecessarily large.

For general purposes a 5-inch centre lathe will be found most handy, the height of centre allowing a wide range in diameter. Then, if the mandrel is moderately light, without back-gear it will be strong enough to take the heaviest work that can be done on a 4-inch lathe, with the advantage of offering facilities for turning wood and light material of much larger size. The bed may be 3 feet 6 inches to 4 feet long, allowing lengths of 2 feet to 2 feet

C

6 inches between the centre points. The convenience of the longer bed consists principally in having the poppit headstock or slide-rest out of the way when either of these is pushed to the end. With short beds it is sometimes necessary to remove the slide-rest or poppit in order to get at the work conveniently, and this is some trouble.

A heavy bed, bolted to substantial standards, is most desirable; the bed for a 5-inch should measure about 4 inches in width and depth; if a double flat the central space may be about $1\frac{1}{4}$ inch wide, leaving each flat a trifle wider. A 4-feet bed should weigh at least $\frac{3}{4}$ of a cwt. The fly-wheel of such a lathe should have series of grooves in steps corresponding with those of the mandrel pulley, so that the band may be shifted to any grooves on a series, and fit taut without any readjustment of length; there should be two series of grooves, for each a special length of band being necessary. The extreme diameter of the wheel may be 24 to 26 inches, with a series of three or four grooves graduated from the largest possible size. The second series would be about half that diameter, and have but two grooves; in cases where the suggestion before made of having a small pulley for slow motion is adopted this may be from 4 to 6 inches in diameter. Fly-wheels are generally too light; $\frac{3}{4}$ of a cwt. is not any too heavy for one 24 inches in diameter. The crank shaft should be $1\frac{1}{4}$ inch diameter, and if 4 feet long, two cranks are advisable, as they support a long treadle better than a single crank, which is, however, quite enough for one 3 feet 6 inches long. The ends should always be plugged with hardened steel, and drilled up properly before being countersunk ; the end should then be turned down conically to meet the edge of the countersink, so that when in position and running the oil applied to lubricate will not be thrown away from the centres by centrifugal force. This is an important point, though constantly neglected by lathe-makers. By observing a crank-shaft with flat ends it will be seen that the oil, applied to the centre, quickly spreads over the face and runs away from the bearing—when the crank is still, by gravity, and when revolving, by centrifugal force. The wheel is usually fixed to the shaft by keying, though sometimes it is secured against a shoulder on the shaft by means of a nut. The points on which the axis revolves should be so adjusted that though the bearing is quite free there is no shake whatever, and the position of these points must be such that the crank shaft runs parallel with the lathe bed. The wheel itself must be fixed perfectly true, and in a vertical line under the mandrel pulley.

The headstock of a plain lathe, in which the mandrel runs—called the mandrel headstock, or fast headstock, to distinguish it from the movable or poppit headstock, which takes the back centre— should have a deep tenon cast on the bottom, to make the casting rigid ; the upper side should be hollowed out to allow freedom for a large pulley, which for a 5-inch lathe may be $8\frac{1}{4}$ inches in diameter. The length of the mandrel adds much to the steadiness in turning, provided always that only the smallest possible amount projects from the collar at the nose end. A mandrel, 8 inches long, is a good proportion, and would be spaced thus: the thread of the nose, $\frac{3}{4}$ inch long, cut with a $\frac{3}{4}$ inch Whitworth thread; cone for front bearing, 1 inch long, the diameter being about $1\frac{1}{8}$ inch, tapering about $1°$; plain part, $1\frac{1}{4}$ inch long, $1\frac{3}{4}$ diameter; pulley, $2\frac{1}{4}$ inch; washer, nut, and plain part behind pulley 2 inches, with a small part $\frac{3}{4}$ inch long, terminating in a cone point. The headstock for such a mandrel would be 10 inches long at the base, with a portion of the boss which holds the tail-pin projecting about $\frac{1}{4}$ inch to the rear, the total length of the hole in which the tail-pin fits being fully 2 inches; the tail-pin should be cylindrical, perfectly true, and fit the hole tightly, being held by a nut on each end. Tail-pins, which are themselves screwed through the casting and fixed with a lock nut should be invariably avoided, as with such the countersunk hole, bored in the centre, is sure to be eccentric when turned in the thread, and thus the axial line of the mandrel would be continually altered. That the headstock casting fits the bed properly is most essential; in many cases it will be found that the casting gets bent on the holding-down bolt being screwed tight, thus throwing the boring of the collar-hole and the tail-pin hole out of continuity. A direct pull by one bolt, near the centre, so often bends the casting that it is advisable to hold it down by two bolts, one near each end.

The back centre headstock should always be bored out quite parallel and in a direct line with the axis of the mandrel, the barrel being cylindrical, with a groove along it in which a T-headed blank screw, dropped into a hole in the casting, fits and prevents the barrel rotating. The screw which actuates the barrel is usually made with a left-handed thread, for convenience in turning, but whether left or right handed is perfectly immaterial, except for the convenience. For turning the screw a hand wheel or a winch handle is used; the former is more convenient for boring with, and the latter offers the advantage of not being so much in the way. An arrangement for clamping the barrel at any desired place always forms part of the poppit head, and if a screw acting direct on to the cylinder is used, a disc of brass or other soft metal should be interposed to save the barrel from being dented. The point of the poppit cylinder is always removable; sometimes it is fitted by screwing into the barrel; but another and far better plan is to fit it in conically. The cone fitting is as tight as any—in fact some lathes have conical noses, on which the chucks fit by simply pressing on, and they then jamb. A cone fitting to the back centre offers great facility for shifting the point, an operation which sometimes has to be done constantly. The screw inside the poppit barrel should be sufficiently long to allow the tail end of the point to be made long enough to touch when the barrel is drawn back, and thus the point is forced out by simply winding back the cylinder. Several points should be fitted to the back centre, and some pieces with flat ends for boring against ; these are, however, spoken of in another chapter. The diameter of the barrel may be an inch, the cylindrical part of the casting into which it fits being about 1¾ inch in diameter. The barrel is bored out from the front end large enough to clear the thread of the screw by which it is moved, to within half an inch or so of the back end ; this part is tapped to fit the screw. The lateral motion of the screw is confined by having a collar on it, which on one side bears against a loose washer resting against the end of the casting, and on the other against the cap screwed on to the casting. The handle on the end of the screw should not confine its lateral motion, and it is often merely pushed on a square or hexagonal fitting, though sometimes secured by a key or a nut.

The hand or T-rest needs but little comment ; the socket should be bored at right angles to the sole, which should be planed with a dovetailed slot. If the lathe bed is double flat the sole of the hand-rest stands direct on it ; if a V-bed it should have a cast-iron foundation plate, shaped to fit the bed on the under side and flat on the top. The screw which clamps the T should have a handle like that of a bench vice fitted to it, as it so often requires to be shifted to suit the work in hand. A "permanent tommy" is also desirable in the screw which clamps the back centre barrel, as it is so much more handy to be able to fix these parts without the trouble of finding the "tommy" on each occasion.

The T itself for general use may be about 2 inches long on the top and should be flat and level; in use it will be continually pitted, and must be filed up smooth again. For turning long cylinders by hand a much longer T is used, measuring as much as 5 or 6 inches. For still longer rods it is customary to use a straight bar as a rest, which is supported near its ends in two T socket-holders; by this plan a rest, reaching the entire length of the bed between the centres, can easily be fitted up. In turning work of short length the T-rest is sometimes found to be in the way, and a ⌐-rest is used instead; this is made of an angle piece, one leg fitted to the rest socket, and the other filed flat on that surface forming the top. The ⌐-rest is often used with the point towards the work, thus giving a rest of about ¾ of an inch in length, very convenient for short work. T and ⌐ rests are usually made of cast iron, but wrought iron is sometimes used, and this is the better material, especially for the latter shape.

A collar-plate is an arrangement in general use for supporting the ends of rods whilst these are being bored up; it consists of a disc of cast iron having a quantity of holes bored near its edge. These holes are very much coned and are graduated in size; in use the largest side is put towards the mandrel, and the bar being turned revolves in the

conical hole as in a collar. The plate is fixed by
its centre by means of a bolt clamping it against a
dwarf casting. The work before being put in the
collar-plate has its end turned true, and the extreme
edge rounded off to prevent its cutting the plate, a
drop of oil being applied to lubricate the bearing.
The axial continuity of the work is preserved by
placing the back centre against it before finally
adjusting and fixing the collar-plate, which is
screwed tight at such a position that the work turns
freely without shake. On removing the poppit head
the centre of the end of the bar may be operated
upon as required ; it may be bored up with a
drill and the hole then enlarged and made true
with a tool in the slide-rest, or otherwise treated.

The chief essential requisites of a good lathe are
that the bed should be sufficiently strong to be
quite rigid, and that the headstocks fit it properly
at all parts of its length; this latter may be tested
by trying them. A bed "in winding" is an abomi-
nation, though sometimes to be met with, being
the result of careless chucking in the planing
machine; through bad bolting to the standards a
bed is sometimes thrown "in winding." For this
defect test with winding strips, which are perfectly
parallel straight edges, by placing them trans-
versely across the bed at various places, and noticing that the top edges of both are level. The entire
framework of the under part of the lathe should be
strong and firmly braced together standing on four
feet, each touching the floor, so that solidity is

imparted to the whole structure. The treadle should be as low as possible, just to be clear of the floor when at its lowest point, rising to about 9 or 10 inches. A narrow strip of wood nailed to the floor just in front of the foot-board of the treadle will serve as a guard to prevent the toes from getting underneath.

That the entire line of centres should be perfectly parallel with the bed is always desirable, and in many cases absolutely essential for producing true work. The two ends of the mandrel should be exactly equidistant from the bed, as should be both ends of the poppit cylinder. The effect of having the axis of rotation of the mandrel at an angle with the bed is not shown when turning between centres, though the carrier and the pin of the driver-chuck will be continually rubbing against each other to an extent proportionate to the error in the line of centres. The mandrel may be differently distanced from the bed at one end than at the other, without affecting the work between centres, though when chucked without any back support the free end of the work will be more or less above, below, or on one side of the back centre point, as work unsupported will naturally take the position of an axial continuity of the mandrel itself.

In order to test the truth of the axis of rotation with the lathe bed itself, the positions of the mandrel bearings must be gauged. The parallelism of these bearings with the top and inside of the bed will be shown by fixing, in a chuck, a bar of metal as long as possible, to allow the back centre to stand on the bed with the point clear. This bar of metal must be centred whilst running in the lathe, and its centre will, if the mandrel is parallel with the bed, coincide with the point ot the poppit; the bar must be strong enough to bear its own weight without drooping at the unsupported end, or the test will show false. Another method of testing the whole of the holes in the headstocks is by putting the mandrel head to the right of the poppit, and reversing the barrel so that it protrudes at its right-hand end ; then if the point of the poppit comes exactly opposite the tail-pin of the mandrel, or its centre if in double bearings, the continuity of the axial line of centres is proved to be in a straight line with the bed.

Another good plan, perhaps the better, is to fit a hard wood mandrel in the bearings, leaving at each end, projecting a few inches from the casting, a cylindrical portion of exactly the same diameter. Make a template or gauge of sheet metal to show the distance of these portions from the bed, and gauge carefully at both ends ; any error will be at once felt, as the sense of touch is marvellously keen. This is proved by the ease with which minute differences, that cannot be detected by the eye, are discovered by the feel in callipering. Unless a good light is on the object it is difficult to see minute errors.

A perfect fit of the mandrel bearings may be

proved by screwing the tail-pin as tight as possible, so that the mandrel may be turned by hand, and if there are no places where the fit is easier than at others you may consider it accurate, providing that there is no side shake whatever. The mandrel must always be kept up to its bearing by the tail-pin, and never allowed to run loose, or the bearings will be worn unequally.

The flange of the nose, against which the chucks screw, ought to be quite flat and perfectly true, so should the thread of the nose, though it is rather the exception to find that it is so. Some makers turn a groove in the mandrel at the back of the thread, reducing the diameter to that at the bottom of the thread, though with what reason is not easily conceivable. The effect is to very materially weaken the mandrel at that part which is, under the most favourable circumstances, its weakest place. The bearing of the mandrel should be of steel and very hard, and the face against which the chucks jamb should also be of steel—in fact, a continuation of the bearing, the usual plan being to shrink a steel collar on a mandrel of fagoted iron.

If the boring of the poppit headstock is anything but absolutely true with the line of centres, the position of the back centre point, relative to the axial continuity of the mandrel, will be constantly varying as the poppit barrel is wound out. The truth of this boring can be tested to a certain extent by winding out the point as far as possible without allowing the barrel to become loose in the hole, and then testing it with a point-chuck. The oppositeness of the points cannot be tested by contact with any degree of accuracy. The best plan is to use a narrow parallel straight edge and adjust the cones to that distance apart which just allows the straight edge to go between them, with its opposite edges resting against the opposite sides of the cones. The straight edge is applied on both sides, above and below, and readily shows the oppositeness of the points. The poppit may be gauged in the same way as described for testing the mandrel bearing with a wooden temporary mandrel; using the barrel, which must fit nicely, projecting at both ends of the casting.

CHAPTER III.

HAND TURNING.

First principles of the art, commencing to practise—Wood turning, the gouge and the chisel—The mode of their application to the cylinder and surface—Easily made objects for beginners—Making a plain wooden box—Metal turning, the graver and triangular tool, and their use—Finishing tools, round nose tools, &c.

WHEN commencing to practise the art of turning it is advisable to begin by using simple tools and appliances, and with them to execute work of the most rudimentary kind, so that the learner may become properly acquainted with the elements of lathe-work, and he will then be able to understand the execution of the more complicated work. It sometimes happens that a fine collection of tools comes into the hands of one who has never had any previous practice in their use, but who will nevertheless boldly essay to use the most complicated machinery before troubling to learn the principles that govern its application, and which are only to be studied in using the simpler tools. A person unacquainted with the conditions under which a hand-tool acts most favourably, only to be learned by practice, cannot correctly judge the best position in which to fix a tool in the slide-rest; and

the art of turning, like all others, to be learned
properly must be begun at the beginning. The
first lesson in turning should, therefore, be at a
plain foot lathe with back-centre and T-rest only, all
the apparatus and attachments which have been
described as adapted for special purposes being
removed entirely, for though the slide-rest may be
very useful to assist a beginner in roughing-down
the work, yet it would be most injudicious to
make use of such an apparatus before acquiring a
thorough mastership over hand-tools.

A plain parallel cylinder is, perhaps, the very
best object for a beginner to try his hand at producing, for its simple form dispenses with all complex manipulation of the tools; yet the production of a true cylinder can only be achieved after
much practice, and such work demands more skill
than would be at first sight imagined. Any slight
slip of the tool causing its point to dig into the
work would, of course, spoil a cylinder nearly
finished to a definite size; but for practice such a
mishap would be of no consequence, only necessitating the reduction of the entire cylinder to the
size of its smallest diameter. For wood turning
the gouge and chisel are the tools most generally
used, and they will be sufficient for our work; a
similar cylinder of metal would be turned with a
graver. Soft wood will do for material, though
hard wood is more pleasant to work, and will not
require driving at a high speed, which is tiring
to the tyro. A chuck will be wanted to carry the

work, and the prong-chuck, described in another chapter, is best suited to the purpose; and we will suppose the rough wood mounted between such a chuck and the back-centre, which is screwed up to take firm bearing and the extreme point oiled.

For soft wood turning, place the band on the pair of grooves giving the quickest motion—that is, from the largest on the fly-wheel to the smallest on the mandrel—and in revolving the work it will be scarcely possible to drive it too quick. The hand-rest is then adjusted so that the top edge of the T is on a level with the lathe-centres, and the work revolves just clear of it. The position for standing at the lathe whilst turning a cylinder is with the shoulders fairly parallel with the lathe-bed, the body upright, resting on one foot, the other being on the foot-board of the treadle, the operator using either leg to support him, and occasionally changing from one foot to the other as he becomes tired; the foot on the ground is placed as far towards the lathe as the treadle-board will allow. With a balanced fly-wheel, that is, one weighted so that the crank always stands, when at rest, slightly inclined forward from its highest point, the treadle will be in the position to receive the pressure of the foot. Under ordinary circumstances the lathe-band is pulled down from the mandrel or the fly-wheel is revolved by the left hand, so as to bring the crank into the position described, and then pressure is exerted on the treadle, and the work revolves. Two or three strokes are given to get up the momentum before the tool is applied to the work.

The turner's gouge is used for roughing out wood-work, and a turner should provide himself with several sizes, according to the work he has to execute. For general use a gouge half-an-inch or so wide will be found most serviceable; the tool is sharpened differently to the carpenter's gouge, so as to leave the cutting edge rounded off instead of square with the shaft of the tool, as in the carpenter's gouge. The grinding is all done from the outside of the semicircle, and forms one continuous bevel, leaving an acute angle for the cutting edge. Gouges should be fitted into long handles to enable the operator to have complete control over the tool when in use. A half-inch gouge may be a foot or so long from end to end of tool and handle combined; larger sizes are much longer, frequently measuring as much as 2 feet, and sometimes even more. The gouge is grasped firmly near the cutting end by the left hand, the knuckles being uppermost, and is laid on the rest with its curved side downwards; the right hand holds the end of the handle, and usually rests against the side of the body, to afford greater steadiness. Thus held, the edge of the gouge is gradually brought sufficiently near the revolving cylinder to touch it in the position known as at a tangent to the circle, that is, so that a line drawn in continuation of the ground bevel will touch but not cut into the cylinder. In this position the tool will not cut, but on raising the end of the handle with the right hand the edge of the tool is depressed, and becomes in the position of a tangent to a smaller circle, then all the material outside of that diameter will be shaved off by the tool. The pressure on the edge during the process tends to force the tool deeper into the work, and, therefore, the end held in the right hand must be kept down till the work has been reduced all round to the new diameter, when the gouge will again cease to cut. A slight elevation of the handle will again throw the edge into the cylinder, and so on till enough has been removed from the work.

Though the elevation of the handle has been described as an intermittant process, yet in practice it is, of course, a continuous one, for it is by raising the handle that the tool is fed into the work, the thickness of the shaving being regulated by the feed thus given. If the theory which governs the cutting of the gouge is properly understood it will be easy to carry out the principle in practice, and thus rapidly acquire proficiency in the use of the tool. By means of the gouge the rough wood is turned to a circular form, all the angles are removed, and the work made as straight as possible. A pair of callipers is used to measure or gauge the size from end to end, and those parts found to exceed the general diameter are reduced, so that the surface will be fairly straight. There will, however, yet remain a series of ridges resulting from the use of the circular-pointed gouge, and these are

D

shaved off by the use of a chisel applied in a similar way.

The turner's chisel is a flat tool similar to the carpenter's paring chisel, but ground very differently. It is bevelled equally from each side, leaving the cutting edge in the centre of the thickness, at an oblique angle with the sides of the shaft, instead of square across, as in the carpenter's chisel, the angles being usually about 70° and 110°. The chisel is held in the same manner as the gouge, with the lower corner of the obtuse angle edge placed on the rest. The chisel is tilted up sufficiently to bring the central part of the cutting edge against the work, leaving both corners free, for should the entire width of the cutting edge be brought to bear on the work the tool will dig in. With the edge lying obliquely against the cylinder the chisel may be slid along the rest with the bottom edge leading, and the cut taken from either end, according to which of the two corners of the tool is laid on the rest. The principles which govern the gouge apply equally to the chisel, and by a proper amount of tilt a shaving of any desired thickness may be removed; the shavings may be so thin as to produce a barely perceptible difference in the diameter of the work. When the ridges left by the gouge have been entirely obliterated the diameter of the cylinder is tested by callipering, and any irregularity can be smoothed off with the chisel.

Capital practice for a beginner will be to take a shaving from end to end of a parallel cylinder, still

leaving it perfectly parallel after the shaving is
removed.   This is not difficult when the manipulation of the tool is quite under control; the thickness of the shaving will be the best guide, and this
may be regulated to the greatest nicety by adjusting the height of the tool handle held in the right
hand.

The directions here given for using the gouge
and chisel on a plain cylinder are equally applicable for turning cones, which are similarly formed
with these tools.

For turning the surface of wood chucked plank-
ways the same tools are used, the T-rest being
placed round to lie parallel with the face of the
work, and the gouge held in a more horizontal
position than when applied to the cylinder. The
chisel is used with its broad surface resting flat on
the top of the T, the whole breadth of the cutting edge against the work, but held so that the
corner on the side towards which the tool is advanced barely touches; the action of the chisel
being scraping rather than cutting, though shavings are produced.

It is curious that beginners at turning are often
at a loss to find an object on which to practise,
so that descriptions of a few that can be easily
made will be suggestive of others.   Ordinary
round rulers, varying from 6 inches to 2 feet in
length, and from $\frac{1}{2}$ inch to $1\frac{1}{4}$ inch in diameter,
are of very simple form.   By following the
directions just given on the use of the gouge

and chisel it will be easy to turn rulers, and so gain experience. A roller on which to hang a jack-towel and a rolling-pin are usually to be found in every household, and capital practice will be afforded in turning exact copies of such things. Cricketers' stumps and bales, tool handles, trenchers, and numerous other common articles are made on the lathe. The production of these will afford variety to the practice and enlarge the range of work without very severely taxing the skill, yet always adding to the capacity of the workman. It is well to remember that an adept at turning such simple objects will find it easy to proceed to the execution of the most complicated work. A plain wooden box affords considerable practice in the use of hand-turning tools, and the method of making one is this :—Having decided on the size of the proposed box, select a piece of wood, almost any kind will do, but preferably use that which has a close even grain. See that the ends are cut tolerably square, and mark a circle on each to serve as a guide for roughing out the circumference as nearly round as possible, first with a hatchet, and afterwards with a rasp. The length of the wood must be :—the height of the box, the height of the rim on which the cover shuts, the height of the cover itself, enough space to allow the parting-tool to be used twice—that is, where the lid is separated from the body of the box, and where the box is cut from the superfluous piece in the chuck—and enough to chuck the wood by. All these measurements added together show the length of wood required to make the box. It is important to measure the rough block to see that there is sufficient material, as it will be a great saving of labour if the complete box, lid, and body are turned from one instead of from several pieces of material.

The roughly-shaped cylindrical block has now to be chucked firmly on the lathe, it may be fixed in a cup-chuck if one of convenient size is to be found; or a boxwood chuck may be hollowed out, to a depth of about a quarter of an inch, sufficiently large in diameter to allow the wood to be driven in firmly by a few smart blows of a mallet. That end which is cut most nearly square with the cylindrical sides should be chosen for driving into the chuck. It should not be made to bottom, that is, the block should be driven into the chuck to touch all the way round. When properly chucked the end of the wood is first operated upon with the gouge and turned true; the tool is held as described in the early part of this chapter, working from the circumference towards the centre. When turned true, the chisel is used to smooth the surface and make it flat; the cylindrical surface of the cylinder is turned true in the manner previously described for such work, and the rough block is thus got to a truly cylindrical form, parallel and square at the end. So far the work has been only preparatory.

The first operation in making the box itself is to shape the lid. On the circumference of the cylinder

mark a ring showing the depth of the intended lid—
this may be done with the angle of the chisel—
then hollow out the front to the required depth, to
leave sufficient thickness of material at the top of
the lid; a side tool will do this part of the work
most easily. The rim of the lid for the box should
be slightly undercut in both directions; a very little
will suffice, so that it will fit closer on to the box.
With a wood-parting tool the lid is cut off from
the rest of the wood; the tool should cut only a
narrow groove, and the direction of this must be
carefully maintained so that the thickness of the
lid will be equal and sufficient for due strength.
Tolerable truth will suffice, as the top of the lid will
be finally finished later on when it is snapped on
the body part, and the top will then face the back
centre. In parting off the wood the groove must
be kept wide enough to allow the tool to be free of
the sides. When getting near the centre extra
care is necessary to guard against the tool catch-
ing in and tearing off the lid, in which case the
probable result would be that the breakage would
spoil the lid.

The wood now left in the chuck is to form the
body of the box; it is first hollowed out to form
the interior, the same tool and the same general
principles as were employed in turning out the
inside of the lid being applicable, the precise
height having first been marked on the outside.
Before removing the entire inside of the box, the
neck part on which the lid fixes must be turned to fit

and the lid snapped on tightly. In turning down the
neck, when it nearly approaches the required size, it
is advisable to frequently try the lid on it, otherwise too much material may be removed and the
job spoilt. With experience, however, it becomes
easy to fit without trying the sizes more than once.
There should not be the slightest play or shake in
the fitting, the rim should be quite true cylin-
drically and the shoulder equally true flatways, so
that when the lid is put on and gently forced to its
place the join should be absolutely imperceptible
but for the appearance of the grain of the wood.
With the lid fitting tightly it can be turned up
true with the chisel, comparatively light cuts will
only be necessary as the work has already been
made true. The cover may be slightly dome-shaped,
and the side of the box should be turned with the
chisel to make it and the lid perfectly coincident.

. With the parting tool the box may be now partially cut off from the remaining piece of waste
wood, but before being entirely detached the exterior ought to be finished. The turning chisel, if
properly handled, will leave a surface that will be
difficult to improve upon, but if any roughness exists
it may be smoothed with fine glass-paper. The
inside of the box is also finished before the parting
tool finally cuts it off; the sides are made straight
and the bottom flat and then the box body is cut off,
the parting tool being held at a slight angle to the
axis of rotation so as to slightly undercut the
bottom which will then stand firmly on its edges,

and requires no further treatment. If it is desired to turn the bottom face, the piece of waste wood can be hollowed out so as to fit the rim on which the lid fits, and chucked by this the bottom may be operated upon as required, leaving it slightly concave. Every time that the box or lid is re-chucked it must run as true as it did in its former position, and to re-chuck work perfectly true is one of the first lessons that a turner should study. There are also the fittings of the lid to the box and the box to the chuck, which will be excellent practice.

It may be assumed that when a plain box, in common wood, can be turned out of hand in every respect well made, the maker has attained sufficient skill in the use of his tools to warrant his undertaking without fear of failure work of far more complicated design and apparently more difficult to execute. The plain box just described is scarcely a piece of work likely to attract the attention of those who have an extensive assortment of tools and appliances; still the care and attention which must necessarily be bestowed on the various operations incidental to its production afford an amount of practice in the use of hand tools on wood which is considerable and varied, and should be prized accordingly.

Turning metal by means of hand tools is a process in every way similar to that just described, modified to suit the nature of the material. It is generally found that an inexperienced hand succeeds better in turning metal than wood; there is, however, no more difficulty in working this latter material, and the circumstance named is due to the more obvious effect produced with wood, making it much easier to see the effect of the tools used, but more difficult to guide them. Wood is turned at a far greater speed than is metal, and the material is much softer, so that whilst the tool more easily penetrates the work and "catches in," this is more liable to be torn than the more tenacious metal revolving at a less velocity.

The same angle is to be preserved in applying the tool to metal, that is, it should form a tangent to the circle being cut, but consequent on the hardness of the material the angles of the cutting edges must be altered to make them stronger; however, the workman who, by practice on wood, makes himself familiar with the most favourable conditions under which the tool acts, will be best able to apply tools to metal to the greatest advantage.

The graver is the most general tool for metal turning. It is a bar of square steel, usually about one-quarter to five-sixteenths of an inch in size, though smaller and larger are used. All the flats are sometimes, but two are always, ground flat and smooth. The end is ground off diagonally, those edges formed by the sides meeting at the point being used for turning. The angle made by the diagonal diamond - shaped end with the shank varies to suit the material that it is intended to act upon, from 60° to 70° being about the usual limit.

The triangular tool is also much used. It is

generally made from a worn-out triangular file, of
the dimensions named as usual for gravers, and
is merely ground on the faces to take out all the
marks of the file teeth, leaving sharp edges at the
angles, all of which are 60°. The end is ground
off obliquely, leaving a point at one angle, but the
tool is generally used to cut with its side edges;
and in this respect it principally differs from the
graver, which is used only at the end.

With the two tools named most of the rough
turning by hand on metal is done. Tools for metal
have short handles. In use the left hand generally
grasps the T-rest and the tool, the fingers encir-
cling the stem of the rest socket and the thumb
clasping the tool to the T. The right hand holds
the handle as described in holding wood-turning
tools; indeed, sometimes both hands are used as
there described, only closer together, a natural
consequence on the reduced length of the handle
and tool itself. A lubricant is used with these
tools on wrought iron and steel; this is necessary
to keep the edge cool and lubricate the cutting.
Water answers the purpose, but soapy water is
better, and perhaps quite as good as oil, though
much cheaper. Cast iron, brass, and gun-metal are
turned dry.

The way in which the graver is applied to the
work is this :—the tool is laid with one angle on the
T-rest, the point being towards the back centre,
and the handle at an angle with the line of centres.
The lathe being set in motion and the graver

brought as near as possible to the work, it is firmly indented on the rest, and by bringing the handle towards the right the point is made to cut the work; the operation is assisted by turning the graver slightly over towards the left. This action makes a narrow groove on the work, and when the handle is so far to the right that the tool is disengaged, the graver is shifted along the rest to recommence the same process. The work turned by this means will consist of a series of grooves, more or less irregular, but the concentric truth will be correct. In the same way the triangular tool may be used to produce a like result.

To further finish the cylinder, after it has been made as straight as can be with the graver, a flat tool is used. This somewhat resembles a carpenter's chisel ground off square at the end so that no bevel exists. This tool is applied, end on, to the cylinder, and cuts away all the ridges reducing the surface to one level. This flat tool may be from about half-an-inch wide and one-eighth thick up to double these dimensions; it can be used indifferently with either edge to cut. Cylinders with straight surfaces, whether parallel or coned, are generally finally finished by filing whilst in rapid revolution in the lathe, a fine file being used. To produce an extra smooth surface emery paper wrapped round the file is afterwards applied, and by this means a very high finish can be given to the work.

Round-nosed tools, which are made of strips of

steel of various widths and thicknesses, having the
ends ground off to a semicircular shape, are used
for hollowing out the exterior of metal work and
turning curvilinear grooves. Tools of a similar
construction with the ends shaped to various patterns are largely used for turning beadings and
mouldings of various kinds. Numerous tools
ground to particular forms are employed for special
purposes, but of these little need be said here.

CHAPTER IV.

SCREW-CUTTING BY HAND.

Striking the thread with outside and inside comb-screw tools—Originating a thread—The method of cutting the thread in a lathe chuck minutely described.

CUTTING screws by means of comb-screw tools guided by hand is a process only to be learnt after considerable practical experience has been attained in the use of hand tools on the ordinary cylindrical work. The tools themselves are made in pairs, one for use on the external the other on the internal thread; they may be bought at all tool shops where turning tools are sold. One pair is of course only applicable to one particular rate of thread, though it may be cut on any diameter. The same screw tool that cuts a thread of, say, fifty turns to the inch on a screw one-eighth of an inch in diameter is also used if the same rate of thread is required, say 2 inches in diameter as in optical instruments. For holes of very small diameter it is very seldom that comb-screw tools are used, and if under certain sizes it is impossible. Taps are generally used for all inside threads that have a thoroughfare hole excepting in optical work; the

workmen in that trade always using comb tools to
cut the fine threads. Holes which cannot be tapped,
through having a bottom, may be cut with a comb
tool, and the process is explained in detail, with
special reference to chasing the screw inside a
chuck, in the latter part of this chapter.

The outside screw tool is very much used for
cutting the threads in bolts and all kinds of work
that can be mounted in the lathe. Frequently the
thread is originated by making a spiral line with
the die stock, the work is then transferred to the
lathe where the screw is cut out with the comb
tool, this cutting faster and better than dies, and
being comparatively easy to keep in the spiral
originated by the dies. If this is not quite true it
is not likely to be improved in the chasing by any
but a skilled screw-cutter. After the bulk has
been removed by the comb tool the dies are used
to finish with. To acquire the habit of traversing
the tool at a uniform rate a beginner should practise
on a cylinder which has a thread already cut on it,
such as one partially cut by dies.

The way in which the screw thread is originated
by hand with the chaser will be easily understood.
It is simply necessary to move the chaser along
the top of the T-rest exactly the same distance that
the teeth are apart whilst the work is turned round
once. If the tool and work have been moved at a
regular speed the thread will be true; if, however,
either motion has been jerky the thread will not
be regular but bent or wavy. It will be seen that

the rate of the screw and the diameter each govern the result, and though the difficulty of striking the true thread may appear very great, yet after careful practice and observation of the result it will be a job that can be done with ease and certainty.

The thread, whether outside or in, is always first struck on the corner of the work, and this is rounded off for the purpose before applying the screw tool. The T-rest, which must have a smooth top, is then placed near to this corner, and having set the lathe going with a regular swinging motion, the comb is brought on to the rest. By a circular motion of the handle, the blade of the tool having a centre of motion on the top of the T, one tooth near the centre is made to cut a spiral line, the depth of which is greatest at its middle and diminishes to nothing at the ends. When once the true helix is struck it is comparatively easy to follow it up, making it deeper and extending it further at each application of the tool.

The thread is thus struck at the end first, and gradually deepened and lengthened till it has reached the distance required; so that during the process of chasing it the thread is always cut deeper at the end, and it is made parallel by giving the final cuts nearer to the back end. The first spiral traced forms a guide, and on repeating the cut the point of a tooth must come in the previously-made groove, or the thread will be damaged and probably spoiled. Those who have cut threads with badly fitting dies have probably had occasion to notice the effect of another thread being originated between the true one; this is what happens if the comb tool is not always put into the first made groove.

The use of the comb-screw tool for inside work is best explained by its application to cutting the thread in lathe chucks, after starting with the tap as described in Chapter VII.

When the thread has been started in the hole and the tap taken out, clean the dust out of the hole and put the hand-rest, which must be quite smooth, at least at that part where the screw tool will take its bearing, close against the hole, at such a height as may be convenient for allowing the chaser to cut. This will be with its edge slightly above the centre, as the rake of the teeth is, in bought screw tools, the wrong way, and in consequence of the thickness of the tool it would, if placed at the correct height—*i.e.* on the line of centres—have the lower points of the teeth in contact with the interior of the hole. If these points were to find their bearing in the spiral groove, the upper cutting edge would not cut at the same spiral line, but a trifle behind it. Thus will be understood the importance of getting the tool to the correct height to let the lower edge escape contact. When all the parts are properly adjusted commence cutting the screw. First get a regular swinging motion to the lathe-treadle; the habit must be acquired of keeping the same regular motion with the foot, independent of the occupation of the hand. Hold the comb-screw tool with the right hand firmly gripping the handle, and the left steadying the tool by having the fingers round the socket of the T-rest, the thumb grasping the chaser near the rest and pressing it firmly into the thread. At first it is advisable to let the tool run in along the thread a few times without cutting, thereby to get the rate of motion impressed on the senses, so that the rate of progression of the tool can be maintained by muscular action as well as being guided by the spiral made by the tap. Having got the rate of motion, take very light cuts at first, but always be sure to have the teeth in the original grooves, otherwise, there is every probability of getting a multifold thread. When the comb is placed near the mouth of the hole with about three teeth projecting inside, the left thumb is used to draw it towards the side of the hole. As soon as it is felt to be in the screw groove a heavy pressure is maintained to keep the chaser up to a full cut, till it has run in right to the bottom of the hole. The tool should be held in such a position as to insure parallelism of the teeth, so that the thread will be cut of equal depth throughout its length. The inexperienced hand runs great risk of coming to grief over screw-cutting, but practice will make perfect, and it is only after repeated trials that an amateur can expect to be able to run in a true thread with the chaser. Care must be exercised not to let the tool go in far enough for its point or end to come in

E

contact with the bottom of the hole whilst the teeth are cutting the thread, or damage more or less serious according to the rigidity with which the tool is held must inevitably follow. The eye and hand will soon become educated to act in unison, so that when the screw tool has gone in to a certain depth, as indicated to the eye, the muscular power of the thumb is relaxed; the teeth of the chaser are gently drawn out of the thread, and when quite clear the tool is drawn outwards, say half an inch or so, and the operation repeated. This is continued till the thread is nearly to size, and it is finally finished with the full tap. There are several points to be considered in cutting the thread. As to its size, if the chaser is too high up it will cut the thread shallower than it should be. If the tool is not run in parallel, the mouth of the hole will not gauge correctly, and consequently it will be impossible to ascertain the exact size of the thread. These points must be studied and acted upon to the best of one's judgment, any definite rules being impossible.

When the thread has been cut out with the chaser to, as near as can be judged, the proper size, the full-sized tap is inserted and screwed home exactly the same way as was the entry tap, using the back centre to keep it square, and working it right in till it " bottoms " in the hole.

CHAPTER V.

BORING AND DRILLING.

Drills, their correct form and uses—How to grind them—Half-round bits—Pin-drills—Bars with movable cutters—Rose cutters and rose bits—Lubrication necessary in boring.

BORING and drilling form a large proportion of the work done on a lathe, and embrace the various methods employed to pierce holes and smooth internal cylinders. Drills, bits, cutters, and many other tools are used for making the holes; slide rest tools, boring bars, broaches, &c., are used to smooth holes already existing.

Drills are the most generally used of all tools for boring holes of all sizes. When these are too large to be made in one drilling, two or more drills each of a size to bore out a proportionate quantity of material are used. It will be found hard work to bore holes larger than half an inch in metal on a foot lathe at one traverse, and it is, therefore, advisable to use three drills for a hole $\frac{7}{8}$ inch in diameter, that being three times the area of the largest size that can be bored without considerable fatigue. The first boring $\frac{1}{2}$ inch, the next $\frac{11}{16}$, and the third full size $\frac{7}{8}$; the work of removing the material will then be

roughly fairly apportioned to each tool. A drawback to the use of drills is that they are liable
to run out of the straight line in which it is intended
to bore, and the drill cutting into the solid material
is most liable to do so. Those which follow on
generally keep fairly true to the original hole, but
they have no tendency to correct any error, and
are sometimes found to increase it. Drills should
always be started in a fairly countersunk hole, and
especial care taken to see that they go correctly in
the spot desired till the entire point angle of the
drill is beneath the surface ; the sides will then
tend to guide it.

Fitted to a chuck such as those described on
page 92, the drill is the most usual form of
borer, as its point will at once find its bearing in a
centre punch mark and follow on fairly concentric,
sufficiently so for the majority of purposes. Thus
for all the general purposes of boring where absolute truth and straightness are not imperative,
drills are the best tools to use. It is only necessary to indent a conical hole with the centre punch,
sufficiently large to allow the flat end formed by
the meeting of the cutting edges across the thickness of the drill to enter well, and the hole will
follow fairly true. If a long cylinder has to be
bored then a drill would be unsuitable, as it would
be sure to deviate from a straight line, and, though
entered perfectly central at one end, on reaching the
other it would come out more or less out of truth
with the centre. This fault is sometimes sought

to be remedied by drilling alternately from both ends and making the holes join in the middle, but here they do so only approximately. Though apparently true from what may be seen at the ends, yet when looked at through the bore will be found to be crooked.

The ordinary form of drill is shown in Fig. 2. The shank part is turned parallel to fit a chuck, and a flat filed to take the point of a clamp-screw. A shoulder, to prevent the drill being forced into the chuck, should be provided as illustrated. The entire drill should be nearly parallel; if small at the point-end it will not bore deep through binding,

Fig. 2.—The Drill for Boring Metal.

and if unnecessarily small at any part behind the point the drill is weakened and liable to break. The blade should be flattened sufficiently far to allow borings to escape. The illustration is intended to convey to the eye an idea of the best general form of a drill for ordinary purposes.

Drills must be ground with their points at an angle of 90°, so that they fit an ordinary right angle square. The extreme point must be in the exact centre, and the flat part of the drill should be nearly parallel on its sides for a short distance from the point, as this will materially assist in guiding; the cutting angle must be small, only sufficient for proper clearance. On taking into consideration what has been said on the cutting edges of tools in another chapter, it will be understood that the proper form of cutting edge for a drill is that of the American twist drills, which act with far superior results to those of the usual form. To grind the cutting edge more acutely by increasing the angle of the bevel, does not produce the same result as when the point is turned up to form a cutting lip, as is the case in the twist drills.

To get the cutting edges to correspond in every respect is essential, so that the drill will act with the best possible results. The point excentric or one edge more prominent than the other will tend to make the drill bore larger than its intended size, and innumerable defects inherent to the tool will develop themselves. The blade must be as thin as is consistent with due strength, so that the material removed in borings may pass along on either side of the drill and not clog the hole. By noticing the quantity and quality of the borings an idea of the relative shape and action of the cutting edges may be formed. Sometimes it is desirable to bore a hole larger inside than at the mouth; this may be done by grinding the drill on one edge only, so as to throw the point out of centre; used in this way the tool will bore larger than its apparent size.

Half-round or D-bits are the sort most generally used for boring holes parallel and straight. These are made by filing a cylinder down to half its diameter and then grinding the end off obliquely.

The description will be found on page 73. These bits are made of all sizes, some used for ornamental work being most minute. They will bore a hole into solid metal, but are more often used to follow a drill and correct any defects left by it. It is only necessary to make a countersink to fit the D-bit correctly ; it will then bore quite straight, but it must itself be straight and be revolved straight. The half-round part must not exceed the semi-diameter, or the bit cannot bore a hole in solid material. An advantage which this form of boring tool has is that it leaves the hole with a flat bottom, not a conical one as drills do. When of large size, these bits usually have a portion wanting to complete the semicircle on the opposite side of the flat. This results from their being made from flat bars of steel not sufficiently thick to form the entire half-round ; it in no way detracts from their utility.

Pin-drills are used to bore a larger size truly concentric with a previously made hole; also for making square countersinks for screw-heads, &c. Somewhat similar to a drill in their action, these tools have a round pin at the end, and the cutting edge is behind this. Generally they have but two cutting lips, but, when made of round steel, pin-drills have usually four cutting edges, as illustrated in Fig. 3. The pin fitting the hole previously made effectually prevents the drill from going excentrically. In order to make one drill serviceable for different-sized holes, collars are

sometimes fitted to the pin, and by this means it is
adapted to larger holes. Pin-drills, often made in
the cutter bar next described, are very useful for
making a level bearing for a nut or a bolt head
against a casting. By using this drill a circle of
any size required may be made quite flat and
smooth, concentric with a hole bored in a rough
casting. By shaping the cutting edges to the
necessary form these tools may be used not only
to face up but also to true the edges of bosses, &c.,
that cannot be turned in the lathe, and even to put
a moulding round them.

Cutters are sometimes used fitted to a bar,
which is revolved between bearings or on the lathe
centres; then the cutter is at some distance from
the end, often near the centre. When near one end
of the bar it forms a kind of pin-drill. These bars
are always for boring large-sized holes, and are
made from motives of economy, one shank or stock
serving for a large number of cutters often having
a wide range of sizes. The cutters to such a bar
can be made in so little time and at such a
very small cost that the advantage is obvious
for all sizes that are not usually required. The
bar itself may be of iron, though preferably of
steel, and after being centred and trued up, it
has a transverse mortice cut through it near the
end. The end is then turned to a certain size to
follow drills or half-round bits of that size. The
cutters for the bar consist of small pieces of steel
wedged into the mortice by a cotter. The cutters

have a groove across them, leaving nibs to fit over the diameter of the bar and ensure their being replaced true. When the blank has been fitted to the bar, it is turned true in its place to the required size, the cutting edges are shaped by filing, and the cutter is hardened and tempered for use. Sometimes the cutters are clamped in the mortice by a set screw.

Rose-bits have several teeth on the end to cut with; some are made quite flat, and are used for cutting recesses of small depth that are required to

Fig. 3.—Pin Drill, with Four Cutting Lips.

have a flat bottom with no hole in the centre. This form of rose-bit does the work of a pin-drill without requiring any thoroughfare hole to guide it. The bit is guided by clamping a piece of sheet metal having a hole in it exactly fitting the rose-bit, and this placed in the hole bores straight away; therefore it is only necessary to place the hole of the plate precisely over the spot that has to be drilled. These rose-bits will not cut into the solid metal, but for some purposes they are indispensable. Fig. 3 without the pin would illustrate a rose-bit.

Rose-cutters made in the same way but with a central hole are used to make pivots. A piece of metal that has been pointed is brought against a cutter of this kind, which then cuts away all the metal within its diameter excepting a cylindrical piece which passes up the central hole and corresponds with it in size. This pivot serves to keep the cutter in position. A hollow rose-bit of this kind fixed into the poppit barrel is a capital tool for making screws with, as at one operation it will cut down the material to a uniform size to take the thread and leave it perfectly cylindrical with the head and shoulder cut in square. For making a projecting pivot-like piece of a casting, that cannot be mounted in the lathe, true and smooth for a bearing, these cutters are also very handy.

Rose-bits with cutting teeth on the end corner only are used for boring holes that are required to be particularly smooth and true. When once entered a bit of this kind cannot go wrong, as the cylindrical part accurately fits the hole bored by the teeth; these are never used except in holes that are very nearly sufficiently large. The hollow rose-bit may be used as a pin-drill by putting a tight-fitting cylindrical plug in the hole with sufficient projecting to answer for a pin. Rose-cutters of all kinds should have the teeth sufficiently large and wide apart to allow of the borings to escape, or they become clogged up if the teeth are fine. Another advantage in large teeth is that they may often be sharpened on the oilstone; this cannot be done with small ones. For half an inch in diameter from four to six teeth will be enough, and when at work they should each do their share of cutting.

Lubricants are required in boring wrought iron and brass, soapy water answering very well, but it is necessary to see that the liquid really reaches the cutting edges. This is sometimes difficult to ensure when boring deep holes horizontally, as they are on the lathe. The borings generally block the way, and even when the hole is clear it is not easy to get any fluid to the bottom of it if deep. A small common syringe is handy for the purpose, but it is only by constantly removing the tool, and with it the bulk of the borings, that the extreme end can be reached even with a syringe. Cast iron can be bored very well quite dry; but with pin-drills and others, that make a bearing as it were of the material into which they are drilling, a lubrication is necessary for all materials to relieve the friction at the bearing part.

CHAPTER VI.

MOUNTING WORK FOR TURNING.

Work between centres — Methods of centring — Necessity of properly preparing the centres—Chucking objects of various forms—False centres—The collar-plate—Chucking on the face-chuck.

WORK is mounted for treatment on the lathe in various ways, consequent on the almost unlimited forms which have to be chucked. There are two broad distinctions, however, by which we may conveniently divide the methods in general use for ease in describing them. First, objects which are supported by the back-centre, cone-plate, or some equivalent contrivance; and second, those which are mounted on the mandrel independent of such support. Amongst the first are generally all objects considerably greater in length than diameter, such as balusters, spindles, and rods of all kinds; the second, embracing short objects, sometimes gripped by their edges, and at others clamped by their surfaces, or held by cement in a similar fashion. In the chapter devoted to chucks much information applicable to this subject will be found.

The method of mounting work by far most generally practised is that of running it between centres.

The extreme facility of so chucking any object capable of such treatment is the chief cause of its extensive use, whilst its effectiveness leaves little to be desired. The indented, shallow, conical recesses to be seen at the ends of nearly all spindles and shafting are evidence of the work having been turned between centres by the aid of such a chuck as the one illustrated in Fig. 9. Work that has been once properly centred may be removed from the lathe, and at any time remounted on any other with the certainty of its running true, that is, providing the centre-points of such lathes are in proper order at the time the work is put between them. Other methods of chucking do not allow of this being done without considerable trouble, and hence all work that has to be often removed and replaced on the lathe should, if possible, be chucked between centres.

The first consideration in preparing work for running between the centres is to get the exact centre-point at each end, so that the entire object will run true on the lathe, and not, by being considerably out of centre, involve a great deal of unnecessary labour in reducing it to a concentric form. It is curious to find that an inexperienced hand seldom attempts to get an accurate centre to his work, and many consider the trouble involved in so doing far outweighs the advantages. It is, however, so easy to centre work absolutely truly that the extra labour is comparatively inappreciable ; in fact, only a slovenly hand would tolerate badly-centred work, involving as it does so much extra labour to no purpose.

Rod metal is, perhaps, the most usual object for centring, and in selecting a piece for a particular object it should be chosen just sufficiently large, both in diameter and length, for the purpose. All superfluous metal will be wasted, and not only that, but the labour which converts the good material into useless waste is itself all lost. The rod should be straight and the ends cut off squarely; these are each in turn filed flat, and at right angles to the axis of the rod. If the end-faces are at a slight angle it is more difficult to judge of the centre of the rod. The try-square will show the inclination of the end-faces with the side of the rod, though a practised eye will, unaided, detect the most minute error appreciable in working.

The actual centring is done with a fine-pointed centre-punch usually. For work of small diameter the punch is placed as near the centre as can be judged by the eye, the work being meanwhile held vertically in the vice, and a light blow of a hammer indents the metal. The rod-end is then carefully examined, and if the dot is found to be out of centre it is driven towards that side of the rod where most metal appears; this is done by holding the punch in a slanting direction when striking it. When the dot is judged to be fairly central the rod is reversed in the vice and the other end treated similarly, the punched centres being only slight. The rod is then placed between

the lathe-centres, and by turning it round with the
thumb and finger, the amount of its eccentricity, if
any, can be noted and the high parts marked with
chalk. The rod is then returned to the jaws of the
vice and the centre-punch applied so as to drive
the indentations towards the centre. The work is
again tested on the lathe-centres and operations
repeated till the rod is found to run true. When
this is accomplished the punch-marks are considerably enlarged by heavy blows, holding and driving
the punch in a straight line with the rod, a stronger
punch being employed.

Drilling in the centres is the next operation, and
an important one it is for work that has to run on
its centres much, though for work
that will never be put on the
lathe a second time it is sometimes dispensed with. Some
workmen, careless of the accu-

Fig. 4.—A properly drilled
Countersunk Centre.

racy of the work they turn out, are content
to use centre-punched centres only. In every
case when the work is liable to be run between
centres on a future occasion, the punch-marks
should be drilled in with a small drill sufficiently
deep to ensure the centre point from bottoming; the
hole should also be slightly countersunk to form a
durable bearing for the centre when running. The
depth of the hole, size of the countersink, &c., will
be dependent on the size of the work, but in all
cases the countersink must bore to the angle corresponding with the centre-point, this being, as

stated in another chapter, 60°. The hole bored in
the work may be very small, but must be deep
enough to clear the centre and allow for a little
wear. Fig. 4 shows how a properly drilled and
countersunk centre-rod should fit the cone-point;
the rod only is shown in section.

Rods of large size, and those objects that have to
be centred at parts where it is difficult to judge of
the precise centre, are usually marked with callipers
or a scribing-tool to show the middle. A gauge
formed of two strips placed at an angle, and having
a straight edge bisecting the angle, can be used
for determining the centre by putting the rod into
the angular opening and scribing on its end two
diametrical lines at somewhere about right angles
to each other, the intersection of these lines showing
the precise centre. A centre-punch sliding in a
barrel at right angles with and forming a continuation of the apex of a hollow cone is also employed,
though not very generally. The cone is placed
vertically over the end of the rod to be centred,
and on bringing down the centre-punch it will
mark the centre of the object within the cone. In
practice this form of centre-finder is confined to the
workshops of amateurs.

A totally different method of centring cylindrical
rods may be adopted, and when many of like
size are to be treated it has advantages over the
centre-punching previously described. By this
method a centre fitted into the poppit barrel, having
its end ground off to a triangular point, is employed

to bore a countersunk hole, its exact central position being ensured by causing the work, which is itself chucked by a temporary punch-mark on the point-chuck, to revolve against some fixed support near its outer end. See illustration, Fig. 5, showing a rod being centred. An L-shaped tool resting on the T-rest, and supporting the work in its angle, will serve every purpose, and by forming a bearing for the rod to work on when the boring-tool is brought up by the poppit head the central position of the hole is ensured. In practice it is usual to

Fig. 5.—Centring Metal Rods on the Lathe.

centre both ends of the rod roughly with a punch, and then by boring only lightly to gradually correct any error by the aid of the L-tool mentioned above, or by a bar fixed in the slide-rest, with a V-slot, in the sides of which the work may take a bearing, and brought up till the rod bears in the slot during the whole of its revolution. The triangular point of the centre, Fig. 6, cutting sideways as well as in the direction of its point, soon cuts towards the highest point of the excentric rod, which is continually pressed towards the centre by the fixed bearing, against which it touches at every

F

revolution. A stiff triangular point is necessary—flexibility would destroy its purpose—and the countersunk hole must be drilled in, as in Fig. 4, with as small drill as has been already described. Work centred by the method last described is, of course, reversed in the chucking when one end is finished, so that the other may be operated upon.

It will be understood that innumerable objects of various forms may be chucked by simply making sound centres in them ; for these, though they may appear but fragile bearings, are really strong enough for every practical requirement if they are only

Fig. 6.—Poppit Centre, with Triangular Cutting-point.

correctly made, as Fig. 4, in the first instance. Square bars that have to be turned with cylindrical parts, as, for example, the ordinary grindstone axis of square section, with a bearing near each end, are easily operated on when running between centres.

In some cases, where work has not a suitable place for centring in a line with the axis on which it should be turned, a piece is put specially to afford a centre bearing. Sometimes the casting or forging is so prepared, and in others a piece is fixed by some means. As an example we may take a crank-shaft, which to be chucked, with the main-shaft excentric and the crank-pin running true, has a piece of metal fastened at each end, projecting sufficiently to allow of a good centre to be made in a line with the crank-pin itself. It may be taken as an axiom that, whenever possible, between centres is the best way of chucking all metal objects in the lathe.

The collar-plate is an appliance for supporting work which cannot be conveniently held in a chuck without support at the outer end, when this outer end has to be operated upon, generally for boring up. The collar-plate, previously mentioned, is a circular plate, usually of cast iron, with a series of conical holes, the sizes of which vary progressively, bored near its circumference equidistant from the centre. This plate is mounted by a central hole on a dwarf casting fitted to the bed, and fixed by the bolt, on which it may be turned when this is slackened for the purpose. The shank of the bolt passing through the casting is square, and sometimes passes through a vertical slot, which allows adjustment for height, but it is better fitted accurately to a square hole in such a position that each coned hole is on a level with the line of centres when at its highest point. For use the collar-plate has simply to be adjusted to the correct distance to form a bearing for the object it has to support, a hole of suitable size having been first determined on and placed uppermost; the extreme edge of the work bears in the hole, and should be slightly bevelled to prevent cutting, a little oil being also necessary for lubrication. In this position the object is ready for being bored up centrally and for similar treatment.

Work mounted for turning on a chuck, and fixed to it, independent of support from the back centre, if of a concentric form is usually held by its edge in a recess turned in the chuck itself. When the fitting is made fairly accurate, and the work is itself tolerably true, this method will secure it firm enough for most purposes. When the work is of angular outline it is best to have three points of contact, which ensure equality of grip if the points are equidistant. In chucking square objects by their angles it is necessary to see that the two diameters across the angles are equal, or the object will be fixed only at two points. When there are but three points all must be in contact; for this reason, three screws in such a chuck as the one numbered Fig. 15 are preferable to four.

The face-plate is, perhaps, the most generally useful chuck for all objects which are capable of being fixed by one side, whether the side itself be sufficiently flat for the purpose, or whether the work be made level by packing. The face-plate chuck is described on page 95, and work to be fixed to it is laid on it and clamped firm, using preferably three points of pressure if that part of the work laid on the chuck has not already been made perfectly flat by turning, planing, filing, &c. Sometimes it is easier to fix work on the face-chuck when this is lying horizontally; at others, *the central* position of an object is maintained by

means of the back-centre point supporting it whilst
being fixed.   Only the peculiarities of the job in
hand can determine the most advantageous manner of placing it on the chuck ; and, in short, every
particular piece of work of an irregular form generally possesses certain special features which at
once offer advantages for chucking it, or the situa-
tion of the part to be operated upon makes the
adoption of certain positions on the lathe essential.
Even two equally competent workmen, who have
been taught—or, perhaps, it would be more correct
to say, have picked up their knowledge—in different
shops, will chuck the same object in totally different
ways.

CHAPTER VII.

FITTING CHUCKS TO THE LATHE-NOSE.

Minute details of the process—Various threads used for lathe-noses —Making taps, &c., for fitting chucks—How the thread should be formed—A truly cut thread necessary on the nose.

CHUCKS are those appliances which, screwed on the nose of the lathe, are used to cause the work to revolve. The variety of work turned on the lathe involves a corresponding variety of chucks, and though the turner who produces only one species of work, as, for instance, stair balusters, only uses one single chuck, yet the amateur turner, who provides a lathe and attachments capable of grappling with work of all descriptions, will find his stock of chucks amount to several score. Those complicated apparatus which involve a lot of mechanism in themselves, such as are used for turning excentrics, ovals, and geometric figures, will not occupy our attention in the present treatise. They are mostly costly tools, and are seldom found in the workshop of the general turner, though an oval chuck is the principal tool of the oval turner, and the engine-turning lathe with geometric apparatus is the every-day tool of watch-case engine-turners.

Chucks are usually added to a lathe by the
turner as occasion occurs, because in making them
the greater part of the work as a general rule has
to be done on the identical lathe on which the
chuck will be used; consequently full details are
here given which will enable those readers who
are able to execute the work to make for themselves. One of the first considerations in a chuck
is that it should be fitted correctly to the nose of
the lathe, and general directions for effecting this
precede the more minute instructions incidental
to each chuck. To fit chucks accurately, as they
should be fitted, it is necessary to have a screw-tap
which cuts the thread identical with that on the
lathe-nose. It is, however, quite impossible to cut
a full thread in a "no thoroughfare" hole with
one tap only, and in consequence of the depth of
the thread usually used for a lathe nose, it is inex-
pedient to cut out a perfect thread by the aid of
taps alone. Therefore, instead of taps a comb screw-
tool is used to cut out the bulk of the material to
form the thread. To use this screw-tool requires a
good deal of practice, but by starting a true thread
by means of a tap, and carefully following up
the spiral scratch made by it with the chaser or
comb, the thread will be cut out with tolerable
truth. Any slight error will be easily rectified
by the full tap when that is put into the hole.
Those who are already provided with taps and
chasers for cutting the threads in their chucks will
not need these details; but as comparatively few

lathe-makers provide these essentials as part of the lathe, it will be advisable to go into minute particulars for making the set of tools requisite for boring and screwing chucks.

With regard to the length of the nose, it is easy to understand that the longer it is the further from the mandrel bearing will the work be, and consequently the more liable to "chatter"; whilst, on the other hand, so long as the nose thread contains enough turns to make it perfectly safe from stripping, there is no other limit to its shortness, providing always that there is enough whereon to screw a chuck. Holtzapffel's and Whitworth's lathes have noses of a length equal to their diameter; and there are scarcely better authorities to be cited on the subject. Having determined so far the proportion of the nose that the chucks are to fit, we will proceed with the description of the tools required for boring and tapping chucks to the $\frac{3}{4}$-inch Whitworth thread.

First a D-bit is wanted to bore out the hole to the exact size required for cutting a full thread, after which must follow the entry-tap. The D-bit will of course be made to bore $\frac{19}{32}$nds diameter. To make this take a piece of cast-steel bar $\frac{5}{8}$ths full by $\frac{5}{16}$ inch, and say 4 inches long. Having softened or annealed this piece proceed to centre one end carefully. Bend the other end over as short and sharp as you can so as to get a good sound centre-punch mark on it, which will allow the bar to run out of true, so that at a short distance from the end

the material will lie all on one side of the line of
centres. Fig. 7 shows the piece of bar chucked
between centres as explained above, A and B being
the centre points, and the dotted lines being the
line of centres. At C, the steel lies all below this
line of centres, and, of course, runs very much out
of truth at that part, so much so that when a cut
is taken along it with the slide-rest, and the diameter reduced to $\frac{16}{32}$nds, the section will form a
semicircle. This will form the cutting part of the
D-bit, the back part of the shank being turned

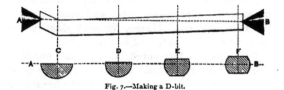

Fig. 7.—Making a D-bit.

down smaller to clear properly, as shown by a
series of sections drawn under the bar. At C is
shown the full-sized part which has to do the
boring. It is turned nearly parallel to the same
size a distance equal to the depth of the hole to be
bored, that will be, allowing $\frac{1}{8}$ inch for clearance,
at the end of the nose, $\frac{7}{8}$ inch. By leaving this part
the exact length, it forms a gauge by which you can
judge of the depth of the hole, and cease boring
when the bit has gone in so far. The remainder of
the bit can be turned parallel, say $\frac{3}{32}$nds or so less
in diameter all the length, and that part, near the

end F, will be fairly flat on both sides, forming a convenient grip for a hand-vice, or hook. When the entire bit has been finished, that part shown to the left of C in the drawing must be cut off, but it is as well to leave just a little piece to form a lip to assist the cutting. Before this end piece with the centre in it is finally cut off, the bit must be smoothed with a superfine file, so that it will bore without tearing away the material. It should also be made to taper very slightly—only a barely appreciable amount is enough, so as to relieve the back part of any cutting, which would be so much unnecessary work, and tend to make the hole tapering. Having finished shaping the D-bit, it must be hardened and tempered.

Two taps will be wanted, an entry and finishing size. Square steel should be used for making these taps, as it is not so liable to warp in the hardening as round steel is. Best cast must be selected, and it may be forged up to shape at a red heat, but on no account must it be overheated or "burnt"; this will spoil the steel, and it had best be thrown on one side at once, for a satisfactory tool cannot be made from burnt steel.

There is not much difficulty in turning down the square stuff in the lathe without any previous preparation, and this will be the best plan when a forge is not easily come-at-able. The length of each tap may be, say, from 3 to 4 inches. For our ¾ Whitworth we shall require one of the rough pieces to be fully ¾ inch, and the other $\frac{11}{16}$ths.

Select two pieces which will finish to these sizes ; centre each quite truly, and test the truth of the centrings before drilling and counter-sinking, then true up the ends. Divide each into three equal lengths, making a nick at each division with a file. That end which is to be the square part of the tap, on which the wrench or spanner will ultimately be placed when the tap is in use, may be left the full size of the square steel, and occupy one-third of the length. The remaining two-thirds will be reduced to $\frac{3}{4}$ inch and $\frac{11}{12}$nds respectively, these being the external diameters of the "full plug" and "entry taps." The method adopted for cutting the thread on the taps is a matter of detail, which will be governed by the appliances at hand. But whenever possible the thread should be cut out very nearly to the full depth by means of a single point tool in the screw-cutting lathe. This ensures a true thread, which is most desirable, though unfortunately not always to be found even on the mandrel nose. Some lathe-makers adhere to a standard size and rate of thread for their lathe noses, which it is in some cases impossible to cut exactly with the ordinary change-wheels. This seems an unaccountable circumstance at first sight, but it is explained by the fact that threads were in extensive use long before screw-cutting lathes were thought of. In the old threads their rate was simply dependent on the caprice of the workman, who had no idea of, or cause to keep in view, a system of aliquot parts when originating a thread.

Thus we find Holtzapffel's threads, which had been
cut before the advent of screw-cutting lathes and
by duplication, have become now almost universal,
are all odd in their rates, and the pitch is usually
given in hundredths of a turn to the inch. For an
example of the irregularity of threads we will cite
those used by Buck, Evans, and Holtzapffel for
their 5-inch lathes.

	Diameter.	Rate.
Holtzapffel . . .	25-32nds.	9·45
Buck	3-4ths.	10·
Evans	13-16ths.	9·5

Whitworth's standard is the one to be recommended in preference to any, as it is comparatively
easy to get any screwing tackle to match his rates;
taps, screw tools, &c., being sold in the tool
shops exactly fitting. The shape of Holtzapffel's
threads differs from Whitworth's, inasmuch as
they are cut with a tool ground to an acute angle,
without any rounding off at all.

The section and elevation of the tap shown in
Fig. 8 is the finishing size, the thread being cut at
the left-hand end to the exact size; so that when
a chuck is tapped with it, it will screw on to the
mandrel nose easily, yet without shake. Chucks
ought to fit too tightly to allow of their being screwed
on with any dirt or metal borings inside the thread.
Most chucks are made so large in the screw that
this is of no consequence, and the result is that
they are screwed on with chips of metal adhering
to the thread, and the chuck is thus made to run

out of truth.   If kept clean, as they must be when
properly fitted, they must always screw home true
to the shoulder, and thus save an immense amount
of trouble.   If a tiny fragment of metal does get
firmly fixed inside the chuck-thread, it can easily
be removed by the aid of the tap, which is the
proper thing to use for the purpose, if a stiff brush
or peg of wood fails ; to mutilate the thread with a
graver or other cutting tool is very bad practice.

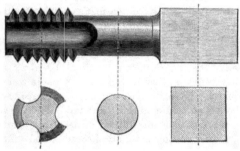

Fig. 8.—Tap for Screwing Chucks.

The length of the screwed part of the tap is just
⅞ inch; so that it screws in to the last turn when
right against the bottom of the hole, bored, as
before directed, ⅞ inch deep.   The round part immediately behind the thread is made to the exact
size of the bottom of the screw, and thus forms a
gauge for the tapping size of chucks.   The square
part is the full size of the steel, from which the tap
is made.   This saves the trouble of reducing the

size by filing, and also gives a larger square to catch hold of. This is convenient in clearing out a chuck, as the large square affords ample grip for the hand, and there is no occasion to use a wrench for that purpose. The sections just beneath the large tap show the shape of it at the thread—the round part—and the square.

The entry tap is precisely similar in shape, only that it is smaller in diameter. The thread is cut to the full depth, and the tap is very nearly parallel. It should have the first two threads filed down on the tops slightly, so as to distribute the amount of work to be done over, say six cutting points. It is a great mistake to leave but one full thread at the commencement to do all the work, as in that case the tap is liable to be made to cut unequally, making a deeper thread at one side of the hole than at the other. If the tap is grooved at three places, then the two first turns of the thread will give six cutting points, and these must be filed down in a series of steps, so that each one does a fair share of the work. This tap is only meant to cut a shallow spiral to guide the comb-screw tool. By this method a true thread—*i.e.*, one which is not drunken—will be originated, and it only requires care on the part of the operator to keep the teeth of the comb in the groove traced by the tap, and a true thread will be maintained till the end, absolute accuracy of parallelism and diameter being insured by the use of the finishing tap, which will also assist in correcting any slight "wobbling" which may be imported into the screw during the chasing by hand.

The illustration Fig. 8 shows the tap to be grooved straight lengthways, and of course these must be made before the taps are hardened. There are several plans for making cutting edges. Semi-circular grooves cut by a circular cutter are perhaps the best, when the necessary tools are within reach. The groove should take up one-sixth of the circumference; there being three grooves, this allows an equal amount of groove and thread. If a milling apparatus is not available, a somewhat similar groove can be cut with a round file, spacing out the divisions by the eye, and filing each groove as nearly equal in size as possible. A better plan is to file them in a spiral direction, making each groove take about half a turn round the tap. This produces a better cutting tool, and the file can be brought to bear on the tap more conveniently in a slanting direction. Some little practice will be required to enable one to make the grooves all of an equal twist and shape, so that the tap will look workmanlike; but so long as the grooves are cut in to a proper depth, there is no necessity to have them all alike, though it improves the appearance. The cutting and back edges must not be left too acute, or they will be liable to be broken off when the tap is in use. The groove should be something like a shallow semicircle in shape.

Having described the method of making the taps and D-bit, we proceed with instructions on their use. Suppose a metal chuck—cast iron, gun metal, or whatever may be the material—is to be fitted, the first operation will be to chuck the casting firmly in the best manner available, according to its shape and the tools or appliances at hand. It should be fixed so as to run as truly as possible and be quite firm, as the process of tapping will strain it very much, and it is very vexatious to get the work thrown out of truth when it is nearly finished. To set it true again is not a difficult job to the experienced hand, but a beginner generally looks upon such a mishap as almost a death-blow to his symmetrical work; therefore, secure the casting so that it will be immovable, and yet not strained to be distorted. Having the casting firmly chucked, and running as true as possible, proceed to face up the shoulder surface all over. The best plan to do this will be first to turn out a sort of counter-sunk hollow in the centre, by means of the graver and hand-rest; then to use the slide rest to turn the face flat.

Probably two or three cuts will suffice to produce a level surface, the last cut being made as fine as possible to leave a smooth shoulder. Now remove the slide rest, and with the graver carefully run a centre to take the point of a drill, say about $\frac{1}{4}$ inch or $\frac{3}{8}$ inch diameter; start the drill truly, and bore down to the depth required for the hole, which will be $\frac{7}{8}$ths of an inch. This small hole having been drilled, it must next be enlarged to a size approaching that of the D-bit. The methods of enlarging are numerous, and the one selected must be left to the workman, who will best know which suits the circumstances of his particular requirements. A small inside or boring tool may be fixed in the slide-rest, and the hole enlarged by this means. This plan is particularly suitable. If the boring has run much out of truth when drilling the first hole, it will be necessary to exercise caution in using a fine tool, such as the limited dimensions of the hole will demand, more especially in getting to the end of the cut at the bottom of the hole, as should the tool be allowed to go but a trifle too deep it will dig in and probably break off. After some little experience with these tender tools they will be found to work well, and a breakage will be of very rare occurrence. Another way of enlarging the hole will be by means of another and larger drill put in to follow the first; this must be started true by turning a chamfer round the edge of the hole to fit the end of the drill. If the first hole has gone in pretty fairly true, the second will follow about the same; but of course if the first hole is crooked, the second drill will not make it straight. This plan must not be adopted if the original hole has run much out of truth in drilling, but instead of a drill a D-bit may be used, and this, if started true, will bore true, without regard to the previous boring; so probably this will be the tool most generally suited to the work.

The D-bit made specially to bore the exact size for tapping is not the tool now meant, but a simi-

G

lar one which bores somewhat smaller in diameter. It would be quite possible—in fact easy—to put this full-sized D-bit in immediately following the small drill ; but to save the tool and ensure greater accuracy, it will be best to only leave a light cut to be taken by this finishing-size D-bit.

The full depth will be accurately determined by this D-bit, which will also cut the bottom out quite square. This is an important consideration, as the points of the drills would leave it very much coned. For many other purposes it is advantageous to have a hole bored with a flat bottom. Numerous instances occur throughout this treatise where explanations that are given with the details applied, more especially for some particular work, may be construed to suit various other processes of an analagous nature. It is easy to fix a collet on to the shaft of the D-bit to form a gauge and prevent the bit boring to too great a depth. This expedient is not necessary when the tool is used by a practised hand, who sees at a glance when the desired depth has been attained. Any slight mark upon the shank of the bit serves as an indication by which to work.

When the hole is bored out to a trifle over $\frac{1}{4}$ inch the finishing D-bit is brought into requisition, and the hole bored to exact diameter and depth, as before described. The next operation, though it is often dispensed with altogether, should be to undercut or turn a ring round the bottom end of *the hole to* the diameter of the outside of the thread.

This groove must be made with an L-shaped slide-rest tool; the breadth is immaterial, about an eighth to three-sixteenths of an inch being the most convenient. The object of this groove is to allow the comb-screw tool, which is used to cut out the thread with, to cut to its proper depth at the inner end, and in fact makes the short hole almost like a thoroughfare for the tool in working, thus conducing greatly to the parallelism of the thread. If the end is not undercut it is practically almost impossible to cut a parallel hole with a hand comb-screw tool. It will be readily understood that, in order to make proper fitting chucks, absolute parallelism of the threads, both in the lathe-nose and in the chucks, is of paramount importance. The sections of chucks show how the thread should be made, being the sectional view of a chuck cut in two diametrically. At the extreme depth of the hole is shown the undercut groove to the full size of the thread.

When the comb-chaser is used, its first tooth will always be felt to pass over the solid metal into the space. Thus every trip will be made all along the thread and not be discontinued at irregular places more or less distant from the bottom, thereby making, of necessity, a conical thread or rather one which is not cut out to a sufficient depth at the bottom part of the hole. The first turn of the thread is shown turned away in all the cuts. This is the best plan to ensure the chuck screwing right home to its shoulder, as it is not possible to get the thread on the mandrel-nose fully cut up against its shoulder.

Sometimes the nose has a groove turned in it close against the shoulder, to allow the chucks to screw up without having the first thread removed. But this is not a commendable system, as it weakens the nose very much at its normally weakest place, which is both undesirable and unnecessary; whereas the removal of the first thread in the chuck has no detrimental effect whatever, and does not practically weaken the chuck in the least.

To return to the screwing process. Having cut out the groove at the back, proceed to start the thread with the small entry tap. Bring the back centre up to support the tail-end of the tap, and ensure its being square with the hole. Hold the square with a spanner or wrench, which may rest against the bed of the lathe to prevent rotation of the tap, and with one hand on the lathe pulley draw it round, the other hand being kept on the back centre winch, so as to keep the point up to its bearing against the tap. By this means the tap will easily be run in to the bottom of the hole, the usual lubricants being used as in ordinary tapping; and on withdrawing the tap there will be a perfectly true spiral thread traced on the inside of the hole. This thread will not be deep, but if the points of the thread on the tap exactly match the points of the teeth of the comb-screw tool, it will be found comparatively easy to follow the shallow spiral with the hand tool, and cut out the thread as true as it was originated by the tap.

Details of the use of the comb-chaser are given in another chapter, and we will suppose that the thread inside the chuck has been cut out fully by that tool. There should, however, still be an appreciable amount to be removed by the tap itself, otherwise there will be no certainty of the fit being accurate. By accurate, a tight fit is not what is meant, but simply a fit which does not allow an unconscionable amount of shake, or permit of a quantity of extraneous dirt being collected in the threads, without causing inconvenience. The tap is used expressly to ensure each chuck being exactly alike in the thread; and of course its object would be defeated if the hole was made too large by the comb-chaser. It seems superfluous to add that the tap must be made of the exact size to tap the chucks to fit the lathe nose exactly. Having completed the thread so far, the first turn or so must be cut away to allow the chuck to shoulder up properly. The best plan is to bore out the thread to a depth of about $\frac{1}{8}$ inch, the full size of the exterior diameter. This can be done with a tool in the slide-rest, and then just taking off the sharp edges with a round-nosed tool by hand. An ordinary chamfer made by means of a graver, cut in at an acute angle, is a very generally adopted method, but not so good as the one first indicated. The thread in the chuck being now finished, it may be screwed on to

the nose of the lathe, and if it shoulders up fair,
and the nose and shoulder of the lathe are true,
the thread and shoulder face of the chuck, in which
the casting is fixed, will run perfectly true also;
but if the nose is " drunken," or the shoulder out of
flat, this will not be the case. Unfortunately the
generality of lathe-noses are defective — either
drunken, crooked, or out of true—and the same
may be said of the shoulders. These defects make
the labour of fitting chucks far more tedious and unsa-
tisfactory, as it is impossible to make a true thread
and true shoulder match an untrue mandrel and fit;
and the difficulty is only increased if *both* chuck and
lathe are untrue. The only plan open for fitting an
untrue nose is to make the chucks considerably
larger in the thread than would be a " fitting" size,
and thus by allowing plenty of shake the chuck,
mandrel, and shoulder are brought together,
forming a " general" bearing, which will be of a
more or less lasting character, according to the
magnitude of the error in the nose. When fitted,
the chuck should go right up against the shoulder,
and take an equal bearing all round. This will
easily be seen on examining the chuck which will
show any points of specially hard contact. Some
people advise that these—what they term " high
parts " of the chuck—should be filed down so as to
allow the other parts to come into contact; but
this is an erroneous idea if the chuck is turned flat
on its shoulder bed. The proper way would be to
correct the lathe nose itself; but this is a job few

would care to undertake, as it involves processes but little used in the general run of workshops.

The method adopted will be dependent on the chief source of error, whether the shoulder of the nose or the thread itself is most out of true; also if the mandrel is hard—*i.e.* too hard to be turned by a graver—or soft enough to be turned true with a hard tool. If the shoulder is out of flat and quite hard, it is best made true by means of a copper lap, running in a drilling spindle and fed with emery. This is driven very rapidly, and the mandrel is revolved at the same time very slowly; thus the high points are soon ground down to a common level and the face of the shoulder made flat and square. This operation will throw all previously fitted chucks out of flat entirely, and they will all have to be turned up true afresh. Some chucks will not stand this, and would therefore be quite useless. If there is already a quantity of chucks fitted to the lathe, it is not very advisable to attempt any correction of the nose; but if a lot of new chucks are to be made, by all means start operations by truing the shoulder and thread as far as possible, making the thread parallel and reducing the length, if necessary, to equal the diameter.

CHAPTER VIII.

VARIOUS USEFUL CHUCKS DESCRIBED.

The point-chuck—The prong-chuck—Different forms of drill-chucks —Taper screw-chucks—Face-chucks—Cup-chucks with three and four screws—Die-chucks with single pairs and movable dies— The four-jaw face-chuck.

THE various chucks used on the lathe are of almost endless variety, and it is here only intended to describe those which are the most useful of the several classes into which they are divided, according to the special uses to which they are most applicable. Appended to the descriptions which follow is a brief indication of the purposes for which the chucks are used. Some chucks are almost duplicates of others that are shown, it being sometimes useful to have a choice of tools for doing some particular work. From the illustrations and details accompanying them, the construction will be made sufficiently explicit to enable the turner to make such chucks for his own use. It is advisable to here point out that chucks will only run absolutely true on one mandrel-nose ; they cannot be used indifferently on other lathes if truth is required. For this reason it is obvious that turners must make their own chucks, or, at least, that these must be turned on the lathe to which they belong.

The chucks that are commonly supplied with a plain lathe by the maker will occupy the first place. They comprise a point-chuck, a prong-chuck, a drill-chuck, and a taper screw-chuck. These will now be described in the order given. These four

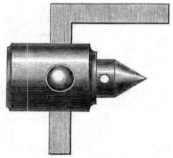

Fig. 9.—Elevation of Point-Chuck.

chucks, at least, should be fitted to the lathe before attempting to undertake any job in the shape of general turning; they are each one useful, and when the range of work is of any extent will require to be supplemented by the addition of other chucks described further on.

The point-chuck, also called a driver, a running-centre, or a take-about-chuck, is shown in Figs. 9 and 10; it is used for metal rods always supported

at the other end by the back-centre. Work turned
by this chuck is said to be turned between centres,
and on account of the facility with which work can
be mounted on the lathe in this manner it is the

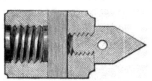

Fig. 10.—Section of Point-Chuck.

one always adopted
when the nature of
the object to be
turned allows it.
The point shown in
the chuck can be re-
placed by one hol-
lowed out to receive
a pointed piece of work. This form, called a
female centre, is used by clockmakers, who turn
all their arbors with pointed ends. Engineers
use the male centre as shown, and centre their
work with a centre-punch. Large lathes usually
have the centres fitted into the mandrel itself,
which is drilled up for that purpose; this keeps the
centre near to the bearing, an advantage that will
be appreciated from what has been said on page 20.
In this case a circular disc of metal, invariably cast
iron, is screwed on to the mandrel-nose, and has a
short, straight driving-pin screwed into it to catch
the tail of the carrier. Usually two or more holes
are drilled and tapped for the pin, at different
radial distances, so that it may be shifted to suit
the work. A modification of this form is used
instead of the one here illustrated, and forms a
stronger chuck, and easier to make, though it is
not so generally employed.

The prong-chuck is used for turning wood supported by the back-centre. This chuck is illustrated in Fig. 11, and is made with the central pip turned true, and the two edges are bevelled from the back only, so as to make them like a carpenter's chisel; thus the two edges do not form a straight diametrical line, as they would if bevelled from both sides. This latter shape is more likely to split the wood, and besides does not hold so firmly as the form first described. The central pip keeps the work central, and the prongs carry it round. The central point must run true, so that if removed the work can be replaced true. To use the prong-chuck the work is put with its centre against the point, and by blows of a mallet driven on sufficiently for the prongs to enter the wood. The poppit-head is then brought up and the centre-point screwed into the centre of the work to support it. Several modifications of the prong-chuck are to be met with, but the form illustrated is the best.

Fig. 11.—Elevation of Prong-Chuck.

The drill-chuck generally supplied is like Fig. 12, without the nozzle, with a steel clamping screw to bite the drills. This is a very good form for large-size drills, say those made from half-inch stuff and upwards, but for facility in changing the drills it is better to use chucks shaped like Fig. 13.

Separate nozzles may be made to fit in the plain chuck first figured, but these are shown as solid pieces of steel driven into cast-iron chucks, so as to be complete in themselves, and consequently

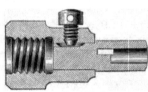

Fig. 12.—Section of Drill-Chuck, with Clamping Screw and Parallel Nozzle.

stronger and less liable to run out of true. The first nozzle is bored with a parallel hole, and the cross mortice is made at the bottom of the hole, all on one side of the diameter. The drills are fitted parallel into the hole, and have half the diameter filed off at the end to form a piece to project into the mortice hole. In some cases the mortice is cut in the form of a slot from the side, which saves trouble, but weakens

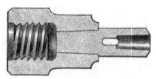

Fig. 13.—Section of Drill-Chuck, with Taper Nozzle.

the chuck by depriving it of the support afforded by the metal shown above the mortice in the figure. The second nozzle is bored out with a taper D-bit, and has the mortice hole cut diametrically across. The drills are fitted tapering, and have flats filed at the end on diametrically opposite sides, leaving a flat piece to enter the mortice hole, where it cannot turn. With the taper socket the drills are wedged in quite tight, and cannot come out of the chuck, as they sometimes do with parallel fitting. For this reason it is to be preferred ; another advantage is that the centre of the drill is preserved. In order to get the drills out it is necessary to use a lever behind the tail of the drill, which projects into the mortice hole. Several drill-chucks, or, at least, nozzles, are wanted to suit different-sized drills, though usually only one is supplied with the lathe. Drill-chucks having a square hole are sometimes used, but, except that they carry any of the square-shanked drills and bits belonging to the carpenter's brace, they are not to be recommended. Though it is as well to point out that the tools fitted to a brace are intended to cut the same way as lathe-cutters, and consequently may be used in the lathe in the ordinary way.

Fig. 14.—Elevation of Taper Screw-Chuck.

The taper screw-chuck shown in Fig. 14 is useful for the purpose of turning wood used plankwise, if a central hole may be made for the screw to enter. Any wooden disc may be fitted to this chuck by boring a hole for the central screw and screwing it into the wood ; this on coming against the face of the chuck will lie fairly flat, and the edge and face may be turned with facility. To hold large discs of beech for chucking work to the taper screw-chuck will be found very useful. The screw itself is made of steel, and ought to be cut with a specially-made chaser, for if the ordinary comb screw-tool is used to cut the cone the thread will be inclined very much, and its hold on the material considerably reduced.

In addition to those already named, plain wooden chucks are generally fitted by the turner himself; these are simply pieces of hard wood, box being much used, screwed to the lathe-nose, as has been described in the previous chapter. They are employed principally to hold work which has been turned true, and may be held by its edge in a recess cut in the face of the wood. For large work beech plank screwed on the taper screw-chuck and turned true is used. The ease with which partially-finished work may be chucked perfectly true, and firmly held without damage, is the great recommendation to wood chucks; also, they are inexpensive, but in use are continually being turned away to fit fresh work, and consequently are lost in shavings. Chalk rubbed on to the edge of the wood which is to hold the work materially increases its bite. As the nose-thread in a wood chuck is liable to be torn out they are often fitted on to a metal flange somewhat resembling Fig. 14, the wood being secured to it by ordinary joiners' screws put through holes in the flange.

A face-chuck is very useful for holding many

kinds of work of irregular form that sometimes
cannot be chucked in any other way. The face-
chuck, also called face-plate, is usually of cast iron,
and as large as the lathe will allow; some have
numerous holes drilled in them, through which
bolts pass to hold the work; in others these holes
are all tapped, and the bolts screw into them.
Some have radial slots, allowing the bolts to slide
to any required distance from the centre. Dogs
and clamps are used with the face-plate, and the
work is laid on it and secured by clamping to its
face, which must always run perfectly true or flat.
Without back-gearing it will be found very difficult
to turn up the surface of a cast-iron chuck the
entire diameter that the lathe will take, but the
face-chuck is so useful for many and indispensable
for some purposes that one should always be fitted
to a lathe intended for general engineering work.
Castings for such chucks are sold by many founders,
it being only necessary to specify the diameter
required when ordering. The clamps used for
holding work to face-chucks should be packed up
at the back end slightly higher than where they
come in contact with the work, or they have a
tendency to force the work away from the holding-
down bolt. In cases where the turning of an
object subjects it to much strain a stop must be
fixed to the face of the chuck to prevent the work
turning. The clamps are not adapted for this purpose, and are only intended to hold the work
against the surface-plate. When the weight of the

objects is much out of balance a counterpoise weight must be bolted on to the chuck; this will check the vibration which in unbalanced work precludes the possibility of satisfactory results.

Cup-chucks fitted with screws to clip the work are employed principally to hold short objects, such as nuts or short rods which are too large to

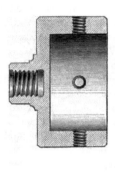

Fig. 15.—Elevation of Cup-Chuck.   Fig. 16.—Section of Cup-Chuck.

go in a grip-chuck. Cup-chucks may be of from 1 to 6 inches internal diameter, and are fitted with three, four, six, or eight screws. The woodcut, Fig. 15, shows one having four screws; if only three were used they would be spaced equidistant, and the work is more easily adjusted if held at three points of contact. Six and eight screws are arranged in two circles, and the screws in one are placed intermediate to those in the other. The object to be held in the chuck is gripped by the points of the screws, and these can each be screwed in as required to centre the work. The projecting screws are often apt to be in the way and cause damage, and their points badly mark the work ; these circumstances are somewhat of a drawback to the use of screw cup-chucks. The construction of cup-

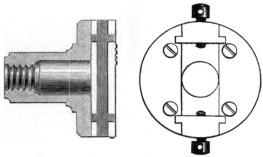

Fig. 17.—Section of Die-Chuck.   Fig. 18.—Front end of Die-Chuck.

chucks is best shown by Fig. 16, a sectional view of Fig. 15.

Grip-chucks are used for holding all kinds of rod-metal, and one with changeable dies, shown in Figs. 17 and 18, is a most serviceable addition to any lathe, and almost indispensable for many things. Though there is more work in its manufacture than in those with only one pair of dies, yet the extra labour is more than compensated for by the convenience and extra range of this chuck. The body

H

nearly the full size that the lathe will carry.   For all
work beyond the range of the previously described
die-chuck the jaw-chuck with its four jaws moved
by independent screws comes in useful, often serving advantageously in the place of the face-plate.
A minute description would occupy more space

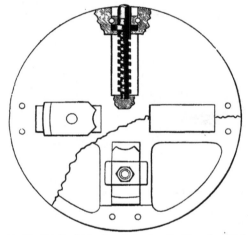

Fig. 20.—Four-Jaw-Chuck: top, Screw in elevation, Chuck in section; left, front
of a Jaw; right, Slot without Jaw; bottom, rear side of Chuck, showing Fillets
and a Jaw.

than can be here allowed, but from the drawing,
which shows details of the principal fittings, the
construction will be sufficiently clear to answer the
purpose of a working drawing in the hands of a
practical man.   The diameter of this chuck should
be as large as possible, and the jaws must not be too

long, or there will be a certain size that cannot be gripped, because it is too small for the stepped part, and too large for the points when opened to their fullest. The jaws, one of which is shown in section at Fig. 21, are made from solid forgings, and must be properly case-hardened.

It is most important that the washers placed on the back of the dies should bear against the casting, or the dies themselves will be twisted upwards directly they are brought against anything to be held.

Fig. 21.—Section of Dog belonging to Four-Jaw-Chuck.

With these principal chucks we must content ourselves; they will be found equal to dealing with most work usually found, and modifications of the various kinds will suggest themselves should occasion require.

CHAPTER IX.

SLIDE-RESTS.

THE slide-rest may be fitted to any lathe and at once greatly enlarges the scope of the tool, as by its aid much work, quite impossible to execute by hand, may be turned easily. Material that is very much out of truth, through being chucked eccentrically or being of irregular form, only reaches the turning tool at intermittent times, and under these conditions it is not easy to hold a tool by hand, so that it acts properly. But in the properly fixed slide-rest a tool is held perfectly rigid and acts equally well on work already made perfectly true, or in turning down only the extreme angles of a square rod chucked between the centres, this latter operation being almost beyond the reach of a hand turner. All work which has a break in the continuity of its cylindrical surface is difficult to turn with hand tools, unless it can be revolved at a very great speed, as may be proved by trying to

true up the teeth of a coarse pitched cast-iron wheel
with a graver. This is intended only as an instance, as such a job would be executed by means
of a file resting against a bar held in the slide-rest.
In turning a parallel cylinder by hand, considerable care and constant gauging is requisite to reduce the material sufficiently and yet guard against
cutting too deep at some part. With a slide-rest
there is no need of such care, for when once properly adjusted a perfectly true and parallel cylinder
or cone is produced by simply feeding the tool up
to the work, and even this is often done automatically.

Slide-rests are of different forms to suit special
purposes. That most generally used for metal turning or miscellaneous work consists of one slide at
right angles to the bed and fixed to it by a bolt at
any suitable place, as in the hand-rest. On the
saddle of this slide another one is fitted at right
angles to the lower one, and on its saddle is an
arrangement for holding the tools used for
turning.

Ornamental slide-rests are made differently. They
usually have one long slide which has a stem at
its centre and fits into a sole like the T-rest sockets;
this allows of the rest being placed at any desired
angle with the line of centres or parallel to the face-
plate. It will be noticed that when this main slide
is in its two positions the end which takes the
winch-handle is reversed, and the leading screw
should therefore have a corresponding projection

at each end, so as to allow the handle to be placed indiscriminately on either.

It is desirable to fit the handles so that they may be removed from one end to the other without trouble; a plain square fitting is the best, made very slightly tapering, so that the handle will wedge on tight enough to remain during manipulation, as it is excessively annoying to have the handle continually dropping off through the vibration of the rest when using overhead gear. A plain milled head fitted to the square is very handy for actuating the screw in special work, and if the screws of both top and bottom slide have their terminations squared off to the same gauge, as they should be, the handles become interchangeable.

The bottom slide, which is the longest, should allow the saddle to travel along a distance about equal to the diameter of the largest face-plate the lathe will carry—that is, double the height of centres. The sole of the rest must be fitted to slide at right angles to the lathe-bed, so that the slide may be placed at any desired distance from the centres, according to the diameter of the work to be operated upon. By these means the top slide may be very short, it being merely required to set in the cut of the tool after it has been placed roughly in position and the slide-rest set fast by means of the main bolt.

There are several ways of fitting the sole to slide squarely; it may be planed up true, and run between two bearers of a saddle fitted to the lathe-

bed, but the most simple plan is to have the dovetail groove planed quite true and fit a piece of iron
to it exactly, the continuation of this iron below
the under surface of the sole-plate being fitted to
the lathe-bed between the bearers. Each piece of
fitting should be as long as convenient to afford
greater bearing surface and consequently accuracy
of adjustment. The whole piece, which may be
either of cast or wrought iron, would appear like a
cross when seen from above, and the two cross
pieces, being on different planes, showing like a T
when seen from the side.

The rest may be shifted with the greatest ease,
when the bottom of the sole has a dovetail groove,
as when the bolt is slackened the piece would
run perfectly free, the sole being drawn square
with the bed on tightening down. With a T-shaped
groove it would be necessary to fit the sliding piece
in a rectangular slot, which, besides being a far
more difficult job, would not allow the freedom in
shifting as above mentioned.

The top slide of an ornamental rest is usually
actuated with a lever instead of a screw, which
enables the operator to throw the tools in and out
of cut more quickly. A leading screw is generally
fitted also, which may be used if occasion requires.
For ornamental work, stops, to confine the travel
of the slides, are requisite to ensure the equality
in length of longitudinal grooves and flutings.
Though it is possible to execute work with tolerable
precision without the aid of these stops, yet they

become almost indispensable to insure absolute accuracy, and are sure preventives against going too far. The general method of holding tools in an ornamental rest is in a rectangular slot to which they are accurately fitted.

It is comparatively seldom that one finds two slide-rests—one for plain metal-turning and the other for ornamentation—belonging to the same lathe, one rest being usually so modified as to suit the requirements of the general run of work.

Tool-holders for clamping the tools in the slide-rests are made in various shapes. The form used in ornamental rests is mentioned elsewhere. For heavy work the chief consideration is that the tools will be held firm, and that they may be fixed in any position on the rest for boring or turning the outside of a cylinder and at any intermediate angle. This is best secured by having the tool-holder to revolve freely on a central stud, or, as is often done, the holder is itself a stud which turns freely in the top plate and has a transverse mortice for the tool to pass through ; the single screw, which clamps the tool, also fixes this stud at the same time. It is advisable to make the tool-holder so that it will take a square bar, the centre of which will come to the height of the lathe centres. The importance of this will be better understood on reference to the drilling spindle described in another chapter.

It is essential for all purposes that the rest should be perfectly rigid under ordinary usage, and that the slides should work quite parallel and true with the lathe centres when the rest is tightened down on the bed. There must be a fair range of traverse in the slides, so as to allow the tool to be applied to an average surface of work without the necessity of shifting the entire rest by moving it on the lathe-bed. For ornamental work, with the drilling apparatus, fly-cutters, and such tools in the slide-rest, and the division plate in use, it is very convenient, and in fact almost necessary, to be able to throw the tool in and out of cut readily, and quickly to replace it with accuracy to the same setting for the next cut ; a lever handle, as before mentioned, is indispensable for this purpose.

In metal-turning or plain work this lever becomes highly objectionable, as it necessitates the undivided attention of one hand at a time when both may be required to actuate the lathe or perform some work in other ways. A leading screw working in a nut and having a fixed lateral bearing therefore becomes requisite in order to afford greater facility in handling. Consistent with the primary consideration—rigidity—a slide-rest may be made as light as possible for elegance in appearance.

The accuracy of the work produced by a slide-rest will depend very much on the way in which this is fitted, and it is therefore necessary that rests should be properly constructed, with all the parts adjusted to each other, the slides level with the lathe-centres and fitting evenly the whole length of

their travel without shake; the strength of the
parts being so proportioned that the whole structure will be quite rigid.

In a self-acting screw-cutting lathe the slide-rest
is fitted to slide on the bed itself, and is moved
along by the leading screw of the lathe usually
extending the whole length of the bed, the nut in
which this engages being split and actuated by a
cam under the control of the turner, who can
disengage the nut from the screw at any time in-
stantaneously, and so arrest the motion of the rest
along the bed without stopping the lathe. Such a
rest fitting on a dovetail slide cannot be removed
from the bed entirely, but may be slid to any convenient place along its length.

The screws used to actuate the slides are called
leading screws; there is no rule as to their size and
pitch, and right and left-handed threads are equally
effective; so also square and angular threads may be
used indifferently. For coarse pitches of small diameter, square threads make a stronger screw than
angular ones. For rate of thread a good proportion is ten to the inch for a 5-inch lathe. Relative
to the adoption of right and left-handed screws
there seems to be much diversity of opinion, and
makers do not seem to agree on the subject. Some
put both screws right-handed, some, though less
often, put left-handed, and some, amongst whom
are numbered the best, put one left and one right-
handed leading screw to the slide-rest. The only
object in having them this last way is to afford the

operator the convenience of producing similar results by similar motions of the handles.

By standing at a slide-rest and making the experiment, it will be found that on turning the two handles in the same direction the motion is really in opposite directions. Supposing both handles of the slide-rests to be in their highest position, on pushing from you the one which is parallel the screw is turned towards the right; when the other handle at right angles to the bed is pushed away the screw is turned towards the left, so that in turning the two handles away from you they really turn in opposite directions.

Therefore, in order to make the same apparent motion produce the same actual effect, a left-handed screw is put in for the top slide, while a right-handed one is used for the bottom one; and though no absolute advantage is gained, yet it is very convenient. In all cases the back centre should be actuated by a screw of the same rake as the one in the top slide, so that motion of the handles in the same direction will produce like results. When the top of the slide-rest and the poppit barrel are actuated by reverse screws, the effect is very embarrassing, so that these two screws had best correspond, whether they be right or left.

The nuts for leading screws may be of wrought iron, brass, gun metal, or almost anything similar; gun metal works more smoothly, and if attention is paid to lubrication will last as long as required. The nuts need not be screwed on to the under

sides of the saddles ; .they may be just let into a
hole drilled for the purpose, a round tail being
turned on each nut to fit. The lateral motion of
the leading screws has to be prevented ; they are
usually fitted with bearings in the respective slide
castings, and to stop endway movement of the
screws when actuating the saddles several methods
are made use of, each having its special claims.

One good plan is to reduce the diameter of the
end of the screw for a length just exceeding the
thickness of the casting, and fit this part in the
hole, allowing it to project say the eighth of an
inch ; a steel washer has to be fitted on to the projecting part so that it cannot turn round indepen-
dently of the screw. A small hole is drilled up the
centre of the screw end ; this hole is tapped, and a
screw fitted with a large head, sufficient to take a
good bearing against the washer, and so keep it in
its place, that is, firm against the casting. When
a plate is put on, as described lower down, to take
the thrust of the screw, the boss cannot well be
used as a divided head, which is often very desirable, and this is why a nut on the rear end of the
screw is preferable. In another plan a boss is left
at the handle end of the screw ; this bears against
the casting, and at the other end a nut is screwed
with a washer fitted on hexagonally, and both are
let into a countersunk hole in the casting, prevent-
ing the screw from being withdrawn. The boss on
the screw may be made to go into a countersink
with its thrust bearing against a small plate held

on by two screws; the other end of the leading
screw is turned down to form a pivot the size of the
diameter of the bottom of the thread, and fits into
the hole in the casting.

Conical bearings are sometimes made to the
screw, but the wear is so very slight that there is
no need for this. Providing the screw is carefully
and well fitted in the first instance, it will last out
the other parts of the rest, and therefore conical
bearings may be considered useless. The motion
of the screw without moving the saddle, caused by
slackness in the fittings of the screw in its bearings
and in the nut, called back lash, does not detract
from the slide-rest's utility when applied to its
legitimate purpose, though this back lash is often
a source of much trouble and annoyance. But it
cannot possibly be eliminated entirely without the
use of double screws, or some such costly contrivance.

For turning cones, the upper slide of the compound slide-rest turns so that it may be placed at
an angle with the bed, some rests being arranged
so that the top side may swivel all round, and
others have only a small angular motion, which is,
however, in most cases, sufficient, as cones are not
generally required very obtuse. The ways in which
the angular motion of the side is obtained are
these :—The best plan, which allows the top slide to
be swung round all the way from right angles to
parallel with the bottom side, is managed by
turning a T-shaped groove in the thickness of the

saddle of the bottom slide into which the heads of
the two bolts fit, and consequently the top slide
may swivel round entirely. The more general plan
is to screw the bolts into a hole in the under saddle,
and cut a circular slot on each side of the circular
base plate of the upper slide, extending as far as
the sides of the slide will allow, and in this case
the length of the curvilinear slots determines the
amount of the angular motion of the top slide.

The first-mentioned plan is, of course, the better,
but it involves more work, and turning the T-groove
requires a great deal more care to ensure the depth
being equal on both sides so that the heads of the
bolts will take a fair bearing. It is seldom required
to set over the top slide more than 30° for ordinary
work, and the second plan of slots allows this.
Being easier of construction it is consequently the
more generally adopted. The top slide swivels on
a steel pin, driven tightly into a hole in one casting
(it is immaterial which), the other casting having a
hole carefully fitted to the projecting piece of the
pin, which forms a pivot at the centre of motion.
The fitting of this pin must be accurate, without
shake, otherwise no dependence can be placed on
the angular setting as shown by the index which
is fitted up, as described further on, to show the
angle at which the rest is set.

The best height for the top plate of the rest, on
which the turning tools fix, will depend on the size
of steel generally employed for these tools; the
usual size of steel should lie wholly beneath the

centres. In order to determine the point, the most suitable size of which to make the tools must be decided. For a 5 inch lathe, square cast steel $\frac{1}{2}$ inch or $\frac{3}{8}$ inch suits very well; tools for light work and fine cuts to be made from the smaller size, and those for roughing down and heavy work generally to be made from the $\frac{1}{2}$-inch bar. In such a case the tools made from the larger stuff will be all the better for having their ends forged with the point or cutting edge low down, and if this is done to the extent of $\frac{1}{8}$ inch all the tools will be $\frac{1}{2}$ inch above the top of the slide-rest. It is easy to pack up tools by placing strips of metal, such as tin plate, under them, and so adjust the cutting edge to its precise point, that is, on the line of centres. Allowing $\frac{1}{16}$ inch for this, the top saddle will be $\frac{9}{16}$ inch below the centres; this is the correct distance for a 5-inch lathe.

When a slide-rest is put to a lathe, the first object is to get it fitted quite true with the line of centres, and the bottom slide must have attention first. The leading screw is removed from the lower slide and the face-plate screwed on the lathe-nose. A centre punch or stiff scribing point is wedged into a hole near the edge of the face-plate, and a flat pointed tool is fixed in the slide-rest. When the lower saddle is at the two extreme ends of its slide, and the point in the face-plate at the near and far side of the lathe, the tool in the rest must just touch it, and will thus show whether the slide is perfectly parallel with the face-plate and at right

I

angles with the bed. Should the slide be at an
angle, the contact of the points will at once show
it, and the bottom of the rest must be filed to bring
it right. The lower slide finished, the upper one is
next treated in a similar manner, using a bar
between the centres with a projecting point in it
instead of the face-plate.

When the two slides are adjusted to the exact
position for turning parallel and flat respectively, a
legible mark should be made to enable the top
slide to be reset at precisely the same angle after
it has been shifted for conical turning. A scale
and index point to show the angular motion of the
slide are sometimes put, and will be found very
convenient. The divisions should always represent
degrees, that is, the 360th part of a circle, or parts
of degrees. Then cones tapering to the amount
required can be turned by setting over the slide-
rest to the necessary distance, and there will be no
need for callipering. The advantages of an index
will best be appreciated when it is required to turn
a cone and a hole for it to fit in. The large end of
the cone will nearly always be towards the mandrel
end, and the hole will be reversed, that is, with
its largest end away from the mandrel. Consequently the slide-rest will have to be set at
reversed angles to turn the hole and the plug;
without a scale it will be most difficult to set the
rest at angles which correspond precisely. In
making such an index the divisions are usually
marked upon the saddle of the slide, and the point

is fixed by a couple of screws to the circular base-plate of the top slide. This point may be itself fixed to read correctly for turning parallel with the index at o°. The best plan for ease in reading is to make the index with a flat end about $\frac{1}{4}$ inch wide, with a line marked in the centre to read against the scale lines, as it is much easier to distinguish the continuity of a line than the position of a pointer with respect to a line.

Spherical slide-rests are sometimes used for producing, but chiefly for ornamenting spherical surfaces; they are seldom met with except on ornamental lathes of the highest class used by amateur turners. The circular motion is produced by fitting a worm wheel and tangent screw to the base of the slide, which is then turned round by means of a handle in precisely the same direction as it would be for conical turning. There are many other additions necessary for the proper use of a spherical slide-rest, and owing to its complicated construction further details would be of little use unless an elaborate description was given, and that would not be within the scope of the present treatise.

The slide-rest is the receptacle for various kinds of apparatus used for wheel-cutting and for shaping material which is held by the mandrel; some of these are described in other chapters. The tools proper consist of square bars of steel having one and sometimes both ends formed into cutters; these solid tools are used for roughing down work and the general run of turning. For special cutters shaped for particular purposes, or those used in certain ways, tools called slide-rest cutter-bars are used. These are bars similar to the ordinary tools with ends shaped to hold small cutters, which may be made with much less trouble than the solid tools mentioned above.

A slide-rest should be strong enough at all parts not merely to resist absolute breakage but to maintain perfect rigidity under the wear and tear of a heavy cut. Several items have to be taken into consideration when judging the strength, or rather inflexibility, of a rest. A certain amount of metal is requisite to make a solid tool, but much more depends on the way in which it is fashioned than appears to be generally understood, judging from the clumsy designs which are sometimes made. Good fitting is also essential to the main object in view. A carefully fitted slide-rest, of neat and elegant design, will stand more hard wear and tear than half-a-dozen of some of the clumsy, heavy, badly-proportioned tools thrown in the market by second-rate manufacturers.

CHAPTER X.

SLIDE-REST TOOLS.

Angles suited for various materials—Useful tools for general purposes
—Cranked tools, knife tools, parting tools, spring tools—Tools
for inside turning—Correct height and adjustment necessary.

SLIDE-rest tools are of numerous forms, some the
result of peculiar individual fancy, others made
to meet the exigencies of the work they have to
perform. In the chapter treating of cutter-bars
much information applicable to solid tools will be
found, and these latter it will be seen, by what is
there stated, are to a large extent superseded by
cutter-bars from motives of economy. The solid
tools are, however, very much used, and in small
workshops they generally do the whole of the
work, cutter-bars being probably not introduced
from a notion that their prime cost would not be
warranted by the work that would be exacted from
them, or that the economy would not be commen-
surate with the cost. Solid tools are usually made
of square steel, though that of varying rectangular section is sometimes used, without any apparent object, however, unless in the case of tools
of particularly broad or narrow width. Cast steel

of special quality should be always used, as the
ordinary material is not adapted to stand the work
required of a slide-rest tool.

The size of the steel used will be determined
according to the height of the slide-rest plate, as
explained on page 113; the length used is optional,
so long as it is sufficient to leave enough shank to
be clamped under the tool-holder. Some tools are
made with each end formed into a cutter, and thus
the number of available cutting edges is doubled
without increasing the number of tools.   This
plan is one that finds little favour, though in some
forms of tool nothing can be said against it.   For
example, screw tools for the slide-rest are always
made with the comb at both ends, they also being
usable either side up.   Tools that are cranked, if
made double ended, must have the cranks at right
angles or on opposite sides, as otherwise the tool
cannot be laid flat on the top of the slide-rest.

The angles best suited for the particular material
to be operated upon are most desirable in slide-
rest tools, and after having had some experience
with hand tools, more especially as applied to
soft-wood turning, anent which some information
is given in another chapter, the advantage . of
various angles will be appreciated.   It will be
understood that the cutting edge will penetrate
best when it is thinnest; other considerations,
however, prevent the adoption of this rule unre-
servedly; and for metal work tools are found to
act best when the faces form the cutting edge at an

angle of from 60° to 90°. The face of the tool
coming next to the work requires to be ground at
a slight angle, leaving the point prominent to prevent the whole face touching the work, and so by
the friction greatly increasing the labour of turning.
When this requirement is satisfied the face should
be as straight as possible, and 3° from the perpendicular suffices. This applies equally to tools with
acute edges used on wood, though when we come

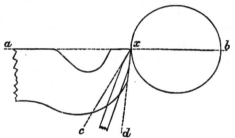

Fig. 22.—Angles of Turning Tools for Wood and Metal.

to knife edges the face of the tool itself usually
rests against the work it has to cut and there
is no angle of clearance.

Fig. 22 herewith shows tools correctly applied
for cutting both wood and steel. By this it is
seen that the slide-rest tool, with a strong cutting
edge suited to dividing the cohesive metal, and the
acute wood-turning chisel, each have the lower
face angle placed in the same position with regard
to the work. Therefore it is only the upper face

which wedges back and curls or breaks off the
shaving that is altered agreeable to the different
nature of the materials. The line of centres is
shown dotted *a b*, and at precisely the height of
this line should be the point of the tool fixed in the
rest. Here it may be advisable to point out that
tools must be packed up with parallel strips, otherwise the relative position of the angles is inter-
fered with. The edge of the metal-turning tool is
formed by the meeting of the faces *a x* and *d x* ;
a x being parallel with *a b*, and *d x* 3° from the
perpendicular, gives the angle of the point as 87°.
This is the most obtuse angle usually employed,
though for some purposes where a scraping action
is required the top face is bevelled off downwards
to make the edge even more blunt. The edge of
the soft-wood chisel is formed by the meeting of
the faces *c x* and *d x*, enclosing 25°, still keeping
the lower face situated precisely alike. The tools
might be applied at any part of the circle even
vertically above it, so long as the same relative
position is maintained; but the slide-rest as ordinarily constructed necessitates the application of
the tool on a level with the centres.

The following illustrations give the forms of
slide-rest tools usually made for general purposes.
Fig. 23 is a straightforward cranked tool for outside work, and is perhaps the most widely used
of all. The form affords great strength and facility for grinding. The face forming the top is
usually nearly triangular in section, though the

form at the inner side is determined by the shape
of the forging, and this is sometimes made by
flattening every angle of the square bar, thus
leaving the point, when ground, diamond shaped.
The front faces meet at an angle of about 90° or a
trifle less, and the arris, which comes near the centre
of the bar, is ground away, leaving a slight face
of from $\frac{1}{32}$ to $\frac{1}{16}$ in. wide. This treatment applies
to all slide-rest tools, for if the acute arris is pre-
sented to the work the edge becomes blunted immediately.

Fig. 24 shows a tool of somewhat similar form,

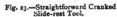

Fig. 23.—Straightforward Cranked   Fig. 24.—Round-nosed Straight-
        Slide-rest Tool.   forward Tool.

though it may be made from a straight bar without
necessitating forging. The face of the cutter is on
a level with the top of the bar, and the metal
behind it is removed to leave a hollow so that there
is less left to grind. This tool is shown with
a semicircular face edge, the form known as round-
nosed, and it is a capital form for real work. The
cranked tool described above may be ground to
the same shape with advantage for certain work.
The two tools, Figs. 23 and 24, are intended for
roughing down plain surface or cylindrical work,
and neither of them will cut into a sharp angle.
Both work from right to left by preference, and the

top face is ground to a slight slope, to leave the left or leading edge a trifle higher. Both may be used in the reverse direction, though in that case the grinding ought to be done accordingly. When such tools are employed indiscriminately in either direction the top surface is ground off square, always, of course, sloping backwards to leave the extreme point highest, and this in accordance with the material to which it is applied.

A left-handed cranked tool is shown next, in Fig. 25. This is very much like Fig. 23, with the point bent sideways, towards the left, so that it is

Fig. 25. — Left - handed Cranked ;Slide - rest Tool.

brought beyond the level of the side of the tool shank; by this means the tool is available for use in the extreme corner of an angle where a cylinder joins a surface. For example, in turning a bolt the front corner would be brought to work on the cylindrical part and the left corner would surface the head. The angle of this point is always less than a right angle, otherwise there would be no clearance and the whole breadth of the edge would be against the work, causing much unnecessary friction; an angle embracing about 80° will be found right. A corresponding tool bent to the opposite side, and called a right-handed cranked tool, is required for working in the reverse direction. Its form is precisely similar, so that no illustration is required; the point is to the right, as Fig. 25 is to the left.

Fig. 26 is a knife-edge side tool used for turning the end surface of a cylinder running between the centres, the form of this tool allowing it to go right up to the point of the poppit head, which the tools hitherto described are not adapted for.   It will be seen that the end of the tool is forged to a narrow blade, and this is ground flat on its face side—that is the one represented as the furthest away in the illustration—but at an angle to clear, and the top and end are bevelled off to form cutting edges.   A corresponding reversed tool for cutting on the left-hand surface of work is sometimes made, but it

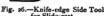

Fig. 26.—Knife-edge Side Tool for Slide-rest.   Fig. 27.—Slide-rest Parting Tool for Metal.

will be readily understood that its use is of most rare occurrence for work on the lathe, though for planing of course both side tools are equally in requisition.

A parting tool for metal is shown in Fig. 27 ; in this the tool is forged with a thin central blade, as shown in the figure, and sometimes, when the width is very slight, it has a much greater depth, occasionally as much as an inch to give the centre tool support.   The length of the blade should be somewhat proportionate to the work it has to do, and it would be absurd to use a blade long enough to part 3-inch stuff for that under an inch in diameter. The tool is ground on both sides, tapering slightly to leave the top edge widest, and the blade must stand accurately upright to be clear of the sides of the groove that it cuts. The front end should be slightly the widest, so that the tool will not rub on its side edges as it proceeds through the work; if quite parallel it will act. Perfect straightness of the blade and its parallelism with the slide by which it is actuated in its forward path are essential. In short, the parting tool, when at work, must cut only with its narrow front edge, which is ground off square; its width may be from $\frac{1}{16}$ to $\frac{1}{8}$ inch, according to the size. Some further information on parting tools is given in the chapter on cutter-bars.

The next illustration shows another tool somewhat out of the usual form; it is called a spring tool, and its object is to present an edge that will to an extent give and take with the irregularities of the work, a property which, despite of all that may be said to the contrary, is a most undesirable one if the object of turning is to produce true cylinders. The form at Fig. 28 places the point of flexure much above the line of centres, and thus when any undue pressure is brought to bear on the edge of the tool it springs from the work, that is, if applied at the exact height of the centres. With a keen edge carefully whetted on an oilstone and a blunt angle, this tool forms a good planisher for long brass rods, but for the most part finishing is done with emery paper on a file. A piece of wood wedged under the spring part will very materially strengthen the tool if less spring is wanted for a special job.

Inside turning with slide-rest tools often takes the place of boring, and *vice versá*, according to the ease with which the work to be operated upon may be mounted on the lathe. The tools used in the slide-rest for this purpose are very similar in their form, and Fig. 29 may be taken as a representative type. The dimensions are varied to suit the size of the hole in which the tool has to go, the size of the tool being generally restricted by that of the

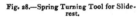

Fig. 28.—Spring Turning Tool for Slide-rest.

Fig. 29.—Inside Turning Tool for Slide-rest.

hole. Referring to the illustration, it will be seen that the shank part is made cylindrical, the length being in accordance with the depth for which the tool is available, short tools being the most rigid, whilst deep holes necessitate the use of long tools. The cutting edge is formed by forging a lip towards the left side of the shank, and this is ground to the form shown, the top face being as nearly as possible on a level with the diametrical centre of the shank. Thus the tool can be introduced into the smallest hole allowable from its size, to cut at the correct height—*i.e.* at the line of centres. The tool shown is intended to cut inwards only, and round-

nosed edges formed like Fig. 24 are useful for
cutting forwards and backwards through a
thoroughfare hole, but are objectionable for holes
that should have a flat bottom, from the circumstances explained in the comments on outside tools
of the same form. With careful usage an inside
tool may be employed of such slight dimensions
that it will bore through a ¼-inch hole 2 inches
deep, and when the depth is not so great the
diameter may be diminished to even less. The
cylindrical part of the shaft of inside tools should
be straight and level, though a slight taper is often
no detriment and strengthens the tool materially.
The projecting lip must be comparatively short, for
all small tools or the leverage it affords will impair
the cutting and spoil the truth of the boring even
if it does not cause a breakage.

As has been shown, it is necessary to apply the
tool to the work at a correct height, or else, no
matter how good and well made it may be, the tool
will fail to perform properly and to the best advantage. A gauge should be made, to be used every
time a tool is fixed in the slide-rest, to test the
height of its cutting point. A plain cylinder or
piece of tube with the ends made perfectly flat, so
that it will stand, and of such a length that when
stood on a particular plane of the slide-rest, or on
the lathe-bed itself, its upper surface is exactly
level with the line of centres, is all that is necessary; and when the tool is finally clamped the
height of its edge should be gauged. The height

is of course adjusted by means of strips of metal; thin bar iron and strips of tin of various thicknesses are best for this purpose, and the gauge is placed in position to afford a guide during this process. The correct adjustment cannot be too strongly urged, and a proper gauge is indispensable. If a tool does not work properly at the correct height, it is sure evidence that it is badly formed; and though a tool may be made to work apparently better above or below the centres, yet in such a position it is at a disadvantage, and should be put right according to the principles explained in this chapter.

CHAPTER XI.

SLIDE-REST CUTTER-BARS.

Advantages over solid tools—Some of those of most general application described—The graver used in the slide-rest—Straightforward tool, parting tool, internal tool—Saving effected by the use of cutter-bars.

In many respects there are advantages in the use of cutter-bars as slide-rest tools in place of the usual form of solid bar steel, in which but a very small fraction of the metal is of any direct use so far as the cutter proper is concerned. The shank of the tool consists of solid metal of the same quality as is the point and cutting edges, and that is invariably the best, and consequently a costly kind. In cutter-bars one shank is used for any number of cutters, just as is the case with boring-bars, and thus only a small piece of metal has to be wrought, hardened, tempered, and ground when a cutter is required. A 6-inch bar of $\frac{3}{8}$-inch square steel, weighing over half a pound, is replaced by an inch length of $\frac{1}{4}$-inch square bar, weighing a quarter of an ounce. In making a dozen of such cutters the saving in metal, which would be a matter of using a quarter of a pound instead of 8 pounds, is only an example of the saving in labour of making, and in the space the finished tools will occupy. As there are no direct advantages in the use of the more expensive tools, the use of cutter-bars has considerably increased. The saving effected by their use in large factories is enormous.

A cutter-bar must be essentially able to hold the cutter perfectly rigid, and so make it, for practical purposes, solid with the bar. In some badly contrived tools this, the chief desideratum, is neglected, and consequently such bars, being of little or no use, are discarded, and gain for cutter-bars, taken as a class, a bad reputation. That the cutters can be removed and replaced with ease and rapidity is, for convenience in use, an important feature, and to this is sometimes sacrificed the firm grip so essential. To the mechanic whose theoretical education has kept pace with his practical experience the arrangement of a thorough firm hold combined with a readily released grip will be easy. The wedge offers a ready and familiar example, and when this contrivance is constructed to be withdrawn easily it is, perhaps, the best of all clamping arrangements, but it requires solid points on which to take its bearings.

Clamping-screws are very good, and if there is sufficient material for a proper allowance of thread, both in respect to diameter and length, then a screw holds firm enough for all things. In cutter-bars, however, the proper size of these parts has usually to be reduced very much, and in many cases

K

the projecting head of a screw is objectionable, if
not absolutely forbidden. Screws applied to draw
parts together and hold the cutters in a vice-like
grip are effective, and when allowable may be used
with most satisfactory results. There are many
ways in which cutters may be held, but they need
not be discussed here; those named will suffice for
the bars of which descriptions are to be given.
The examples are offered as types on which it is
quite possible to effect alterations and modifications to suit special requirements. The illustrations may serve as working drawings to those
desirous of constructing
facsimile tools.

The ordinary graver
used for hand turning
may be fixed in the slide-

Fig. 30.—Slide-rest Cutter-bar, for
holding Gravers.

rest by means of the holder shown in Fig. 30, which
gives a sectional and top view of the arrangement. In
this case the cutter-bar consists of two strips of metal
with an angular groove running lengthwise, into
which the graver fits. The sides of this groove are
inclined so as to bring the tool to the best position
for cutting, which may be best seen in the sectional
view. The angles are 60° and 30° respectively,
making together a right angle fitting the square
tool. The two halves of the bar do not quite come
into contact; they, however, take a fair bearing on
the tool, and are so kept sufficiently rigid for all
practical purposes. In making a bar of this description a piece of metal of double the intended

length, and in section twice as wide as thick, is
selected.   On one side of this the angular groove is
cut from end to end; the bar is then divided in the
middle and the two halves laid one over the other,
as shown in the drawing.   Though the ordinary
graver is perfectly suited for use in this bar, yet
practically it is more economical to use a piece of
square bar steel properly hardened and tempered,
both ends of which may be ground for cutting.
The angle which forms the point should be somewhat rounded off to make
the tool stand better. This
forms an excellent tool for
roughing - down purposes;
and a trial of its capabilities,
which may be easily made
by using hard wood for the
clamping - bar,   generally
leads to the ultimate adop-

Fig. 31.—Slide-rest Cutter-bar,
for straightforward tool.

tion of this form of cutter-bar for the purposes to
which it is specially suited.

A straightforward tool for general purposes is
frequently made as in Fig. 31, which shows a top
and side view.   In this the bar is cranked down at
the end, the metal is split by the saw-kerf terminating in the round hole. The cutter is of triangular
section, one angle forming a point at the end of the
bar. This cutter fits into a groove of corresponding section drifted through the bar at an angle
with its horizontal faces, and the transverse screw,
passing freely through one-half and tapped into

the other, draws the jaws together and grips the
cutter firmly. In the top illustration of Fig. 31 it
will be seen that the cutter has facets ground on
its front faces. From this view it will also be seen
that the height of the cutting edge may be adjusted
by clamping the cutter at the required height, and
thus obviating the necessity of gauging the height
of the tool each time it is put in the slide-rest.
The clamping-bolt has a washer under its head in
the drawing, but this may be dispensed with if
desired.

In parting off metal of large diameter the bar

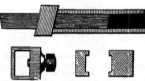

shown in Fig. 32 is
very serviceable, as
in it the blade may
be held as short as
possible to cut
through the work in
hand. This bar is
made by cutting a

Fig. 32.—Slide-rest Cutter-bar, for parting
tools.

groove along the side of a piece of metal bar fitting
the slide-rest; into this groove a strip of cast
steel is fitted, and this forms the cutter. Sections of the bar in the woodcut show the form at
all parts of its length, the smaller section in the
centre being the extreme end reduced, as shown,
to receive the strap drawn on the left. This strap
is put at an angle, as shown in the upper illustration, so that the cutter-blade is supported as far
under the cut as possible. The set screw and form
of the strap is shown by the figure on the left, its

extreme left representing the edge, of which the face is seen in the top figure. In this cutter-bar the blades used may be of different thicknesses, according to the work to which they are applied; the width should always fit the groove accurately. The blades are ground to taper from top to bottom, so as to leave the cutting edge, that is the top, wide enough to cut a channel, in which the lower part is free. The groove in the bar is at a slight angle to keep the blade upright, and to give it a fair bearing; the strap is also shaped slightly angular at that part where the blade comes. It will be readily seen that the blade is drawn out to any desired extent, and there fixed by the set screw in the strap, and thus the length is regulated according to the depth that has to be cut. The blade itself may be tempered far more precisely than if part of a solid tool; and, moreover, the cutting edge may be left much harder than usual by tempering from the lower edge, which by being softened lends toughness and support to the hard cutting edge.

It may not be inappropriate here to point out that when a metal bar is severed by means of a parting tool in the lathe, the channel cut invariably terminates in a square flat bottom, and those who have had experience will know that in such condition the metal is comparatively difficult to break. If the channel ends in an acute angle the metal separates much easier. With this object one end of the blade may be ground to an acute point and

used to make the final cut before breaking, and so
save much labour.   Sharpness of the point is most
important to ensure an easy break.

For internal work, when the hole being operated
upon is of small size, the bar shown in Fig. 33
takes the place of a solid tool of similar outline.
In that the small piece forged up from the solid
to form the cutting-point soon gets ground away in
the sharpening process, and the tool has to go
through the fire again to be made serviceable.   In
the cutter-bar illustrated the bar has a portion of
its length turned cylindrical to a size suited to the

Fig. 33.—Slide-rest Cutter-bar, for inside turning.

usual requirements of such a tool.   Into the end
of this cylindrical part, starting from the diametrical edge, and at an angle of 45°, a hole is drilled,
as shown by the dotted outline in the lower figure;
this hole is made tapering and a flat facet filed on
the bar at its mouth.   Small pieces of cylindrical and
tapering steel are fitted to it, and the ends of these
are fashioned into cutters, as shown in Fig. 33, where
three distinct views are given.   The hole is sometimes made square by drifting and filing and the
cutters of a corresponding section, but a properly
fitted round cone is easier to make and answers

the purpose equally well.   In grinding these cutters it is preferable to hold them in a tool made by
drilling a conical hole in a bar, from which they
project more than when in the cutter-bar itself;
the grinding may then be done with greater ease
and certainty. When a cutter is worn too short
for use it is cast on one side, and a new one that
costs but an inconsiderable fraction for material,
and that may be made in a few minutes, is put in
place of it.

Speaking generally of the four cutter-bars described, it is scarcely necessary to point out the
great saving of material effected by their use; that
is to say, the small cost at which the worn-out tool
can be rendered as new, as compared with a similar
process on the solid tool. Apart from this, each
form of bar has peculiar advantages over the solid
tool that it is intended to replace. Fig. 32 is,
perhaps, the most obvious instance of this, but each
has an advantage. Again, by making numerous
cutters to these bars they are rendered equivalent
to an equal number of solid tools, that is, providing only one is to be used at a time, at a very
small fraction of the cost. For example, three
blades fitted to the parting-tool, Fig. 32—a wide,
a medium, and a narrow one—would make that
tool equal in its range to three solid tools of corresponding dimensions. Small cutters of various
forms adapted to particular purposes, fitted to the
inside tool, Fig. 33, take the place of complete solid
bars. The value of material and workmanship of

each of these would suffice for, perhaps, twenty
small cutters, each of which would be equally
efficacious. A direct saving in the cost of material
is made by using iron for the bars in place of
steel for the solid tools. In most cases good iron
answers all the purposes of a cutter-bar, though
occasionally it is better to use steel; that is, in
cases where the material has to be reduced to small
dimensions, as it would be in Fig. 33 if made to go
into a hole ¼ inch in diameter.

CHAPTER XII.

OVERHEAD GEARING.

Fixed and portable—Single bands and compound gearing—Fixed bars —Swinging bars —Revolving shafting—Screw-cutting by band- gearing—Shape of grooves for the bands.

OVERHEAD gear designates the apparatus rigged up to drive drilling spindles, vertical cutters, and many other appliances of a similar kind. There are innumerable modifications of gearing used, and it would be impossible to give anything like an adequate description even of those commonly employed, the arrangement adopted depending so much on purely local facilities and requirements. Often a wall, ceiling, beam, or other substantial support is available for the attachment of the gear, and such a circumstance should be turned to every possible account. Those lathes which are intended to be easily movable have the overhead gear, if any, fitted to standards rising from the frame of the lathe itself, sometimes cast in one piece with the standards on which the bed rests, though more often made separately and bolted to them. Such supports are somewhat in the way, and their recom- mendation is the fact of their being permanent attachments to the lathe and available for use wherever it may be. Stability necessitates comparatively bulky castings, which obscure the light and in other ways impede the workman in various operations.

Overhead gearing may be divided into two classes : one in which a single band from the fly-wheel, or other source of motion, is led over pulleys to the mandrel it has to drive ; the other in which the band from the source of motion turns a shaft from which another band, occasionally through the intervention of other shafts, goes to the object to be driven. The first method is simple, but admits of comparatively little variety in, and no accurate adjustment in the relative velocity of, the driving and driven pulleys. The second method is more elaborate, and admits of adjustments so fine that screw-cutting, with all the accuracy of a screw-cutting lathe, can be performed by its aid. The process of regulating velocities by means of bands is one that appears to have received very little attention as applied to extremely accurate speeding, but it is a subject well worthy of investigation.

The first class of overhead gear in its most simple form consists of a plain bar of rod iron, fixed paralled to and in a line vertically above the lathe centres. On the bar are fitted two pairs of pulleys, one receiving the band from the fly-wheel, the other leading the band to the cutter. The first pair of pulleys are usually fixed vertically above the

driving-wheel, whilst the second are moved along
the bar to suit the position of the apparatus to be
driven. The driving-band having various lengths
to suit is then put in position, and the movable
pulleys are finally fixed at that point where they
keep the band at proper tension for working. If the
band leads fairly on to the apparatus that it is to
drive, or this latter is fitted with proper guide
runners as described in the chapter on the Vertical
Cutter Frame, the gear will work. If, however, the
band leads at too great an angle it will be liable
to slip off, hence the necessity of having various
lengths of band. By judicious arrangement a few
pieces of band suffice for all wants. First cut a
length to fit the shortest workable distance, that is
from the slow motion groove of the fly-wheel to
the drill spindle close to the headstock; this may
be about 18 to 20 feet. Then cut a length of
6 inches, another of 1 foot, another of 2 feet.
With these three pieces only the band can be increased by 6, 12, 18, 24, 30, 36, or 42 inches, giving
a choice of seven lengths as may be found most
convenient, all within only a difference of 6 inches,
which is near enough for almost anything.

Another very simple form is that of a bar jointed
to a standard rising from the lathe-frame near the
headstock. This bar takes two pairs of pulleys as
first described, and the left-hand end has a weight
attached to it to keep the band taut; this weight is
increased in proportion to the work being performed. Fig. 34 illustrates such an apparatus; the

vertical bar, shown broken off at its lower end, is of
wrought or cast iron. It has a collar, shown just
under the lower part of the bracket, on which this
rests, or the upper end is shaped pivot-like and the
upper bearing of the bracket is fitted to it. The
bracket itself is of cast iron having bosses bored to
fit the upright loosely so that it turns freely. The
projecting end of the bracket has a lug cast in
with a vertical mortice hole which forms the bearing of the rod, a pin shown in the illustration being

Fig. 34.—Swinging Bar overhead Gear.

the axis. The tail end of the bracket has another
upright piece cast with a slot in it, in which the rod
rests when weighted, as shown. This slot also forms
a guide for the bar, when drawn down by the
bands on the pulleys, confining its horizontal
motion which is all made with the vertical bar as
axis, the bracket being quite free to turn round
on this.

The horizontal bar taking the two pairs of
pulleys is shown round at that part where the
pulleys slide. This is an advantage over a square

bar in allowing the pulleys to be canted over, which is sometimes necessary to let the band lead freely on when running at an angle. That portion to the left of the first pulleys is flattened to make it better for the bearing, and the continuation beyond the vertical slot has holes, two of which are shown, by which to suspend the weight. When easily managed it is well to make the suspension long so as to bring the weight near the ground, in which position it will be less likely to do damage in case of a breakdown. The point at which the bar is centred leaves the right-hand end heaviest, and it is advisable to put a guard on it so that it will not fall in the event of the weight being removed. A piece of wire fastened round the bracket and rod sufficiently slack to leave enough motion for working will answer this purpose, and many other ways will suggest themselves.

The swinging bar overhead gear is brought into operation by passing the driving-band round the lathe fly-wheel, bringing the two ends over the first pulleys, then over the second and round the pulley of the apparatus to be driven. The first pair of pulleys are adjusted to receive and deliver the band fairly on to the driving-wheel, the second being adjusted to perform the same functions with regard to the driller or other cutter which is to be driven. To assist in this latter adjustment the arm is swung round to come perpendicularly over the pulley, and when all is ready to start the bar should be tilted downwards, so that the whole of the weight being on the short arm bears on the band and keeps it taut. The length of the band should be so arranged that it will when working leave the bar nearly in its normal horizontal position, though of course it must be drawn down sufficiently to lift the weight quite clear of the bottom of the back slot in the bracket. It will be obvious that this form of overhead apparatus has many advantages over the plain bar first described.

The pulleys used in both the gearings are generally made with the two wheels running side by side on the same axis. The fork in which they go being pivoted on to the cannon, which slides on the bar at right angles to it, allows the pulleys to move freely and place themselves in line with the band. It is very necessary for pulleys such as these to be free to adapt themselves to the direction in which the band runs, or this will soon be worn out by cutting against the edges. A plain pulley, such as may be bought at most ironmongery shops, if attached to a piece cord of an inch or so in length, so that it is perfectly free to move in every direction but one, will answer admirably on the apparatus just described, and is a very cheap way of fitting up overhead gear. It is, however, advisable to knock out the iron pin on which the pulley revolves, and, after carefully broaching out the hole, to fit a steel pin to form the axis.

The second form of overhead gear, in which revolving shafts are used with various bands to transmit the motion, is shown in its most simple form in Fig. 35. The illustration represents a lathe, cut through vertically in the plane of the mandrel pulley. The bed is shown in section, surmounted by the headstock which carries the mandrel and pulley, from one of the middle steps of which a band passes to a stepped pulley above. This pulley is on an axis which revolves between fixed centres so that its distance from the lathe pulley is unalterable. Moving on the same centres is a light frame in which is fitted, to run perfectly parallel with the first-named shaft, another shaft shown in section on the right-hand top corner of the figure. This shaft, being in a frame only free to oscillate on the same centres as the shaft driven from the mandrel, remains constantly at the same distance from it. The second revolving shaft may be raised or lowered, thereby making considerable

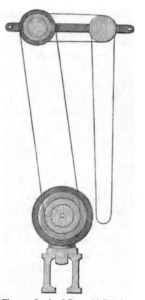

Fig. 35.—Overhead Gear, with Revolving Shafts.

alteration in the distance between it and the lathe-bed, and consequently with any apparatus fixed in the slide-rest. A grooved pulley fixed on to the leading screw of the slide running parallel with the lathe-bed, and actuated by the gearing illustrated, will traverse at a uniform rate and cut an accurate screw-thread. Of this more hereafter.

The front shaft of the gear, Fig. 35, is usually made with a parallel roller extending the whole length of the lathe-bed likely to be used with circular cutting apparatus, one end only being fitted with a stepped cone corresponding with one on the shaft driven from the mandrel. By means of this pair of stepped cones, three or four different rates of speed can be got with the single intermediary band. The plain cylindrical part will drive the band going to the cutter-frame at any point of its length, and thus all distances along the bed become equally within range. The up and down motion of the frame is sufficient to make up for any adjustment necessary through using large or small pulleys, and hence the one set of bands suffices for all purposes within the range of the pulleys. The band driving the main shaft may be led straight from the lathe fly-wheel.

Though the illustration is only intended to convey an idea of how the gear is fitted up, still the practical details can be easily filled in. The first consideration is to get rigid supports for the main shaft, on which and about the same centre the frame oscillates. Hanging standards fixed to the ceiling or an overhead beam are perhaps the best. The frame is conveniently made of two pieces of flat bar iron, braced together with stretcher bars at each end by the holes shown in the illustration, with a locking nut on both sides, and with centred screws to form bearings for the pointed ends of the shafts. To support the front side of the frame and keep the driving-band taut it must be attached overhead, and springs of some kind or weights are very handy to keep up the required tension at all times. These and other minor details are not shown, as they are entirely dependent on local circumstances which it is quite impossible to anticipate.

Accurate speeding, for screw-cutting purposes, such as mentioned before, is arranged by using a particular groove of the mandrel pulley, and making a pulley for the main shaft of precisely the same diameter. It is not difficult to turn a wooden pulley to size so near that the difference is not perceptible in a thousand revolutions. On the main shaft a cone pulley of three or four steps is placed exactly opposite a corresponding one reversed, so that the same band serves for all speeds alike. Thus three or four varieties of speed are obtained, and each must be made accurately proportional. The band from the front shaft to the grooved disc on the slide-rest screw must come from an accurately gauged pulley, and if these two are of equal size, then the rate of thread cut will depend on the ratio of the pulleys connecting the two shafts; if these are

L

equal, then the thread cut will be the same rate as that of the leading screw.

Any number of pulleys may be fitted to the slide-rest screw, each to suit a special rate which by the cone pulleys already described will be available for three or four others, according to the number of steps in the cones. The pulleys for speeding with gut bands must not have the ordinary V-form of groove, but a semi-circular one exactly fitting the band. The band must have hooks and eyes that are of precisely equal diameter, or each time they pass over a pulley there will be a jerk in the speed. Grooves of V-shape jam the band and allow it to act on a smaller diameter if put on tighter; hence they cannot be depended on for speeding, even if once got to size, and this is very hard to accomplish from the difficulty in determining the diameter for callipering. Grooves turned with a round nose tool of the same radius as the band can be callipered to a nicety, and their working diameter is exactly what they calliper plus two semi-diameters of the gut band.

CHAPTER XIII.

DIVIDING APPARATUS.

Its object and use—Dividing the lathe pulley—Numbers most useful for dividing purposes—Originating and making a division plate—Drilling the holes—Index pegs of various kinds.

DIVIDING apparatus is used on the lathe for many purposes, wheel-cutting being perhaps the most important, though also the most rare. Its chief uses on the foot lathe are to space out divisions on work which is turned, such as the bolt-holes of a cylinder cover, and for marking equidistant lines on cylinders which have to be made prismatic in shape, such as bolt-heads and nuts. In conjunction with the drilling or the upright spindle and overhead gear, which are described elsewhere, the dividing apparatus is used to hold the lathe mandrel while the driller or upright cutter is used in any of their numerous applications. The apparatus consists of a division plate drilled with a series of concentric circles of equidistant holes, bored either in the face of the pulley itself or in a ring attached to it, and an index which is a point arranged to fit into the holes, and so hold the pulley from revolving.

The holes in the division plate are usually drilled

in circles of numbers which afford the largest
variety of useful divisions. For general purposes
the numbers best suited are 360, 200, 96, and 84, if
the number of rows is limited to four. When the
number of rows is not so restricted, the holes in
each of course are selected to afford the largest
number of extra divisions, and in deciding these it
is necessary to have due regard for the purposes
for which the divisions will be used. Three
hundred and sixty is a very desirable number to
have, as it enables the degrees of a circle to be
marked, besides giving a wide range of numbers.
This large number cannot well be got on a pulley
of less diameter than those fitted to $5\frac{1}{2}$-inch lathes ;
but for very fine work 360 holes are sometimes
drilled in the pulley of a 5-inch lathe. The
proportion between the size of hole and space
between is about as two to one, calculating on
the outside circle, which is usually the most
crowded.

The pulley of a 5-inch lathe should be large
enough to allow a dividing circle, say 23 inches in
circumference. With 360 holes, this would give
their distance apart as ·0639 inch and the diameter of
the hole, say ·0426 inch, which is less than $\frac{1}{21}$ inch.
Such small holes answer their purpose very well for
fine ornamental work on ivory, &c., but will not do
to hold the pulley by when taking a cut on metal.
With 200 holes in the same diameter the size would
be ·0766, or $\frac{1}{13}$ inch; this is a strong hole, and
if a properly fitted index is used, the pulley may

be held perfectly stiff during any of the ordinary operations. For four rows of strong holes, 200, 180, 96, and 84 will be about the most useful; this is just the same as the numbers given above with the 360 halved. The largest circle should always contain the greatest number of holes, and the distance between two rows may be enough to allow the diameter of a hole as clear space between each.

Several forms of index are in common use; some are plain springs without adjustment, and others have arrangements for vertical adjustment. In these the peg can be raised or lowered to bring any particular part of the work to correspond with certain holes in the division plate. Altering the height of the index peg will cause the pulley to revolve, and thus bring a fresh point of the work before the tool. Adjustable indexes may be used to divide a number which cannot be got on the division plate; this is done by moving the index a certain distance between each division, and thus adding to or diminishing the number of divisions as shown by the division plate. Thus, suppose it is required to cut 101 teeth in a wheel, using the 200 circle, then the division peg would be put into every alternate hole. Also at every stoppage for cutting a tooth the index itself would be moved downwards a distance equal to one-hundredth part of the distance between the two holes. By the time the entire circle was divided the peg would have been moved through a space equal to a one-hun-

dredth part of the circle, and so the divisions would
be 101.

By adjusting the movable peg only once, and
placing it just half-way between where the holes
have been, the number of divisions will be doubled,
so by this means the 180 circle may be used for
dividing the degrees of a circle. For many purposes an adjustable index will be found more convenient to use than a plain one, though this latter
is very useful and somewhat easier to make. The
dividing apparatus which gives the greatest number
of divisions is an arrangement of a worm-wheel
fixed to the mandrel, with a tangent screw to
actuate it. This tangent screw is adapted to take
change-wheels, which will allow the screw to be
turned to any extent with certainty. This form
of dividing apparatus is often fitted to expensive
ornamental turning lathes, but is very seldom seen
on foot lathes of an ordinary kind.

A dividing apparatus may be fitted to a plain
headstock without very great difficulty, and as the
job is quite within the range of this treatise full
details are given. The number of holes for the
division plate should be decided according to requirements, and in order to see at a glance the
practical value of particular numbers a table should
be prepared similar to the one here given. Twelve
of the most useful numbers are taken, but any
others may be substituted to suit the purposes
wanted.

÷	360	240	216	200	192	168	144	140	136	135	112	104
20	18	12		10				7				
19												
18	20		12				8					
17								8				
16		15			12		9				7	
15	24	16								9		
14						12		10			8	
13												8
12	30	20	18		16	14	12					
11												
10	36	24		20				14				
9	40		24				16			15		
8	45	30	27	25	24	21	18		17		14	13
7						24		20			16	
6	60	40	36		32	28	24					
5	72	48		40				28		27		
4	90	60	54	50	48	42	36	35	34		28	26
3	120	80	72		64	56	48			45		
2	180	120	108	100	96	84	72	70	68		56	52
1	360	240	216	200	192	168	144	140	136	135	112	104

The top line shows the numbers up to 20, and the prime numbers, 11 and 19, are not given with either of the dividing numbers in the table, 13 is given only by 104, and 17 only by 136. If it is required to divide 11 and 19 multiplicands of these numbers must be drilled in the dividing plate. The best way to deal with these prime numbers, 11, 13, 17, and 19, if they are particularly wanted, is to drill specially for them; that is, make one row to contain 13 and 17 equal to 221, and another 11 and 19 equal to 209. As these rows will be of no practical use except for the numbers named, it is best to drill only those holes, and not the entire number; this makes the divisions clearer to read, and saves the trouble of drilling 370 holes. The way to originate these divisions is to get a circle of the number given, say 221, and, starting from a marked hole, mark every 13th hole, then re-start from the first hole and mark every 17th, and drill the holes at these marked places; thus, instead of 221, only 30 holes will be wanted. They will come at irregular intervals, and each series must be distinctively marked to avoid mistakes in use.

To originate a dividing plate it is first necessary to have a primitive circle, which is readily made of a band of metal, a small clock mainspring being, perhaps, the most convenient. The largest possible diameter should be used for this originating circle, so as to get the holes as far apart as can be, and so make any errors proportionately less. A

wooden disc is used to wrap the band on, and this,
being made as large as the lathe will allow, gives
the length of the band, which for a 5-inch lathe
would be 30 inches if the disc was sawn carefully
as circular as possible before being turned. The
disc should be made of sound wood and firmly
mounted on the mandrel, the face should be turned
true as well as the edge, and the dividing plate
which is to be drilled may be chucked direct on the
disc by recessing it out in the centre and laying
the plate in with its edge held by the wood.

Suppose that four rows of 200, 180, 96, and 84
respectively are to be drilled, the band to encircle
the disc must first have 200 equidistant holes
made in it on a length of not more than the circumference of the disc, viz. 30 inches ; the holes
will, therefore, be ·15, or a trifle over $\frac{1}{7}$th of an inch
apart. A template for drilling the holes perfectly
equidistant has to be made; this consists of two
pieces of stout sheet steel, each about 2 inches long,
and, for convenience, just three times the width of
the band. File them up straight, and mark a central
line very truly ; on this central line drill two small
holes at the precise distance apart that is wanted.
Drill holes through the steel to rivet them together
by, and break off two pieces from the metal band to
put between the templates, which will have to be
riveted together so as to allow the band itself to
pass through freely, but without shake. A reference to the accompanying illustration will show
the construction of the template (see Fig. 36). To

allow the band to pass it will be necessary to put an extra thickness of material between the plates where riveted, a piece of writing-paper being about sufficient. The two gauge holes first mentioned must be broached out carefully, quite upright and exactly the same size; they should also be made quite in a line with the centre of the aperture through which the band is to pass. The exact distance apart of these holes must be got most carefully, for the error of only $\frac{1}{100}$th part of an inch will make a difference of 2 inches in the length of the band. The diameter of these holes

Fig. 36.—Template for making Dividing Band.

may be about $\frac{1}{16}$ inch. The steel plates should be hardened before riveting together.

The 200 holes have now to be made in the band; they are all drilled through the template. The first hole is made at about 1 inch from the end; this allows the band to go quite through the aperture. When drilled the hole is broached out through the template to the same size, and a steel pin is put through to hold the band firm. The next hole is drilled through the second hole, and is broached out to size without removing the pin till the hole is finished. Then the pin is taken out and the band passed on for the last-made hole to come under the first hole in the template, the pin is put through, another hole is drilled, and the operations are repeated till 200 holes are made. Take a piece of metal exactly like the band and drill in it two or four equidistant holes, then cut the band half a space between the 200th hole and half a space from the 1st hole, lay it on the bench with the extra piece in the inside, and put pins through the holes next the join, so as to get the first and last hole of the band equidistant with the others. The band is then joined by soldering a strip of metal on each side of the row of holes and so kept in position. Now remove the short piece used to justify the holes with, and the band is ready to go on the disc.

Care must be taken to see that the correct number of holes, 200, are in the band, and the disc is then turned down, to allow the circle to fit on it tightly, a groove being turned in the wood so as to allow the point of the division peg to come through the band without impinging on the disc. At this stage the primitive dividing ring is ready for use on the 200 circle when the index peg has been fitted as described further on. It is here advisable to give the method of altering the ring to suit the other divisions. It is only necessary to cut the length of the band to contain the number required, and then resolder it, turn the disc down to fit the reduced diameter, and the dividing ring is again ready. Practically it is better to work differently in the case under notice, for if the band were cut off to 84 holes, the diameter of the disc would be only a trifle over 12¼ inches, whilst by using the band with 168 holes in it and taking every second hole the same result is attained with a diameter of over 25 inches. The same reasoning applies to the 96 circle, so that the band will be best cut with 200, 192, 180, and 168 holes respectively. This will save a lot of trouble in turning down the disc, besides affording a much better hold for the division peg, and a proportionate reduction of any errors that there may be in the originating circle. With the 192 circle, each alternate hole is used. The third row, from the outside of the plate being drilled, is bored second, and the 180 circle, though outside of it, is drilled third, in order to use the 192 circle instead of the 96.

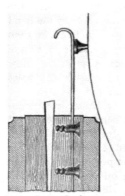

Fig. 37.—Division Peg for temporary use.

A division peg for temporary use with the dividing band may be fitted up in the socket of the hand-rest, as shown in Fig. 37. It consists of a plain steel spring with the top end bent over hook-shaped, to afford a hold for the fingers, and a taper steel peg riveted to it. The lower end is shown wedged into the T-socket; this is shown as a specimen of an easy way in which to improvise the index. It has been used and found to answer all the requirements.

For drilling the holes the drilling spindle, described in another chapter, is mounted on the slide-rest 'and driven from the overhead motion. The drill used is of peculiar shape; it cuts at the point and also on both its sides, so that it drills a conical hole tapering about 15°; the depth may be from $\frac{1}{12}$th to $\frac{1}{8}$th of an inch, according to the diameter. The drill must be fitted quite tight in the drilling spindle; it must be short and stiff, so as not to bend in use. It is carefully sharpened before commencing to bore the holes, and should not be reground till the whole of them are drilled, or the shape may be altered. Every hole must be bored to precisely the same depth, and a stop must be put to the slide-rest to ensure this. If the holes are unequal in depth the divisions made with the plate cannot be accurate. The circles of holes must also run perfectly concentric with the mandrel, or the spacing will be unequal.

The holes in the division plate should be drilled, at the place where they commence, with each circle starting in a diametrical line, and the numbers should be marked by punching in the figures or otherwise. The peg which goes into the holes must be turned to a corresponding cone so as to fit; it must not reach the bottom, and the point requires to be rounded off so that it will not scratch the face of the dividing plate. When in the hole the peg ought to stand quite square and be about mid-

way up the pulley. A large sectional view of the
peg in one of the holes, showing the correct proportions of the parts, is illustrated in Fig. 38. The
peg is here shown apart from the index spring. It
should be as short as can be conveniently used; if
too short the light is kept from the point by the
spring, and it is difficult to see the hole when
inserting the peg.

The illustrations show three kinds of division
pegs. Fig. 37 is the most simple, having no adjustment. It is a plain steel spring with the conical
stalk riveted to the lower end; this stalk fits a

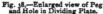

Fig. 38.—Enlarged view of Peg   Fig. 39.—Knob for Division Peg.
  and Hole in Dividing Plate.

hole in the spherical knob which is screwed into the
side of the headstock, and allows angular motion
to the peg, so that it can be put into either row of
holes. The end of the spring is wrought over in a
hook shape to afford a grip for the fingers; in the
others a small button is riveted to the springs for
that purpose. The knob screwed into the headstock is generally made like Fig. 39, and gun-metal
is a suitable material. The centre of the sphere
where the hole is should be so placed that the
spring will stand upright when the peg is in the
centre row of holes and level with the lathe centres.

The division peg illustrated in Fig. 40 has a screw fitted after the plan of the poppet headstock barrel screw, by turning which the peg may be

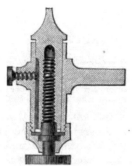

Fig. 40.—Adjustable Division Peg.

shifted to the greatest nicety. The construction is shown in the sectional drawing, and needs no further description. This is one of the best forms of adjustable division pegs.

CHAPTER XIV.

THE DRILLING SPINDLE.

Its use and how to make—Making the mandrel—Making the collars, grinding the bearings—Lead grinders—Fitting the collars, grinding the cones—Hardening and tempering—Putting together.

A DRILLING SPINDLE will be found very useful for many purposes. Apart from drilling simple holes, it may be used for grooving taps, making drifts or punches to make triangular, square, hexagonal, octagonal, and other shaped holes ; also for squaring the flats of bolt-heads and shaping up prismatic pieces of all descriptions in wood or metal. On surfaces it may be used for cutting slots and grooves of all shapes ; indeed to so many purposes is the drilling-spindle applied that it would scarcely be possible to enumerate them. Overhead gear and a dividing apparatus are required when using a drilling spindle. The following particulars will make its construction clear. It is not very difficult to make, and by following the drawings a serviceable tool will be produced.

Fig. 41 is a sectional drawing of the complete apparatus, in which the principles of construction may be seen at a glance. The exterior shape may

be altered to suit special circumstances, but the
form shown, a plain square bar, will usually be
found the most convenient for use. It is held in
position on the top of the slide-rest by means
of the usual tool-holder. The only reason for
adopting another pattern would be when the tool-
holder is of such a shape as to necessitate it, as is
the case in some which have not sufficient space in
the usual tool receptacle to admit the shank of the
spindle.

Before constructing any piece of apparatus it is

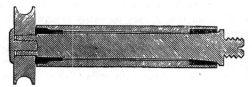

Fig. 41.—Sectional view of Drilling Spindle.

always best to make working drawings as guides
during the progress of the work, then by continual
reference it is easy to guard against errors, and so
save much time. The size of the drilling spindle
will depend for diameter on the height of the
lathe-centres above the top plate of the slide-rest,
and for length on the size of this same plate. A
piece of square iron which will finish up to double
the difference between the height of centres and
top of rest, and a trifle longer than the widest way
of the top plate, will be required for the shank,
through which the mandrel or spindle runs. This

M

piece of iron must be mounted between the lathe-centres to have the ends turned true, and at the same time a very light cut may be taken along its entire length to just round off the corners ; the bar is then made quite square and flat on each side by filing. To turn the corners off of a piece of $1\frac{1}{4}$-inch square iron would be by many considered a very difficult if not an impossible job for a light foot lathe, but it may be done without trouble if set about in a workmanlike manner. When the bar has been filed up it is well to select the truest surface for the bottom to rest on the slide-rest, and mark it so that it may be easily recognised afterwards.

The piece has to be bored through as nearly as possible central. This may be done with ordinary drills, working from both ends; the centre marks left from the turning will serve as a guide in starting. A small hole is drilled first, and larger ones subsequently, till the hole is about half the diameter of the square bar. If this hole is tolerably true centrally, and straight from end to end, it may be further enlarged by drilling, but if much out of truth the hole must be got central by using a boring bar between the lathe-centres. The square shank, being fixed in its place on the slide-rest, is traversed along the bar so that the hole is made to exactly coincide with the line of centres. The boring bar has to be just over twice the length of the hole, and, therefore, it is necessary to have it as stout as can be, so as to get the greatest pos-

sible rigidity. A bar of round cast steel will serve
for the boring bar; it need only be truly centred
at both ends, and must have a transverse hole at
the middle of its length to take the cutter. The
bar must be straight, and as large as may be to
run clear of the boring. The cutter is wedged in
the transverse hole to project enough to take a
light cut, and the square bar fixed on the rest is
traversed along it. The cutter is set out for subse-
quent cuts, and the boring continued till the hole
in the bar is quite truly in line with the centres,
and large enough for the intended spindle.

The size of the spindle to be used will depend
greatly on the work to which it is to be applied.
A mandrel $\frac{3}{8}$ inch in diameter will serve the purpose for light drilling, whilst for actuating cutters
on metal one as large as 1 inch in diameter is
used for a 5-inch lathe. To suit the requirements
of this particular work the maker must select an
appropriate size. Large ones have threads cut on a
nose, as is illustrated in Fig. 41, and sometimes
internal threads, by which chucks may be screwed
to the spindle; small ones are generally made like
the drill-chuck figured on page 92, Fig. 13. Small
cutters, drills, &c., may be fitted into this form of
spindle very firmly, but for heavy work the thread
will be found necessary. The spindle runs in two
collars, one at each end of the shank, which is
bored out to receive them. The end-motion is confined by an abrupt cone at the nose end and the
pulley bearing against the face of the back collar.

The collars must, therefore, have shoulders to prevent them being forced into the shank by the
lateral pressure on the spindle.

For the mandrel select a piece of round cast steel,
cut it to the correct length, anneal carefully, then
centre both ends truly, and mount on the lathe to
run true. Drill the hole for the screw in the tail-
end, and turn the steel roughly to the correct
shape. If from the working of the steel it is
thought desirable it may be again thoroughly annealed at this stage. Whether the mandrel shall
be hardened when finished or left perfectly soft is a
question which is not readily answered. In the
process of hardening the spindle is almost certain
to warp, probably it will crack as well, and generally, from one or the other cause, the mandrel will
be rendered useless, and all the labour spent on it
wasted. A soft mandrel will answer every purpose,
and may be used for an indefinite time, and for
general purposes there is very little cause for
troubling about hardening at all.

The two collars are made from round cast steel
of the requisite diameter. Large collars are generally forged roughly to shape, but when only one
or two are required it is easier to make from the
solid; and for small collars, say those under 1
inch in diameter, this is always the better plan.
A short length of steel is mounted in a chuck,
such as the two-die chuck, Fig. 17, or the four-
screw cup-chuck, Fig. 15; the end is turned flat
and a small hole bored up the centre; this is

enlarged to nearly the intended size, the depth being a little more than the length of the collar; a deep groove is turned on the outside, and the rough collar can then be broken off. A second piece is prepared just in the same way, and the two blanks are thoroughly annealed before being further worked. They are then chucked, one at a time, for boring out conically; the outside should run quite true; the boring is done with an inside tool in the slide-rest. The top slide is set over, as described on page 111, to 30″, this being the correct amount of taper for cone-bearings. At this angle bore out one collar to very nearly the size, as shown by the working drawing. See that the last cut is a light one, and done with a sharp tool, to leave a smooth inside to the collar, which is then taken out of the chuck and the other one bored. The front collar has its largest end turned to a bevel inside, as shown in the various woodcuts.

The two collars bored, next mount the mandrel on the lathe, and turn the parts where the bearings will come conical to correspond with the insides of the collars. Turn as smoothly as possible, and fit the collars on at some distance from their ultimate places. Thus the mandrel answers the purpose of an arbor for turning the outsides of the collars on, which is the next operation, the collars being turned to shape on the outside and made nearly small enough to go into the recessed borings in the ends of the iron shank. The ends of the collars must be turned true; they will hold on to the man-

drel tight enough to allow a fairly heavy cut to be
taken, the principal care being required to guard
against cutting the mandrel when turning the ends
of the collars ; these are next carefully annealed,
so that the thick parts are made quite red-hot without burning the thin.

The next process will be to grind out the collars.
Lead grinders will answer all the purposes, though
brass or gun-metal ones are sometimes used.   The
lead grinders are made in this way :—Prepare a
piece of round or square iron rod three or four inches
long by centring the ends and tinning with pewter
solder a part near the end.   Roll up very smoothly
a cylinder of writing-paper, tying a piece of string
round to prevent its unrolling.   Stand this cylinder
on a metal surface, with the tinned part of the rod
in its centre, pour in some melted lead, which will
melt the pewter and solder itself to the iron rod.
Mount the rod between the centres, and turn the
lead to fit the largest collar, carefully keeping it
to the same cone.

The collar must be driven into a chuck so that it
will be quite true.   The grinding is then done by
supplying the lead grinder freely with rather coarse
emery and oil; the emery imbeds itself in the soft
metal, and soon grinds the steel smooth.   An ordinary carrier is screwed on to the tail end of the
grinder by which to hold it.   Whilst the lathe is
revolving the grinder is continually drawn to and
fro, so that rings will not be cut in the collar.   In
this way the collar will be made very smooth,

though possibly it may be necessary to recast the lead, so as to turn the grinder to size afresh when it has been used for some time. Emery will produce a sufficiently fine surface in the collar; that on the grinder will become finer as it is used, so that it is only necessary to refrain from putting fresh emery in order to get the requisite fineness. The back collar must be ground out in the same way, and both are then cleaned to remove all the abraded particles.

When the collars are now put on the mandrel they will, of course, go further on the cone than before being ground out, but the cone will have to be reduced to allow them to come very nearly to the place they will ultimately occupy; a very fine flat file will be found very useful for this purpose. The collars are finally fitted by grinding on the mandrel itself with oilstone dust and oil, still leaving a trifle for fitting when the collars are driven into the shank. The oilstone dust is cleaned off and the collars finally turned to fit the shank. The small holes through which the oil to lubricate the bearings is supplied have to be drilled in the collars so that they will coincide with holes drilled for the same purpose in the iron shank. The inside of the collars must have a small groove leading from the oil holes to distribute the oil along the bearing. These channels must be cut with a round file; if with an angular one the collars will most likely split in hardening.

Considerable attention must be paid to the

hardening of these collars, or they will be burned in some parts whilst not hot enough in others. When red hot plunge into cold water, and they will not crack if the previous annealing process is done properly, and there are no sharp angular nicks in them. There is hardly any necessity to temper the collars; anyhow, they should be heated only sufficiently to just show a change of colour. The back end of the smaller collar, which takes the bearing of the pulley, must be made quite flat by grinding. A sheet of emery paper laid on a flat surface will do this.

To get the collars into the shank they are put in the right position for the oil holes to come uppermost and correspond with holes drilled through the iron. Drive them in slightly with a mallet, then put a bolt through the two collars, screw on the nut to draw them together. See that the head and nut of the bolt bed fair and that it pulls straight, then screw up. If the collars are very tight and do not go by this means, drive them with a heavy hammer, giving only light blows, and keeping the pressure on the bolt; by these means the two collars will be got into their places right home to the shoulder.

With the collars driven fast into the shank, the next process is to grind in the mandrel-bearings. The soft spindle is reduced by filing with a fine file, whilst it is revolved quickly in the lathe, till the bearings nearly reach the intended point. The mandrel is then taken from the lathe-centres and ground in by hand, using oilstone dust and oil for *the abrading* material. The insides of the collars

will be ground quite bright, and the spindle
will become a dull lead-colour when the bearings are ground right home, so that the front cone
touches the face of the front collar. The spindle,
collars, and the entire shank must be thoroughly
cleaned to remove all trace of the grinding material. The tail end of the spindle, which projects
from the back collar, will have to be turned down
to receive the pulley, which coming up to form the
back-bearing, prevents endshake. The pulley is
to be made as large as possible to clear the
slide-rest. It can be of cast iron, and is bored
slightly smaller than the size of the tail of the
spindle, which is then fitted to go in tight. The
pulley may be turned up true, and the gut-groove
made in it when driven tight on to the spindle ; but
the final fit of the pulley should not be quite so
tight as that, because the screw which goes into
the tail is intended to force the pulley against the
shoulder, which it cannot do if the fitting is very
tight. The hole is tapped, and a screw fitted having
a head of greater diameter than the tail of the mandrel. The pulley projects slightly beyond the end,
and on screwing in the screw forces it against the
shoulder on the spindle, and so holds it firm. It
will be understood that the face of the pulley
against the shoulder forms the bearing to prevent
the endshake. There is not any appreciable wear
here, as the action of nearly all the tools used in the
drilling spindle is to press it backwards against
the front cone.

The nose-end may next be finished ; it can have

a thread cut upon it as shown in Fig. 41, or may be drilled up like the chuck, Fig. 13. It is rather difficult to cut such a short thread true and parallel with dies, so it ought to be cut in a screw-cutting lathe. The thread ought to be cut right up to the shoulder, and the remarks already made relative to the nose of the lathe-mandrel, page 27, are equally applicable to this one. To get the thread right up to the shoulder, it is necessary, whether cutting it with dies or a tool in the lathe, to nick in the termination of the thread as soon as the point where it ends is apparent. A crossing file is the best to use for this purpose, and the nicking in should be done progressively, to keep pace with the screw-cutting. With a nick cut in, the last shaving or chip of metal cut out of the screw-thread breaks off; but it does not do so in the ordinary way; consequently the metal accumulates, and the thread is cut shorter at each trip of the screw-cutter.

In describing the way in which to make a drilling spindle numerous practical processes have to be explained in detail, and it will be easy for the intelligent reader to apply them to purposes for which they are suited as occasion may require. As an example, lead grinders are used for grinding out fittings of all kinds, and the description of their make and use, as specially applied to grinding out the conical collars of the drilling spindle, will serve equally well in innumerable other cases.

CHAPTER XV.

VERTICAL CUTTER-FRAME.

Its use and construction—Circular-cutters for wheel teeth—Cutters for
general purposes—Fly-cutters—Making the frame and spindle.

A CUTTER-FRAME, in which the spindle revolves
vertically instead of horizontally as in the drilling
spindle already described, is used for many purposes where the latter cannot be employed; as for
cutting longitudinal grooves and slots, the sectional
form of which is such as can be easily shaped by
means of circular cutters having their edges turned
to a counterpart shape and teeth formed on them,
to cut the material being wrought. These circular
cutters may be home-made, and for peculiar forms
it is often necessary for the workman to make
a special cutter. Unless sufficient quantities are
used to warrant the fitting up of special apparatus
for their manufacture, these home-made cutters
will not as a rule be found anything like equal to
those sold at the tool-shops, and which are manu-
factured in large quantities by the aid of specially
designed machinery.

The apparatus illustrated in this chapter may be

used for wheel-cutting. It is scarcely necessary
to say that the cutters required for removing the
material from the interspaces of the wheel-teeth are
to be bought in all shapes and sizes, suited for small
work, at the tool shops, such cutters being made
by templates to cut the correct epicycloidal form
of tooth. A very large number of cutters would be
necessary to correctly form the teeth of wheels
varying in size; that is to say, each diameter of
wheel should be cut with a cutter formed slightly
differently, though the teeth would be ostensibly
the same. Practically, however, the difference in
the form is so slight that in the most accurate sets
eight cutters are considered sufficient to cut from
pinions of twelve leaves to wheels of infinite
radius, as typified by a rack; and not unusually
four cutters serve all the purposes.

For general purposes cutters having square and
circular edges are most generally in request; the
former, as the most easily made, being very similar
to circular saws, though usually much thicker, and
always having coarser teeth. Cutters of an inch to
an inch and a half diameter should have about
twelve to eighteen teeth; that will make them
about a quarter of an inch apart. They may
then be ground when blunted, and, moreover, the
coarse teeth will not become clogged with shavings as do the fine teeth. For cutters that are not
likely to see much service three or four teeth will
answer, and are easier to form than a larger
number. The single tooth or fly-cutter, however, is

still less trouble to make, and when sufficiently durable is generally used. Square-edged cutters of various thicknesses are useful for cutting out rectangular grooves, though a properly formed drill in the drilling spindle will do the same work often quite as well and in some cases better. Circular-edged cutters are used for grooving taps and cutting channels of semi-circular section, the diameter of which is equal to the thickness of the cutter employed. The grooves in taps are made to remove one-half of the thread, measuring circumferentially, so that for three grooves the width of the cutter should be just a semi-diameter of the tap. Four or six cutters of different widths will suffice for grooving all taps ranging from a quarter to three-quarters of an inch diameter. The larger sizes will absorb all the power that can be brought to bear on them in a cutter-frame of the kind here described, so that the range of work is somewhat limited.

Fly-cutters are single cutters fitted to the cross mortice hole with one projecting end shaped to the requisite form. Small brass wheels such as are used in English clocks have the teeth cut by means of a single-tooth fly-cutter, so that their effectiveness is proved. In consequence of the ease with which they can be made, fly-cutters are used for innumerable jobs requiring a cutter of special form, such as moulding, &c. It is only necessary to fit a piece of steel to the mortice hole in the spindle, leave one end projecting, file it up to the desired shape, leaving plenty of clearance, harden and temper, and the cutter is ready for work. The cutting edges should be made as smooth as possible if a smooth finished cut is desired, and the bulk of the material should be removed by circular cutters before applying the fly. These are driven at great speed, and practically it is not possible to drive fly-cutters too fast With quick speed and slow feed the work that can be done with a fly is almost incredible.

The accompanying illustrations show a very good form of cutter-frame. The main part to which the fittings are attached may be a gun-metal casting or forged of iron. It is essential that it should be rigid, so as to withstand the vibration caused by quick speed ; this is liable to throw a fragile instrument into a state of tremor, in which condition it is impossible to produce good work. In working with quick-speed cutters, subject to vibration, it is often easy to place a stay from some substantial point to support the most unstable part of the work, and this gives surprising additional power. For example, by placing a wooden stay from the back part of the lathe-bench to catch the head of the top centre screw in this cutter-frame, the entire slide-rest and apparatus will be made inconceivably more rigid.

The top view, Fig. 42, shows a small portion of the shank part by which the apparatus is held in the slide-rest. It is only necessary to point out that when designing the pattern for the frame, the

shank must be placed at the correct height to
bring the mortice groove in the spindle on a level
with the lathe-centres. The shank may be of
square section, about ¾ inch for a 5-inch centre
lathe, the width of the frame part corresponding as
seen by the front view, Fig. 43. The arms that
project to take the centre screws may be shaped
off to fancy as shown in Fig. 42. A frame made to

Fig. 42.—Top view of Vertical Cutter Frame.

the proportions given in the illustration will be
found to be sufficiently strong without being
clumsy for all the purposes to which it is likely to
be applied. The upright spindle must run truly
vertical to produce accurate work; if slanting, the
cutters revolving in it will not cut grooves precisely
corresponding with their edges. In use the cutters
are often made to serve a purpose to which they

are not really adapted by tilting the frame slightly.

The cutter-spindle is seen in Fig. 43. It is made of steel, and has a large-sized pulley fitted to it, to

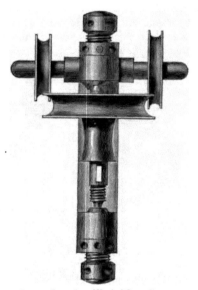

Fig. 43.—Front view of Vertical Cutter-Frame.

be driven from the overhead gear. This pulley must have a wide groove for the band which has to pass entirely round it, so that half of its diameter is encircled by two breadths of band. For this reason the two guide pulleys, or runners, are of different sizes, so that the driving band is led on and taken off at different heights, the difference being the thickness of the band used, and thus the band is prevented from over riding, as it probably would do if the guide pulleys were of equal size. Precisely the same effect is produced by using runners of equal diameter and placing the pins on which they revolve at different heights. These runners must have wide semicircular grooves, so as to receive the band fairly when running at an angle. Narrow grooves will wear out the band by cutting with their edges, and angular grooves will absorb power detrimentally by jambing. Pulleys which are to be driven by a single band require to be grooved out angularly, but those serving merely as runners are best made with wide semicircular grooves in which the band runs as freely as possible.

The spindle has pointed ends, as should all revolving arbors in preference to centred ends, which owing to the usual flatness of the end drive the oil from the actual point of friction by centrifugal force. It is necessary to see that the top bearing is lubricated when working, as the oil applied to it is apt to run down the cone point away from the screw end. The lower bearing is of course arranged to the best advantage; but if the upper end of the spindle were centred like the bottom screw, and thus offered a receptacle for the oil, it would be driven off by centrifugal force as explained above. Though apparently a very trivial matter, yet practically proper arrange-

N

ments for lubrication are of primary consideration.

The form of the spindle is of little moment so
long as strength is not sacrificed.
The shoulder against which cutters
are jambed by the nuts should be
broad and flat. The thread for the
locking nut being as fine as may
be consistent with strength, the
diameter being but the merest shade less than
that of the plain part on which the cutters should
fit. In Fig. 44 the locking nut is shown in plan
and section ; a hexagonal nut is used in preference

Fig. 44.—Locking Nut
of Vertical Cutter-
frame.

Fig. 45.—Hooked Tommy.

to a circular one with holes drilled radially, such
as those shown as lock-nuts on the screws forming
the bearings, as it is more easy to clamp in the
vice for tightening, though the other form will
answer all the purposes. To actuate these nuts,
which have but comparatively shallow holes, a
"tommy" of the ordinary form will not do, and
one of special shape, illustrated in Fig. 45, and
called a "hooked tommy" has to be provided.
This tool has simply to be bent to the curve, and
then filed out to accurately fit the half circumference of the nut; the small pin at the end of the
hook is then inserted. In use the hooked tommy

must always be turned in the direction of the curve, and of course is available for screwing up or un-screwing by simply turning it over to the side required. Hooked tommys are employed to actuate all those capstan headed screws and nuts which from insufficiency in the depth of the holes do not afford a hold for the ordinary straightforward tommy.

The stud-pins on which the runners revolve are of round steel, being screwed into the frame. The runners are shown loose, that is free to drop off; but a pin may be put diametrically through each stud near the ends to prevent such an occurrence. The runners must, however, have plenty of freedom along the pins, so that they may adjust them-selves to positions suited to the angles at which the driving-band is led on and off of the overhead

Fig. 46.—Screw Collet of Vertical Cutter-frame.

gear. If quite free and made with wide open grooves, the runners will lead a band at almost any angle in reason, and so obviate a lot of trouble in making several lengths of band to suit particular positions of the vertical cutter-frame along the lathe-bed.

The cross mortice hole in the spindle is useful for single-tooth cutters as previously described. These are fitted to the opening and are held by a set screw from the side. The substance of the spindle itself is not enough to afford a hold for the set screw, and the collet shown in Fig. 46, which gives end and sectional views, has to be used. The mortice hole in this collet should be slightly less

than the corresponding mortice through the
spindle in all its dimensions; so that the cutters
fitted to it will pass free in the spindle hole. The
set screw, which is tapped in the collet, must pass
clear through the spindle; this will necessitate
boring a hole to the size of the diameter of the
thread in the spindle. In use the collet is fixed by
the clamp-nut just as a circular cutter would be;
always taking the precaution to see that the
mortice holes correspond and the set screw is opposite the hole in the spindle. The head of this set
screw should be as flat as may be so as to clear
the work when in use. The diameter of the spindle
where the cutters fit is regulated by the size of
hole in the circular cutters as usually made, that
is about $\frac{3}{8}$ inch. It is advisable to procure a
circular cutter to fit by when making the spindle,
if bought cutters are likely to be used; if home-
made ones are to be solely employed, then the
holes in them can be made to suit the size of the
spindle whatever may be the diameter.

CHAPTER XVI.

SCREW-CUTTING BY SELF-ACTING MOTION.

Theoretical principles—Wheels usually supplied—Preparing a table of rates that can be cut—Screw-threads, how described—Rules for calculating change-wheels—Examples proving the calculation—Multiple threads.

SCREW-CUTTING is performed in lathes specially arranged for the purpose, as described in the second chapter, by self-acting feed-motion. This automatically moves the tool along in the direction of the axis of the work whilst this is revolving, and thus a spiral is cut on the cylinder, forming of it a screw. To fully understand the theoretical principles of screw-cutting in the lathe:—suppose a cylindrical rod turned true and running between the lathe-centres; a cutting-tool attached to a nut working on a screw which revolves in fixed bearings parallel to the cylinder, and properly placed for cutting, will, when the rotary motion of the cylinder is imparted to the screw, traverse longitudinally and cut a spiral groove. It is evident that if the cylinder and guide-screw make equal revolutions, the thread on the cylinder will be of the same rate or pitch as that of the screw, and if the guide-screw and the cylinder revolve in the same direction the threads will be in the same direction, but if the rotation is in contrary directions the thread will be reversed, that is, one will be right-handed and the other left-handed. When the relative velocity of guide-screw and cylinder is varied, the ratio between the respective threads is varied in the same ratio; or when the cylinder makes two revolutions to one of the guide-screw, the thread traced will have twice the number of threads in a given length. These conditions once understood, screw-cutting by change-wheels will be no longer the mystery that it is to some.

In the ordinary screw-cutting lathe the mandrel itself has a projecting tail, as shown in Fig. 1, on which change-wheels of various sizes are put as required. The guide-screw is put in bearings inside, or just in front, of the lathe-bed, and has a projecting piece at the left-hand end precisely the same diameter as the mandrel tail, so that wheels fitting one are interchangeable. The slide-rest fitting the bed has a clamp-nut, which may be engaged and disengaged with the screw by means of a handle within easy access, and under the control of the operator. The threads that may be cut are both right and left-handed, and limited in their number only by the variety of change-wheels that are available. The relative velocity of the mandrel, and with it the work to be threaded, and the guide-screw, and with it the traverse of the cutting-tool, is regulated by putting on each wheels duly proportionate to the work required. When the pitch of the leading screw is known, the production of threads of any desired ratio becomes merely a matter of calculation.

Change-wheels for heavy screw-cutting lathes, and, indeed, most of those in general use, are made of cast iron ; and are very cheap and effective. They may be bought in sets or singly of various pitches, *i.e.* number of teeth to a given diameter, suited to the size of the lathe for which they are to be used. The set usually consists of 22 wheels, including one pair, the smallest having 20 teeth, and the largest 100 or 120. Gun-metal and brass engine-cut wheels are supplied with high-class lathes made for amateurs' use; these are from about 16 to 20 pitch, *i.e.* have about that number of teeth per inch diameter. The set generally consists of 19 wheels, including two pairs, having from 24 to 120 teeth. The difference in ratios is explained by the fact of the wheels being in one case multiples of 5 and in the other multiples of 6.

When placed in position for working, a simple train of wheels consists of three only, two of which have to be of definite proportions, the third being merely an idle wheel. One is called the " driver," that is, it conveys the motion, being fixed to the mandrel ; one is the " driven," that is, it is fixed to the guide-screw, and is driven by the mandrel-wheel. The intermediate wheel, called a " stud-wheel," is of any size convenient for connecting the driver with the driven. A compound train consists in its simplest form of four wheels, and is different from the set just described only inasmuch that the stud-wheel is replaced by two wheels. These are fixed on the same axis and revolve together, one driven by the mandrel-wheel, the other driving the screw-wheel. The relative size of these two wheels form elements in the calculation, the driver becoming part of the mandrel-wheel and the driven part of the screw-wheel.

A table of the threads which may be cut on the particular lathe should be the first consideration to the possessor of a screw-cutting lathe. This must be prepared specially agreeable to the rate of the leading-screw and the wheels available, and, once made, all trouble of calculating for particular jobs is obviated. In order to avoid complication, every whole number from 1 to 100 that can be cut should be written down, and opposite to it the numbers of the wheels requisite. Pitches that may occasionally be met with involving the use of fractions are easily calculated by a glance at this table, and it is easy to see whether any number that may be required can be cut or not. In the latter case the next pitch nearest, whether coarser or finer, is seen, and whether it is sufficiently accurate for the purpose may be determined off hand.

Whether the nearest pitch will serve the purpose will depend on the purpose for which the screw is required; for accurate work nothing short of the exact pitch should suffice. It is satisfactory to note that first-class work is now put together with

screws of a definite rate, which can be cut with
the wheels usually accompanying a screw-cutting
lathe. The cause of the origin of some of the
threads involving such peculiar fractions is explained in another chapter. For some work the
error of a few hundredths of a turn per inch is of
no consequence, and is, in fact, much nearer accuracy than could be depended upon in the work produced by dies which are self-guiding.

When preparing and calculating a screw-cutting
table, it must be remembered that the number of
teeth in the wheels required to cut a given rate of
threads is governed by the pitch of the leading-
screw. The wheels themselves must, however, be
considered in relation to the peculiarities of the
machine on which they are to be placed, as well as
to the number of their teeth ; and from these rea-
sons it is impossible to adopt one table common to
all lathes having a leading screw at the same
pitch.

There are various ways of describing screw-
threads, *e.g.* the same thread might be said to be
¼-inch pitch, meaning that the distance apart of
the threads is ¼ inch, measuring in a straight line
from one thread to a corresponding part of the
next; or to have four threads or turns per inch,
meaning that if the screw were turned round four
complete revolutions in its nut it would have
moved longitudinally the space of 1 inch; or,
again, it might be termed ·25-inch pitch, which is
the same as the first example, the fraction being

expressed in decimal parts. This explanation of the terms used will enable the uninitiated to understand what is meant when speaking of threads technically. There are almost innumerable formulæ for calculating wheels, and it is hard to decide on one of universal application, for the explanation which is perfectly clear to one mind may be incomprehensible jargon to another of equal culture.

Expressed in a simple rule-of-three sum, the calculation is this:—The pitch of the guide-screw is to the pitch of the screw to be cut as the diameter of the wheel on the mandrel is to the diameter of the wheel on the guide-screw. This rule may always be used to prove a doubtful calculation. The diameters of the wheels are, of course, most easily expressed by the number of teeth they contain. When a pair of wheels are used on the intermediate stud, then the wheel on the mandrel is multiplied by that driving on the stud, and the driven wheel has to be multiplied by the wheel on the guide-screw; thus the wheels are more correctly expressed by the terms drivers and driven.

The easiest possible rule is probably this:— Write down in the form of a vulgar fraction the number of threads in a given length of the guide-screw and the threads in the same length of the screw to be cut. Multiply both by a number that will produce a numerator and denominator equal to some two of your set of change-wheels. Put the quotient of the guide-screw on the mandrel, or as drivers, and that of the pitch required on the guide-screw, or as driven; arranged in this way the desired result will be attained. The knowledge of arithmetic necessarily involved in the calculation is of the most elementary and simple character, and few can fail to work out the simple rule.

Examples afford the best means of showing the working, and we will suppose that calculations are required for a lathe having a guide-screw of four threads per inch, or $\frac{1}{4}$ pitch. To cut five threads per inch we calculate according to the rule last given thus :—Put down the two rates in the form of a vulgar fraction, $\frac{4}{5}$; multiplying both by a number, say 10, we get $\frac{40}{50}$; by 15, $\frac{75}{60}$; by 20, $\frac{100}{80}$. Every one of these numbers is to be found in the usual set of change-wheels, and in practice we simply select those two which are most convenient in size. In the last three, putting the 100 on the guide-screw and the 80 on the mandrel, and any wheel on the stud to form an intermediary to reverse the motion, we shall cut a right-handed thread of 5 turns to the inch. With two studs and two idle intermediary wheels the thread will be the same rate, but left-handed.

To calculate the wheels for cutting an odd pitch, as $4\frac{3}{4}$ per inch, offers no more trouble whatever when once understood. By the example we see that the first fraction consists of the number of threads in equal lengths of guide-screw and screw required. In 4 inches of the rate now required there are 19 turns, and in the same length of guide-screw

16, so we put down $\frac{16}{16}$, and multiplying by 5 get $\frac{80}{80}$, the wheels required. Suppose we want to cut $6\frac{3}{4}$ threads per inch, then we get as the first fraction $\frac{27}{4}$, which multiplied by 5 gives $\frac{135}{20}$. If there is a wheel of 135 teeth the calculation is finished, but if 120 is the largest wheel available, then we must find some means of reducing the large number. This is easily done by breaking up the fraction, as shown in the next example.

Suppose we want to cut 40 threads per inch, then the fraction stands $\frac{40}{1}$. To get the small number to equal one of the smallest of the change-wheels it must be multiplied by 10 at least, and this gives 400 as the size of the wheel wanted on the guide-screw. This number is, of course, beyond the range altogether; however, we proceed as before, and get $\frac{400}{10}$; this is equal to $\frac{80 \times 5}{20 \times 2}$. Here the first numerator and denominator are to be found amongst our wheels, and the second pair multiplied by 10 give $\frac{50}{20}$. This involves the use of two wheels of 20, and as these are not usually found we use 15 as the multiplicand, and get $\frac{75}{30}$, the complete fraction standing thus, $\frac{80}{20}-\frac{75}{30}$. In case the wheels do not gear well together it may be changed by multiplying, always remembering to serve one numerator and one demoninator alike, thus by adding $\frac{1}{4}$ to the 80 and 20 we get $\frac{100}{25}-\frac{75}{30}$. With these the gearing can probably be mounted, always remembering that the products of the screw to be cut, viz. 100 and 75, represent the driven wheels; and putting one of these on the guide-screw, and one of the products of the guide-screw on the mandrel, the other two are put on the stud, one driving the guide-screw, the other driven from the mandrel. In the same way several studs with compound wheels may be introduced, and thus the capacity of screw-cutting gear extended.

To prove whether a calculation is correct, the most simple plan is to multiply all the driving wheels together and all the driven wheels together, divide the greater number by the less, and the quotient will show the ratio between the guide-screw and the screw to be cut. As example, take the last calculation, $100 \times 75 = 7500$, and $30 \times 25 = 750$, then dividing 7500 by 750 the product is 10, and the ratio between the guide-screw and the one to be cut is as 40 : 4, hence the accuracy of the wheels is proved.

Double, triple, quadruple, and multiple threads generally may be cut on the lathe, the slide-rest being made to traverse along the bed at the correct speed representing the pitch. If a single point is used for cutting the thread the several different ones are made equidistant by so arranging the train of wheels that the one on the mandrel contains an exact multiple of the number of threads. This wheel is marked at equidistant parts, say on the teeth, and one space in the wheel that it drives is also marked, chalk serving all ordinary purposes if care is exercised to avoid rubbing it off. When one thread has been fully cut out the mandrel wheel is employed as a division plate to start the next equidistant from the first. A comb-screw tool may be used having the teeth in it to correspond with the several threads taken collectively; thus, with a comb-tool cutting 10 threads per inch and the slide-rest travelling at the rate of 5 per inch a double screw of 5 pitch will be cut at one operation.

Square, angular, and any form of screws may be cut both inside and outside with the screw-cutting motion, it being only necessary to form the point of the tool to cut the shape required. Single points will answer most purposes, and are always to be preferred for removing the bulk of the material, the comb-chasers serving to smooth and finish the thread.

INDEX.

THE END.

PRINTED BY J. S. VIRTUE AND CO., LIMITED, CITY ROAD, LONDON

LONDON, *May*, 18_1.

A Catalogue of Books

INCLUDING MANY NEW AND STANDARD WORKS IN

ENGINEERING, ARCHITECTURE, AGRICULTURE, MATHEMATICS, MECHANICS, SCIENCE, ETC.

PUBLISHED BY

CROSBY LOCKWOOD & CO.,

7, STATIONERS'-HALL COURT, LUDGATE HILL, E.C.

ENGINEERING, SURVEYING, ETC.

Humber's New Work on Water-Supply.

A COMPREHENSIVE TREATISE on the WATER-SUPPLY of CITIES and TOWNS. By WILLIAM HUMBER, A-M. Inst. C.E., and M. Inst. M.E. Illustrated with 50 Double Plates, 1 Single Plate, Coloured Frontispiece, and upwards of 250 Woodcuts, and containing 400 pages of Text, Imp. 4to, 6*l.* 6*s.* elegantly and substantially half-bound in morocco.

List of Contents:—

I. Historical Sketch of some of the means that have been adopted for the Supply of Water to Cities and Towns.—II. Water and the Foreign Matter usually associated with it.—III. Rainfall and Evaporation.—IV. Springs and the water-bearing formations of various districts.—V. Measurement and Estimation of the Flow of Water.—VI. On the Selection of the Source of Supply.—VII. Wells.—VIII Reservoirs.—IX. The Purification of Water.—X. Pumps.—XI. Pumping Machinery.—XII. Conduits.—XIII. Distribution of Water.—XIV. Meters, Service Pipes, and House Fittings.—XV. The Law and Economy of Water Works.—XVI. Constant and Intermittent Supply.—XVII. Description of Plates.—Appendices, giving Tables of Rates of Supply, Velocities, &c. &c., together with Specifications of several Works illustrated, among which will be found:—Aberdeen, Bideford, Canterbury, Dundee, Halifax, Lambeth, Rotherham, Dublin, and others.

" The most systematic and valuable work upon water supply hitherto produced in English, or in any other language . . . . Mr. Humber's work is characterised almost throughout by an exhaustiveness much more distinctive of French and German than of English technical treatises."—*Engineer.*

Humber's Great Work on Bridge Construction.

A COMPLETE and PRACTICAL TREATISE on CAST and WROUGHT-IRON BRIDGE CONSTRUCTION, including Iron Foundations. In Three Parts—Theoretical, Practical, and Descriptive. By WILLIAM HUMBER, A-M. Inst. C.E., and M. Inst. M.E. Third Edition, with 115 Double Plates. In 2 vols. imp. 4to, 6*l.* 16*s.* 6*d.* half-bound in morocco.

" A book—and particularly a large and costly treatise like Mr. Humber's—which has reached its third edition may certainly be said to have established its own reputation."—*Engineering.*

B

Humber's Modern Engineering.

A RECORD of the PROGRESS of MODERN ENGINEER-
ING. First Series. Comprising Civil, Mechanical, Marine, Hydraulic, Railway, Bridge, and other Engineering Works, &c. By
WILLIAM HUMBER, A-M. Inst. C.E., &c. Imp. 4to, with
36 Double Plates, drawn to a large scale, and Portrait of John
Hawkshaw C.E., F.R.S., &c., and descriptive Letter-press, Specifications, &c.   3*l.* 3*s.* half morocco.

List of the Plates and Diagrams.

Victoria Station and Roof, L. B. & S. C. R. (8 plates); Southport Pier (2 plates); Victoria Station and Roof, L. C. & D. and G. W. R. (6 plates); Roof of Cremorne Music Hall; Bridge over G. N. Railway; Roof of Station, Dutch Rhenish Rail (2 plates); Bridge over the Thames, West London Extension Railway (5 plates); Armour Plates; Suspension Bridge, Thames (4 plates); The Allen Engine; Suspension Bridge, Avon (3 plates); Underground Railway (3 plates).

" Handsomely lithographed and printed. It will find favourwith many who desire
to preserve in a permanent form copies of the plans and specifications prepared for the
guidance of the contractors for many important engineering works."—*Engineer*.

HUMBER'S RECORD OF MODERN ENGINEERING. Second
Series. Imp. 4to, with 36 Double Plates, Portrait of Robert Stephenson, C.E., &c., and descriptive Letterpress, Specifications,
&c.   3*l.* 3*s.* half morocco.

List of the Plates and Diagrams.

Birkenhead Docks, Low Water Basin (15 plates); Charing Cross Station Roof, C. C. Railway (3 plates); Digswell Viaduct, G. N. Railway; Robbery Wood Viaduct, G. N. Railway; Iron Permanent Way; Clydach Viaduct, Merthyr, Tre-degar, and Abergavenny Railway; Ebbw Viaduct, Merthyr, Tredegar, and Aberga-venny Railway; College Wood Viaduct, Cornwall Railway; Dublin Winter Palace Roof (3 plates); Bridge over the Thames, L. C. and D. Railway (6 plates); Albert Harbour, Greenock (4 plates).

HUMBER'S RECORD OF MODERN ENGINEERING.   Third
Series. Imp. 4to, with 40 Double Plates, Portrait of J. R. M'Clean,
Esq., late Pres. Inst. C.E., and descriptive Letterpress, Specifica-
tions, &c.   3*l.* 3*s.* half morocco.

List of the Plates and Diagrams.

MAIN DRAINAGE, METROPOLIS. — *North Side.*—Map showing Interception of Sewers; Middle Level Sewer (2 plates'; Outfall Sewer, Bridge over River Lea (3 plates); Outfall Sewer, Bridge over Marsh Lane, North Woolwich Railway, and Bow and Barking Railway Junction; Outfall Sewer, Bridge over Bow and Barking Railway (3 plates); Outfall Sewer, Bridge over East London Waterworks' Feeder (2 plates); Outfall Sewer, Reservoir (2 plates); Outfall Sewer, Tumbling Bay and Outlet; Outfall Sewer, Penstocks. *South Side.*—Outfall Sewer, Bermondsey Branch (2 plates); Outfall Sewer, Reservoir and Outlet (4 plates); Outfall Sewer, Filth Hoist; Sections of Sewers (North and South Sides).

THAMES EMBANKMENT.— Section of River Wall; Steamboat Pier, Westminster (2 plates); Landing Stairs between Charing Cross and Waterloo Bridges; York Gate (2 plates); Overflow and Outlet at Savoy Street Sewer (3 plates); Steamboat Pier, Waterloo Bridge (3 plates); Junction of Sewers, Plans and Sections; Gullies, Plans and Sections; Rolling Stock; Granite and Iron Forts.

HUMBER'S RECORD OF MODERN ENGINEERING.   Fourth
Series. Imp. 4to, with 36 Double Plates, Portrait of John Fowler,
Esq., late Pres. Inst. C.E., and descriptive Letterpress, Specifica-
tions, &c.   3*l.* 3*s.* half morocco.

List of the Plates and Diagrams.

Abbey Mills Pumping Station, Main Drainage, Metropolis (4 plates); Barrow Docks (5 plates); Manquis Viaduct, Santiago and Valparaiso Railway (2 plates); Adam's Locomotive, St. Helen's Canal Railway (2 plates); Cannon Street Station Roof, Charing Cross Railway (3 plates); Road Bridge over the River Moka (2 plates). Telegraphic Apparatus for Meso-potamia; Viaduct over the River Wye, Midland Railway (3 plates); St. German's Viaduct, Cornwall Railway (2 plates); Wrought-Iron Cylinder for Diving Bell; Millwall Docks (6 plates); Milroy's Patent Excavator, Metropolitan District Railway (6 plates); Harbours, Ports, and Break-waters (3 plates).

Strains, Formulæ & Diagrams for Calculation of.

A HANDY BOOK for the CALCULATION of STRAINS in GIRDERS and SIMILAR STRUCTURES, and their STRENGTH ; consisting of Formulæ and Corresponding Diagrams, with numerous Details for Practical Application, &c. By WILLIAM HUMBER, A·M. Inst. C.E., &c. Third Edition. With nearly 100 Woodcuts and 3 Plates, Crown 8vo, 7s. 6d. cloth.

"The arrangement of the matter in this little volume is as convenient as it well could be. . . . The system of employing diagrams as a substitute for complex computations is one justly coming into great favour, and in that respect Mr. Humber's volume is fully up to the times."—*Engineering.*
"The formulæ are neatly expressed, and the diagrams good."—*Athenæum.*

Strains.

THE STRAINS ON STRUCTURES OF IRONWORK ; with Practical Remarks on Iron Construction. By F. W. SHEILDS, M. Inst. C.E. Second Edition, with 5 Plates. Royal 8vo, 5s. cloth.

"The student cannot find a better little book on this subject than that written by Mr. Sheilds."—*Engineer.*

Barlow on the Strength of Materials, enlarged.

A TREATISE ON THE STRENGTH OF MATERIALS, with Rules for application in Architecture, the Construction of Suspension Bridges, Railways, &c. ; and an Appendix on the Power of Locomotive Engines, and the effect of Inclined Planes and Gradients. By PETER BARLOW, F.R.S. A New Edition, revised by his Sons, P. W. BARLOW, F.R.S., and W. H. BARLOW, F.R.S. The whole arranged and edited by W. HUMBER, A·M. Inst. C.E. 8vo, 400 pp., with 19 large Plates, 18s. cloth.

"The best book on the subject which has yet appeared. . . . . We know of no work that so completely fulfils its mission."—*English Mechanic.*
"The standard treatise upon this particular subject."—*Engineer.*

Strength of Cast Iron, &c.

A PRACTICAL ESSAY on the STRENGTH of CAST IRON and OTHER METALS. By THOMAS TREDGOLD, C.E. Fifth Edition. To which are added, Experimental Researches on the Strength and other Properties of Cast Iron, by E. HODGKINSON, F.R.S. With 9 Engravings and numerous Woodcuts. 8vo, 12s. cloth.   *** HODGKINSON'S RESEARCHES, separate, price 6s.

Hydraulics.

HYDRAULIC TABLES, CO-EFFICIENTS, and FORMULÆ for finding the Discharge of Water from Orifices, Notches, Weirs, Pipes, and Rivers. With New Formulæ, Tables, and General Information on Rain-fall, Catchment-Basins, Drainage, Sewerage, Water Supply for Towns and Mill Power. By JOHN NEVILLE, Civil Engineer, M.R.I.A. Third Edition, carefully revised, with considerable Additions. Numerous Illustrations. Cr. 8vo, 14s. cloth.

"Undoubtedly an exceedingly useful and elaborate compilation."—*Iron.*
"Alike valuable to students and engineers in practice."—*Mining Journal.*

River Engineering.

RIVER BARS : Notes on the Causes of their Formation, and on their Treatment by 'Induced Tidal Scour,' with a Description of the Successful Reduction by this Method of the Bar at Dublin. By I. J. MANN, Assistant Engineer to the Dublin Port and Docks Board. With Illustrations. Royal 8vo. 7s. 6d. cloth. [Just published.

Levelling.

A TREATISE on the PRINCIPLES and PRACTICE of LEVELLING; showing its Application to Purposes of Railway and Civil Engineering, in the Construction of Roads; with Mr. TELFORD's Rules for the same. By FREDERICK W. SIMMS, F.G.S., M. Inst. C.E. Sixth Edition, very carefully revised, with the addition of Mr. LAW's Practical Examples for Setting out Railway Curves, and Mr. TRAUTWINE's Field Practice of Laying out Circular Curves. With 7 Plates and numerous Woodcuts. 8vo, 8s. 6d. cloth. *₊* TRAUTWINE on Curves, separate, 5s.

"The text-book on levelling in most of our engineering schools and colleges."—*Engineer.*

Practical Tunnelling.

PRACTICAL TUNNELLING: Explaining in detail the Setting out of the Works, Shaft-sinking and Heading-Driving, Ranging the Lines and Levelling under Ground, Sub-Excavating, Timbering, and the Construction of the Brickwork of Tunnels with the amount of labour required for, and the Cost of, the various portions of the work. By F. W. SIMMS, M. Inst. C.E. Third Edition, Revised and Extended. By D. KINNEAR CLARK, M.I.C.E. Imp. 8vo, with 21 Folding Plates and numerous Wood Engravings, 30s. cloth.

"It has been regarded from the first as a text-book of the subject. . . . Mr. Clark has added immensely to the value of the book."—*Engineer.*

Steam.

STEAM AND THE STEAM ENGINE, Stationary and Portable. Being an Extension of Sewell's Treatise on Steam. By D. KINNEAR CLARK, M.I.C.E. Second Edition. 12mo, 4s. cloth.

Civil and Hydraulic Engineering.

CIVIL ENGINEERING. By HENRY LAW, M. Inst. C.E. Including a Treatise on Hydraulic Engineering, by GEORGE R. BURNELL, M.I.C.E. Sixth Edition, Revised, with large additions on Recent Practice in Civil Engineering, by D. KINNEAR CLARK, M. Inst. C.E. 12mo, 7s. 6d., cloth. [*Just published.*

Gas-Lighting.

COMMON SENSE FOR GAS-USERS: a Catechism of Gas-Lighting for Householders, Gasfitters, Millowners, Architects, Engineers, &c. By R. WILSON, C.E. 2nd Edition. Cr. 8vo, 2s. 6d.

Bridge Construction in Masonry, Timber, & Iron.

EXAMPLES OF BRIDGE AND VIADUCT CONSTRUCTION OF MASONRY, TIMBER, AND IRON; consisting of 46 Plates from the Contract Drawings or Admeasurement of select Works. By W. DAVIS HASKOLL, C.E. Second Edition, with the addition of 554 Estimates, and the Practice of Setting out Works, with 6 pages of Diagrams. Imp. 4to, 2l. 12s. 6d. half-morocco.

"A work of the present nature by a man of Mr. Haskoll's experience, must prove invaluable. The tables of estimates considerably enhance its value."—*Engineering.*

Earthwork.

EARTHWORK TABLES, showing the Contents in Cubic Yards of Embankments, Cuttings, &c., of Heights or Depths up to an average of 80 feet. By JOSEPH BROADBENT, C.E., and FRANCIS CAMPIN, C.E. Cr. 8vo, oblong, 5s. cloth.

Tramways and their Working.

TRAMWAYS: their CONSTRUCTION and WORKING.
Containing a Comprehensive History of the System; an exhaustive Analysis of the Various Modes of Traction, including Horse Power, Steam, Heated Water, and Compressed Air; a Description of the varieties of Rolling Stock; and ample Details of Cost and Working Expenses, with Special Reference to the Tramways of the United Kingdom. By D. KINNEAR CLARK, M. I. C. E., Author of 'Railway Machinery,' &c., in one vol. 8vo, with numerous Illustrations and thirteen folding Plates, 18*s*. cloth.

"All interested in tramways must refer to it, as all railway engineers have turned to the author's work 'Railway Machinery.'"—*The Engineer.*
"Mr. Clark's book is indispensable for the students of the subject."—*The Builder.*

Pioneer Engineering.

PIONEER ENGINEERING. A Treatise on the Engineering Operations connected with the Settlement of Waste Lands in New Countries. By EDWARD DOBSON, A.I.C.E. With Plates and Wood Engravings. Revised Edition. 12mo, 5*s*. cloth.

"A workmanlike production, and one without possession of which no man should start to encounter the duties of a pioneer engineer."—*Athenæum.*

Steam Engine.

TEXT-BOOK ON THE STEAM ENGINE. By T. M. GOODEVE, M.A., Barrister-at-Law, Author of "The Principles of Mechanics," "The Elements of Mechanism," &c. Third Edition. With numerous Illustrations. Crown 8vo, 6*s*. cloth.

"Professor Goodeve has given us a treatise on the steam engine, which will bear comparison with anything written by Huxley or Maxwell, and we can award it no higher praise."—*Engineer.*
"Mr. Goodeve's text-book is a work of which every young engineer should possess himself."—*Mining Journal.*

Steam.

THE SAFE USE OF STEAM: containing Rules for Unprofessional Steam Users. By an ENGINEER. 4th Edition. Sewed, 6*d*.

"If steam-users would but learn this little book by heart, boiler explosions would become sensations by their rarity."—*English Mechanic.*

Mechanical Engineering.

MECHANICAL ENGINEERING: a Practical Treatise on. Comprising Metallurgy, Moulding, Casting, Forging, Tools, Workshop Machinery, Mechanical Manipulation, Manufacture of the Steam Engine, &c. By FRANCIS CAMPIN, C.E., Author of "Materials and Construction," &c. With Numerous Illustrations. 12mo, 3*s*. cloth boards.   [*Just published.*

Works of Construction.

MATERIALS AND CONSTRUCTION: a Theoretical and Practical Treatise on the Strains, Designing, and Erection of Works of Construction. By FRANCIS CAMPIN, C.E., Author of "A Practical Treatise on Mechanical Engineering, &c." 12mo, 3*s*. 6*d*. cloth boards.

Iron Bridges, Girders, Roofs, &c.

A TREATISE ON THE APPLICATION OF IRON TO THE CONSTRUCTION OF BRIDGES, GIRDERS, ROOFS, AND OTHER WORKS. By F. CAMPIN, C.E. 12mo, 3*s*.

Oblique Arches.

A PRACTICAL TREATISE ON THE CONSTRUCTION of
OBLIQUE ARCHES. By JOHN HART. 3rd Ed. Imp. 8vo, 8s. cloth.

Oblique Bridges.

A PRACTICAL and THEORETICAL ESSAY on OBLIQUE
BRIDGES, with 13 large Plates. By the late GEO. WATSON
BUCK, M.I.C.E. Third Edition, revised by his Son, J. H. WATSON
BUCK, M.I.C.E. ; and with the addition of Description to Dia-
grams for Facilitating the Construction of Oblique Bridges, by
W. H. BARLOW, M.I.C.E. Royal 8vo, 12s. cloth.
"The standard text book for all engineers regarding skew arches is Mr. Bu_k's
treatise and it would be impossible to consult a better."—*Engineer.*

Gas and Gasworks.

THE CONSTRUCTION OF GASWORKS AND THE
MANUFACTURE AND DISTRIBUTION OF COAL-GAS.
Originally written by SAMUEL HUGHES, C.E. Sixth Edition.
Re-written and much Enlarged, by WILLIAM RICHARDS, C.E.
With 72 Woodcuts. 12mo, 5s. cloth boards.

Waterworks for Cities and Towns.

WATERWORKS for the SUPPLY of CITIES and TOWNS,
with a Description of the Principal Geological Formations of England as influencing Supplies of Water. By S. HUGHES. 4s. 6d. cloth.

Locomotive-Engine Driving.

LOCOMOTIVE-ENGINE DRIVING ; a Practical Manual for
Engineers in charge of Locomotive Engines. By MICHAEL
REYNOLDS, M.S.E., formerly Locomotive Inspector L. B. and
S. C. R. Fourth Edition, greatly enlarged. Comprising A
KEY TO THE LOCOMOTIVE ENGINE. With Illustra-
tions and Portrait of Author. Crown 8vo, 4s. 6d. cloth.
"Mr. Reynolds has supplied a want, and has supplied it well. We can confidently
recommend the book not only to the practical driver, but to every one who takes an
nterest in the performance of locomotive engines."—*Engineer.*

The Engineer, Fireman, and Engine-Boy.

THE MODEL LOCOMOTIVE ENGINEER, FIREMAN,
AND ENGINE-BOY : comprising a Historical Notice of the
Pioneer Locomotive Engines and their Inventors, with a project
for the establishment of Certificates of Qualification in the Running
Service of Railways. By MICHAEL REYNOLDS, Author of
"Locomotive-Engine Driving." Crown 8vo, 4s. 6d. cloth.
"From the technical knowledge of the author it will appeal to the railway man of
o-day more forcibly than anything written by Dr. Smiles."—*English Mechanic.*

Stationary Engine Driving.

STATIONARY ENGINE DRIVING. A Practical Manual fcr
Engineers in Charge of Stationary Engines. By MICHAEL REY-
NOLDS ("The Engine-Driver's Friend"), Author of "Locomo-
tive-Engine Driving," &c. With Plates and Woodcuts, and Steel
Portrait of James Watt. Crown 8vo, 4s. 6d. cloth.

Engine-Driving Life.

ENGINE-DRIVING LIFE ; or Stirring Adventures and Inci-
dents in the Lives of Locomotive Engine-Drivers. By MICHAEL
REYNOLDS. Crown 8vo, 2s. cloth.   [*Just published.*

Construction of Iron Beams, Pillars, &c.

IRON AND HEAT; exhibiting the Principles concerned in the construction of Iron Beams, Pillars, and Bridge Girders, and the Action of Heat in the Smelting Furnace. By J. ARMOUR, C.E. 3s.

Fire Engineering.

FIRES, FIRE-ENGINES, AND FIRE BRIGADES. With a History of Fire-Engines, their Construction, Use, and Management; Remarks on Fire-Proof Buildings, and the Preservation of Life from Fire; Statistics of the Fire Appliances in English Towns; Foreign Fire Systems; Hints on Fire Brigades, &c., &c. By CHARLES F. T. YOUNG, C.E. With numerous Illustrations, handsomely printed, 544 pp., demy 8vo, 1l. 4s. cloth.

"We can most heartily commend this book."—*Engineering.*

"Mr. Young's book on 'Fire Engines and Fire Brigades' contains a mass of information, which has been collected from a variety of sources. The subject is so intensely interesting and useful that it demands consideration."—*Building News.*

Trigonometrical Surveying.

AN OUTLINE OF THE METHOD OF CONDUCTING A TRIGONOMETRICAL SURVEY, for the Formation of Geographical and Topographical Maps and Plans, Military Reconnaissance, Levelling, &c., with the most useful Problems in Geodesy and Practical Astronomy. By LIEUT.-GEN. FROME, R.E., late Inspector-General of Fortifications. Fourth Edition, Enlarged, and partly Re-written. By CAPTAIN CHARLES WARREN, R.E. With 19 Plates and 115 Woodcuts, royal 8vo, 16s. cloth.

Tables of Curves.

TABLES OF TANGENTIAL ANGLES and MULTIPLES for setting out Curves from 5 to 200 Radius. By ALEXANDER BEAZELEY, M. Inst. C.E. Second Edition. Printed on 48 Cards, and sold in a cloth box, waistcoat-pocket size, 3s. 6d.

"Each table is printed on a small card, which, being placed on the theodolite, leaves the hands free to manipulate the instrument."—*Engineer.*

"Very handy; a man may know that all his day's work must fall on two of these cards, which he puts into his own card-case, and leaves the rest behind."— [*Athenæum.*

Engineering Fieldwork.

THE PRACTICE OF ENGINEERING FIELDWORK, applied to Land and Hydraulic, Hydrographic, and Submarine Surveying and Levelling. Second Edition, revised, with considerable additions, and a Supplement on WATERWORKS, SEWERS, SEWAGE, and IRRIGATION. By W. DAVIS HASKOLL, C.E. Numerous folding Plates. In 1 Vol., demy 8vo, 1l. 5s., cl. boards.

Large Tunnel Shafts.

THE CONSTRUCTION OF LARGE TUNNEL SHAFTS. A Practical and Theoretical Essay. By J. H. WATSON BUCK, M. Inst. C.E., Resident Engineer, London and North-Western Railway. Illustrated with Folding Plates. Royal 8vo, 12s. cloth.

"Many of the methods given are of extreme practical value to the mason, and the observations on the form of arch, the rules for ordering the stone, and the construction of the templates, will be found of considerable use. We commend the book to the engineering profession, and to all who have to build similar shafts."—*Building News.*

"Will be regarded by civil engineers as of the utmost value, and calculated to save much time and obviate many mistakes"—*Colliery Guardian.*

Survey Practice.

AID TO SURVEY PRACTICE: for Reference in Surveying, Levelling, Setting-out and in Route Surveys of Travellers by Land and Sea. With Tables, Illustrations, and Records. By LOWIS D'A. JACKSON, A-M.I.C.E. Author of "Hydraulic Manual and Statistics," &c. Large crown, 8vo, 12s. 6d., cloth.

"Mr. Jackson has produced a valuable *vade-mecum* for the surveyor. We can recommend this book as containing an admirable supplement to the teaching of the accomplished surveyor."—*Athenæum.*

"A general text book was wanted, and we are able to speak with confidence of Mr. Jackson's treatise. . . . We cannot recommend to the student who knows something of the mathematical principles of the subject a better course than to fortify his practice in the field under a competent surveyor with a study of Mr. Jackson's useful manual. The field records illustrate every kind of survey, and will be found an essential aid to the student."—*Building News.*

"The author brings to his work a fortunate union of theory and practical experience which, aided by a clear and lucid style of writing, renders the book both a very useful one and very agreeable to read."—*Builder.*

Sanitary Work.

SANITARY WORK IN THE SMALLER TOWNS AND IN VILLAGES. Comprising :—1. Some of the more Common Forms of Nuisance and their Remedies ; 2. Drainage ; 3. Water Supply. By CHAS. SLAGG, Assoc. Inst. C.E. Crown 8vo, 3s. cloth.

"A very useful book, and may be safely recommended. The author has had practical experience in the works of which he treats."—*Builder.*

Locomotives.

LOCOMOTIVE ENGINES, A Rudimentary Treatise on. Comprising an Historical Sketch and Description of the Locomotive Engine. By G. D. DEMPSEY, C.E. With large additions treating of the MODERN LOCOMOTIVE, by D. KINNEAR CLARK, C.E., M.I.C.E., Author of "Tramways, their Construction and Working," &c., &c. With numerous Illustrations. 12mo. 3s. 6d. cloth boards.

"The student cannot fail to profit largely by adopting this as his preliminary text-book."—*Iron and Coal Trades Review.*

"Seems a model of what an elementary technical book should be."—*Academy.*

Fuels and their Economy.

FUEL, its Combustion and Economy ; consisting of an Abridgment of "A Treatise on the Combustion of Coal and the Prevention of Smoke." By C. W. WILLIAMS, A.I.C.E. With extensive additions on Recent Practice in the Combustion and Economy of Fuel—Coal, Coke, Wood, Peat, Petroleum, &c. ; by D. KINNEAR CLARK, C.E., M.I.C.E. Second Edition, revised. With numerous Illustrations. 12mo. 4s. cloth boards.

"Students should buy the book and read it, as one of the most complete and satisfactory treatises on the combustion and economy of fuel to be had."—*Engineer.*

Roads and Streets.

THE CONSTRUCTION OF ROADS AND STREETS. In Two Parts. I. The Art of Constructing Common Roads. By HENRY LAW, C.E. Revised and Condensed. II. Recent Practice in the Construction of Roads and Streets : including Pavements of Stone, Wood, and Asphalte. By D. KINNEAR CLARK, C.E., M.I.C.E. Second Edit., revised. 12mo, 5s. cloth.

"A book which every borough surveyor and engineer must possess, and which will be of considerable service to architects, builders, and property owners generally."—*Building News.*

Sewing Machine (The).

SEWING MACHINERY; being a Practical Manual of the Sewing Machine, comprising its History and Details of its Construction, with full Technical Directions for the Adjusting of Sewing Machines. By J. W. URQUHART, Author of "Electro Plating: a Practical Manual;" "Electric Light: its Production and Use." With Numerous Illustrations. 12mo, 2s. 6d. cloth boards.

Field-Book for Engineers.

THE ENGINEER'S, MINING SURVEYOR'S, and CONTRACTOR'S FIELD-BOOK. By W. DAVIS HASKOLL, C.E. Consisting of a Series of Tables, with Rules, Explanations of Systems, and Use of Theodolite for Traverse Surveying and Plotting the Work with minute accuracy by means of Straight Edge and Set Square only; Levelling with the Theodolite, Casting out and Reducing Levels to Datum, and Plotting Sections in the ordinary manner; Setting out Curves with the Theodolite by Tangential Angles and Multiples with Right and Left-hand Readings of the Instrument; Setting out Curves without Theodolite on the System of Tangential Angles by Sets of Tangents and Offsets; and Earthwork Tables to 80 feet deep, calculated for every 6 inches in depth. With numerous Woodcuts. 4th Edition, enlarged. Cr. 8vo. 12s. cloth.

"The book is very handy, and the author might have added that the separate tables of sines and tangents to every minute will make it useful for many other purposes, the genuine traverse tables existing all the same."—*Athenæum.*

"Cannot fail, from its portability and utility, to be extensively patronised by the engineering profession."—*Mining Journal.*

Earthwork, Measurement and Calculation of.

A MANUAL on EARTHWORK. By ALEX. J. S. GRAHAM, C.E., Resident Engineer, Forest of Dean Central Railway. With numerous Diagrams. 18mo, 2s. 6d. cloth.

"As a really handy book for reference, we know of no work equal to it; and the railway engineers and others employed in the measurement and calculation of earthwork will find a great amount of practical information very admirably arranged, and available for general or rough estimates, as well as for the more exact calculations required in the engineers' contractor's offices."—*Artisan.*

Drawing for Engineers, &c.

THE WORKMAN'S MANUAL OF ENGINEERING DRAWING. By JOHN MAXTON, Instructor in Engineering Drawing, Royal Naval College, Greenwich, formerly of R. S. N. A., South Kensington. Fourth Edition, carefully revised. With upwards of 300 Plates and Diagrams. 12mo, cloth, strongly bound, 4s.

"A copy of it should be kept for reference in every drawing office."—*Engineering.*
"Indispensable for teachers of engineering drawing."—*Mechanics' Magazine.*

Weale's Dictionary of Terms.

A DICTIONARY of TERMS used in ARCHITECTURE, BUILDING, ENGINEERING, MINING, METALLURGY, ARCHÆOLOGY, the FINE ARTS, &c. By JOHN WEALE. Fifth Edition, revised by ROBERT HUNT, F.R.S., Keeper of Mining Records, Editor of "Ure's Dictionary of Arts." 12mo, 6s. cl. bds.

"The best small technological dictionary in the language."—*Architect.*
"The absolute accuracy of a work of this character can only be judged of after extensive consultation, and from our examination it appears very correct and very complete."—*Mining Journal.*

MINING, METALLURGY, ETC.

Metalliferous Minerals and Mining.

A TREATISE ON METALLIFEROUS MINERALS AND
MINING. By D.C. DAVIES, F.G.S., author of "A Treatise on
Slate and Slate Quarrying." With numerous wood engravings.
Second Edition, revised. Cr. 8vo. 12s. 6d. cloth.

"Without question, the most exhaustive and the most practically useful work we
have seen ; the amount of information given is enormous, and it is given concisely
and intelligibly."—*Mining Journal.*

"The volume is one which no student of mineralogy should be without."—*Colliery
Guardian.*

"The author has gathered together from all available sources a vast amount of
really useful information. As a history of the present state of mining throughout
the world this book has a real value, and it supplies an actual want, for no such information has hitherto been brought together within such limited space."—*Athenæum.*

Slate and Slate Quarrying.

A TREATISE ON SLATE AND SLATE QUARRYING,
Scientific, Practical, and Commercial. By D. C. DAVIES, F.G.S.,
Mining Engineer, &c. With numerous Illustrations and Folding
Plates. Second Edition, carefully revised. 12mo, 3s. 6d. cloth boards.

"Mr. Davies has written a useful and practical hand-book on an important industry,
with all the conditions and details of which he appears familiar."—*Engineering.*

"The work is illustrated by actual practice, and is unusually thorough and lucid.
. . . Mr. Davies has completed his work with industry and skill."—*Builder.*

Metallurgy of Iron.

A TREATISE ON THE METALLURGY OF IRON : con-
taining Outlines of the History of Iron Manufacture, Methods of
Assay, and Analyses of Iron Ores, Processes of Manufacture of
Iron and Steel, &c. By H. BAUERMAN, F.G.S., Associate of the
Royal School of Mines. With numerous Illustrations. Fourth
Edition, revised and much enlarged. 12mo, cloth boards, 5s.

"Has the merit of brevity and conciseness, as to less important points, while all
material matters are very fully and thoroughly entered into."—*Standard.*

Manual of Mining Tools.

MINING TOOLS. For the use of Mine Managers, Agents,
Mining Students, &c. By WILLIAM MORGANS, Lecturer on Practical Mining at the Bristol School of Mines. Volume of Text.
12mo, 3s. With an Atlas of Plates, containing 235 Illustrations.
4to, 6s. Together, 9s. cloth boards.

"Students in the Science of Mining, and Overmen, Captains, Managers, and
Viewers may gain practical knowledge and useful hints by the study of Mr.
Morgans' Manual."—*Colliery Guardian.*

Mining, Surveying and Valuing.

THE MINERAL SURVEYOR AND VALUER'S COM-
PLETE GUIDE, comprising a Treatise on Improved Mining
Surveying, with new Traverse Tables ; and Descriptions of Im-
proved Instruments ; also an Exposition of the Correct Principles
of Laying out and Valuing Home and Foreign Iron and Coal
Mineral Properties. By WILLIAM LINTERN, Mining and Civil
Engineer. With four Plates of Diagrams, Plans, &c., 12mo, 4s. cloth.

"Contains much valuable information given in a small compass, and which, as fa
as we have tested it, is thoroughly trustworthy."—*Iron and Coal Trades Review.*

*** The above, bound with THOMAN'S TABLES. (See page 20.)
Price 7s. 6d. cloth.

Coal and Coal Mining.

COAL AND COAL MINING: a Rudimentary Treatise on. By WARINGTON W. SMYTH, M.A., F.R.S., &c., Chief Inspector of the Mines of the Crown. Fifth edition, revised and corrected. 12mo, with numerous Illustations, 4s. cloth boards.

"Every portion of the volume appears to have been prepared with much care, and as an outline is given of every known coal-field in this and other countries, as well as of the two principal methods of working, the book will doubtless interest a very large number of readers."—*Mining Journal.*

Underground Pumping Machinery.

MINE DRAINAGE; being a Complete and Practical Treatise on Direct-Acting Underground Steam Pumping Machinery, with a Description of a large number of the best known Engines, their General Utility and the Special Sphere of their Action, the Mode of their Application, and their merits compared with other forms of Pumping Machinery. By STEPHEN MICHELL, Joint-Author of "The Cornish System of Mine Drainage." 8vo, 15s. cloth. [*Just published.*

NAVAL ARCHITECTURE, NAVIGATION, ETC.

Pocket Book for Naval Architects & Shipbuilders.

THE NAVAL ARCHITECT'S AND SHIPBUILDER'S POCKET BOOK OF FORMULÆ, RULES, AND TABLES AND MARINE ENGINEER'S AND SURVEYOR'S HANDY BOOK OF REFERENCE. By CLEMENT MACKROW, M. Inst. N. A., Naval Draughtsman. With numerous Diagrams. Fcap., 12s. 6d., strongly bound in leather.

"Should be used by all who are engaged in the construction or design of vessels.' —*Engineer.*

"There is scarcely a subject on which a naval architect or shipbuilder can require to refresh his memory which will not be found within the covers of Mr. Mackrow's book."—*English Mechanic.*

"Mr. Mackrow has compressed an extraordinary amount of information into this useful volume."—*Athenæum.*

Grantham's Iron Ship-Building.

ON IRON SHIP-BUILDING; with Practical Examples and Details. Fifth Edition. Imp. 4to, boards, enlarged from 24 to 40 Plates (21 quite new), including the latest Examples. Together with separate Text, also considerably enlarged, 12mo, cloth limp. By JOHN GRANTHAM, M. Inst. C.E., &c. 2l. 2s. complete.

"Mr. Grantham's work is of great interest. It will, we are confident, command an extensive circulation among shipbuilders in general. By order of the Board of Admiralty, the work will form the text-book on which the examination in iron ship-building of candidates for promotion in the dockyards will be mainly based."—*Engineering.*

Pocket-Book for Marine Engineers.

A POCKET-BOOK OF USEFUL TABLES AND FOR MULÆ FOR MARINE ENGINEERS. By FRANK PROCTOR, A.I.N.A. Second Edition, revised and enlarged. Royal 32mo, leather, gilt edges, with strap, 4s.

"A most useful companion to all marine engineers."—*United Service Gazette.* "Scarcely anything required by a naval engineer appears to have been forgotten."—*Iron.*

Light-Houses.

EUROPEAN LIGHT-HOUSE SYSTEMS; being a Report of a Tour of Inspection made in 1873. By Major GEORGE H. ELLIOT, Corps of Engineers, U.S.A. Illustrated by 51 Engravings and 31 Woodcuts in the Text. 8vo, 21s. cloth.

Surveying (Land and Marine).

LAND AND MARINE SURVEYING, in Reference to the Preparation of Plans for Roads and Railways, Canals, Rivers, Towns' Water Supplies, Docks and Harbours; with Description and Use of Surveying Instruments. By W. DAVIS HASKOLL, C. E. With 14 folding Plates, and numerous Woodcuts. 8vo, 12s. 6d. cloth.
" A most useful and well arranged book for the aid of a student."—*Builder.*
" Of the utmost practical utility, and may be safely recommended to all students who aspire to become clean and expert surveyors."—*Mining Journal.*

Storms.

STORMS: their Nature, Classification, and Laws, with the Means of Predicting them by their Embodiments, the Clouds. By WILLIAM BLASIUS. Crown 8vo, 10s. 6d. cloth boards.

Rudimentary Navigation.

THE SAILOR'S SEA-BOOK: a Rudimentary Treatise on Navigation. By JAMES GREENWOOD, B.A. New and enlarged edition. By W. H. ROSSER. 12mo, 3s. cloth boards.

Mathematical and Nautical Tables.

MATHEMATICAL TABLES, for Trigonometrical, Astronomical, and Nautical Calculations; to which is prefixed a Treatise on Logarithms. By HENRY LAW, C.E. Together with a Series of Tables for Navigation and Nautical Astronomy. By J. R. YOUNG, formerly Professor of Mathematics in Belfast College. New Edition. 12mo, 4s. cloth boards.

Navigation (Practical), with Tables.

PRACTICAL NAVIGATION: consisting of the Sailor's Sea-Book, by JAMES GREENWOOD and W. H. ROSSER; together with the requisite Mathematical and Nautical Tables for the Working of the Problems. By HENRY LAW, C.E., and Professor J. R. YOUNG. Illustrated with numerous Wood Engravings and Coloured Plates. 12mo, 7s. strongly half bound in leather.

WEALE'S RUDIMENTARY SERIES.

The following books in Naval Architecture, etc., are published in the above series.

MASTING, MAST-MAKING, AND RIGGING OF SHIPS. By ROBERT KIPPING, N.A. Fourteenth Edition. 12mo, 2s. 6d. cloth.
SAILS AND SAIL-MAKING. Tenth Edition, enlarged. By ROBERT KIPPING, N.A. Illustrated. 12mo, 3s. cloth boards.
NAVAL ARCHITECTURE. By JAMES PEAKE. Fourth Edition, with Plates and Diagrams. 12mo, 4s. cloth boards.
MARINE ENGINES, AND STEAM VESSELS. By ROBERT MURRAY, C.E. Seventh Edition. 12mo, 3s. 6d. cloth boards.

ARCHITECTURE, BUILDING, ETC.

Construction.

THE SCIENCE of BUILDING: An Elementary Treatise on the Principles of Construction. By E. WYNDHAM TARN, M.A., Architect. With 47 Wood Engravings. Demy 8vo, 8s. 6d. cloth.
"A very valuable book, which we strongly recommend to all students."—*Builder*.
"No architectural student should be without this hand-book."—*Architect*.

Villa Architecture.

A HANDY BOOK of VILLA ARCHITECTURE; being a Series of Designs for Villa Residences in various Styles. With Detailed Specifications and Estimates. By C. WICKES, Architect, Author of "The Spires and Towers of the Mediæval Churches of England," &c. 31 Plates, 4to, half morocco, gilt edges, 1l. 1s.
. Also an Enlarged edition of the above. 61 Plates, with Detailed Specifications, Estimates, &c. 2l. 2s. half morocco.
"The whole of the designs bear evidence of their being the work of an artistic architect, and they will prove very valuable and suggestive."—*Building News*.

Useful Text-Book for Architects.

THE ARCHITECT'S GUIDE: Being a Text-book of Useful Information for Architects, Engineers, Surveyors, Contractors, Clerks of Works, &c. By FREDERICK ROGERS. Author of "Specifications for Practical Architecture," &c. Cr. 8vo, 6s. cloth.
"As a text-book of useful information for architects, engineers, surveyors, &c., it would be hard to find a handier or more complete little volume."—*Standard*.

Taylor and Cresy's Rome.

THE ARCHITECTURAL ANTIQUITIES OF ROME. By the late G. L. TAYLOR, Esq., F.S.A., and EDWARD CRESY, Esq. New Edition, thoroughly revised, and supplemented under the editorial care of the Rev. ALEXANDER TAYLOR, M.A. (son of the late G. L. Taylor, Esq.), Chaplain of Gray's Inn. This is the only book which gives on a large scale, and with the precision of architectural measurement, the principal Monuments of Ancient Rome in plan, elevation, and detail. Large folio, with 130 Plates, half-bound, 3l. 3s.
. Originally published in two volumes, folio, at 18l. 18s.

Vitruvius' Architecture.

THE ARCHITECTURE OF MARCUS VITRUVIUS POLLIO. Translated by JOSEPH GWILT, F.S.A., F.R.A.S. Numerous Plates. 12mo, cloth limp, 5s.

The Young Architect's Book.

HINTS TO YOUNG ARCHITECTS. By GEORGE WIGHTWICK, Architect. New Edition, revised and enlarged. By G. HUSKISSON GUILLAUME, Architect. 12mo, cloth boards, 4s.
"Will be found an acquisition to pupils, and a copy ought to be considered as necessary a purchase as a box of instruments."—*Architect*.
"A large amount of information, which young architects will do well to acquire, if they wish to succeed in the everyday work of their profession."—*English Mechanic*.

Drawing for Builders and Students.

PRACTICAL RULES ON DRAWING for the OPERATIVE BUILDER and YOUNG STUDENT in ARCHITECTURE. By GEORGE PYNE. With 14 Plates, 4to, 7s. 6d. boards.

The House-Owner's Estimator.

THE HOUSE-OWNER'S ESTIMATOR; or, What will it Cost to Build, Alter, or Repair? A Price-Book adapted to the Use of Unprofessional People as well as for the Architectural Surveyor and Builder. By the late JAMES D. SIMON, A.R.I.B.A. Edited and Revised by FRANCIS T. W. MILLER, A.R.I.B.A., Surveyor. Third Edition, carefully Revised. Crown 8vo, 3s. 6d., cloth. [*Just published.*

" In two years it will repay its cost a hundred times over."—*Field.*
" A very handy book for those who want to know what a house will cost to build, alter, or repair."—*English Mechanic.*

Boiler and Factory Chimneys.

BOILER AND FACTORY CHIMNEYS ; their Draught-power and Stability, with a chapter on Lightning Conductors. By ROBERT WILSON, C.E., Author of " Treatise on Steam Boilers," &c., &c. Crown 8vo, 3s. 6d. cloth.

Civil and Ecclesiastical Building.

A BOOK ON BUILDING, CIVIL AND ECCLESIASTICAL, Including CHURCH RESTORATION. By Sir EDMUND BECKETT, Bart., LL.D., Q.C., F.R.A.S., Chancellor and Vicar-General of York. Author of "Clocks and Watches and Bells," &c. Second Edition, 12mo, 5s. cloth boards.

" A book which is always amusing and nearly always instructive. Sir E. Beckett will be read for the raciness of his style. We are able very cordially to recommend all persons to read it for themselves. The style throughout is in the highest degree condensed and epigrammatic."—*Times.*
" We commend the book to the thoughtful consideration of all who are interested in the building art."—*Builder.*

Architecture, Ancient and Modern.

RUDIMENTARY ARCHITECTURE, Ancient and Modern. Consisting of VITRUVIUS, translated by JOSEPH GWILT, F.S.A., &c., with 23 fine copper plates; GRECIAN Architecture, by the EARL of ABERDEEN; the ORDERS of Architecture, by W. H. LEEDS, Esq.; The STYLES of Architecture of Various Countries, by T. TALBOT BURY; The PRINCIPLES of DESIGN in Architecture, by E. L. GARBETT. In one volume, half-bound (pp. 1,100), copiously illustrated, 12s.

⁎ *Sold separately, in two vols., as follows—*
ANCIENT ARCHITECTURE. Containing Gwilt's Vitruvius and Aberdeen's Grecian Architecture. Price 6s. half-bound.
N.B.—*This is the only edition of VITRUVIUS procurable at a moderate price.*
MODERN ARCHITECTURE. Containing the Orders, by Leeds ; The Styles, by Bury ; and Design, by Garbett. 6s. half-bound.

House Painting.

HOUSE PAINTING, GRAINING, MARBLING, AND SIGN WRITING : a Practical Manual of. With 9 Coloured Plates of Woods and Marbles, and nearly 150 Wood Engravings. By ELLIS A. DAVIDSON, Author of "Building Construction," &c. Third Edition, carefully revised. 12mo, 6s. cloth boards.
" Contains a mass of information of use to the amateur and of value to the practical man."—*English Mechanic.*

Plumbing.

PLUMBING; a Text-book to the Practice of the Art or Craft of the Plumber. With chapters upon House-drainage, embodying the latest Improvements. By W. P. BUCHAN, Sanitary Engineer. Second Edition, enlarged, with 300 illustrations, 12mo.   4s. cloth.

" The chapters on house-drainage may be usefully consulted, not only by plumbers, but also by engineers and all engaged or interested in house-building."—*Iron.*

Handbook of Specifications.

THE HANDBOOK OF SPECIFICATIONS; or, Practical Guide to the Architect, Engineer, Surveyor, and Builder, in drawing up Specifications and Contracts for Works and Constructions. Illustrated by Precedents of Buildings actually executed by eminent Architects and Engineers. By Professor THOMAS L. DONALDSON, M.I.B.A. New Edition, in One large volume, 8vo, with upwards of 1000 pages of text, and 33 Plates, cloth, 1l. 11s. 6d.

" In this work forty-four specifications of executed works are given. . . . Donaldson's Handbook of Specifications must be bought by all architects."—*Builder.*

Specifications for Practical Architecture.

SPECIFICATIONS FOR PRACTICAL ARCHITECTURE: A Guide to the Architect, Engineer, Surveyor, and Builder; with an Essay on the Structure and Science of Modern Buildings. By FREDERICK ROGERS, Architect. 8vo, 15s. cloth.

** A volume of specifications of a practical character being greatly required, and the old standard work of Alfred Bartholomew being out of print, the author, on the basis of that work, has produced the above.—*Extract from Preface.*

Designing, Measuring, and Valuing.

THE STUDENT'S GUIDE to the PRACTICE of MEASURING and VALUING ARTIFICERS' WORKS; containing Directions for taking Dimensions, Abstracting the same, and bringing the Quantities into Bill, with Tables of Constants, and copious Memoranda for the Valuation of Labour and Materials in the respective Trades of Bricklayer and Slater, Carpenter and Joiner, Painter and Glazier, Paperhanger, &c. With 43 Plates and Woodcuts. Originally edited by EDWARD DOBSON, Architect. New Edition, re-written, with Additions on Mensuration and Construction, and useful Tables for facilitating Calculations and Measurements. By E. WYNDHAM TARN, M.A., 8vo, 10s. 6d. cloth.

" Well fulfils the promise of its title-page. Mr. Tarn's additions and revisions have much increased the usefulness of the work."—*Engineering.*

Beaton's Pocket Estimator.

THE POCKET ESTIMATOR FOR THE BUILDING TRADES, being an easy method of estimating the various parts of a Building collectively, more especially applied to Carpenters' and Joiners' work, priced according to the present value of material and labour. By A. C. BEATON, Author of "Quantities and Measurements." Second Edition. Waistcoat-pocket size. 1s. 6d.

Beaton's Builders' and Surveyors' Technical Guide.

THE POCKET TECHNICAL GUIDE AND MEASURER FOR BUILDERS AND SURVEYORS: containing a Complete Explanation of the Terms used in Building Construction, Memoranda for Reference, Technical Directions for Measuring Work in all the Building Trades, &c. By A. C. BEATON. 1s. 6d.

Builder's and Contractor's Price Book.

LOCKWOOD & CO.'S BUILDER'S AND CONTRACTOR'S PRICE BOOK, containing the latest prices of all kinds of Builders' Materials and Labour, and of all Trades connected with Building, &c., &c. The whole revised and edited by F. T. W. MILLER, A.R.I.B.A. Fcap. half-bound, 4s.

CARPENTRY, TIMBER, ETC.

Tredgold's Carpentry, new and cheaper Edition.

THE ELEMENTARY PRINCIPLES OF CARPENTRY : a Treatise on the Pressure and Equilibrium of Timber Framing, the Resistance of Timber, and the Construction of Floors, Arches, Bridges, Roofs, Uniting Iron and Stone with Timber, &c. To which is added an Essay on the Nature and Properties of Timber, &c., with Descriptions of the Kinds of Wood used in Building ; also numerous Tables of the Scantlings of Timber for different purposes, the Specific Gravities of Materials, &c. By THOMAS TREDGOLD, C.E. Edited by PETER BARLOW, F.R.S. Fifth Edition, corrected and enlarged. With 64 Plates (11 of which now first appear in this edition), Portrait of the Author, and several Woodcuts. In 1 vol., 4to, published at 2l. 2s., reduced to 1l. 5s. cloth.

"Ought to be in every architect's and every builder's library, and those who do not already possess it ought to avail themselves of the new issue."—*Builder.*
"A work whose monumental excellence must commend it wherever skilful carpentry is concerned. The Author's principles are rather confirmed than impaired by time. The additional plates are of great intrinsic value."—*Building News.*

Grandy's Timber Tables.

THE TIMBER IMPORTER'S, TIMBER MERCHANT'S, and BUILDER'S STANDARD GUIDE. By RICHARD E. GRANDY. Comprising :—An Analysis of Deal Standards, Home and Foreign, with comparative Values and Tabular Arrangements for Fixing Nett Landed Cost on Baltic and North American Deals, including all intermediate Expenses, Freight, Insurance, &c., &c. ; together with Copious Information for the Retailer and Builder. 2nd Edition. Carefully revised and corrected. 12mo, 3s. 6d. cloth.

"Everything it pretends to be: built up gradually, it leads one from a forest to a treenail, and throws in, as a makeweight, a host of material concerning bricks, columns, cisterns, &c.—all that the class to whom it appeals requires."—*English Mechanic.*

Timber Freight Book.

THE TIMBER IMPORTERS' AND SHIPOWNERS' FREIGHT BOOK : Being a Comprehensive Series of Tables for the Use of Timber Importers, Captains of Ships, Shipbrokers, Builders, and all Dealers in Wood whatsoever. By WILLIAM RICHARDSON, Timber Broker. Crown 8vo, 6s. cloth.

Tables for Packing-Case Makers.

PACKING-CASE TABLES ; showing the number of Superficial Feet in Boxes or Packing-Cases, from six inches square and upwards. By W. RICHARDSON. Oblong 4to, 3s. 6d. cloth.

"Will save much labour and calculation to packing-case makers and those who use packing-cases."—*Grocer.*   "Invaluable labour-saving tables."—*Ironmonger.*

Horton's Measurer.

THE COMPLETE MEASURER; setting forth the Measurement of Boards, Glass, &c.; Unequal-sided, Square-sided, Octagonal-sided, Round Timber and Stone, and Standing Timber. With just allowances for the bark in the respective species of trees, and proper deductions for the waste in hewing the trees, &c.; also a Table showing the solidity of hewn or eight-sided timber, or of any octagonal-sided column. By RICHARD HORTON. Third edition, with considerable and valuable additions, 12mo, strongly bound in leather, 5s.

Horton's Underwood and Woodland Tables.

TABLES FOR PLANTING AND VALUING UNDERWOOD AND WOODLAND; also Lineal, Superficial, Cubical, and Decimal Tables, &c. By R. HORTON. 12mo, 2s. leather.

Nicholson's Carpenter's Guide.

THE CARPENTER'S NEW GUIDE; or, BOOK of LINES for CARPENTERS: comprising all the Elementary Principles essential for acquiring a knowledge of Carpentry. Founded on the late PETER NICHOLSON'S standard work. A new Edition, revised by ARTHUR ASHPITEL, F.S.A., together with Practical Rules on Drawing, by GEORGE PYNE. With 74 Plates, 4to, 1l. 1s. cloth.

Dowsing's Timber Merchant's Companion.

THE TIMBER MERCHANT'S AND BUILDER'S COMPANION; containing New and Copious Tables of the Reduced Weight and Measurement of Deals and Battens, of all sizes, from One to a Thousand Pieces, also the relative Price that each size bears per Lineal Foot to any given Price per Petersburgh Standard Hundred, &c., &c. Also a variety of other valuable information. By WILLIAM DOWSING, Timber Merchant. Third Edition, Revised. Crown 8vo, 3s. cloth.

"Everything is as concise and clear as it can possibly be made. There can be no doubt that every timber merchant and builder ought to possess it."—*Hull Advertiser.*

Practical Timber Merchant.

THE PRACTICAL TIMBER MERCHANT, being a Guide for the use of Building Contractors, Surveyors, Builders, &c., comprising useful Tables for all purposes connected with the Timber Trade, Essay on the Strength of Timber, Remarks on the Growth of Timber, &c. By W. RICHARDSON. Fcap. 8vo, 3s. 6d. cl.

Woodworking Machinery.

WOODWORKING MACHINERY; its Rise, Progress, and Construction. With Hints on the Management of Saw Mills and the Economical Conversion of Timber. Illustrated with Examples of Recent Designs by leading English, French, and American Engineers. By M. POWIS BALE, M.I.M.E. Large crown 8vo, 12s. 6d. cloth.

"Mr. Bale is evidently an expert on the subject, and he has collected so much information that his book is all-sufficient for builders and others engaged in the conversion of timber."—*Architect.*

"The most comprehensive compendium of wood-working machinery we have seen. The author is a thorough master of his subject."—*Building News.*

"It should be in the office of every wood-working factory."—*English Mechanic.*

MECHANICS, ETC.

Turning.

LATHE-WORK: a Practical Treatise on the Tools, Appliances, and Processes employed in the Art of Turning. By PAUL N. HAS-LUCK. With numerous Illustrations drawn by the Author. Crown 8vo, 5s. cloth. [*Just published.*
"Evidently written from personal experience, and gives a large amount of just that sort of information which beginners at the lathe require."—*Builder.*
"Expounds the art and mystery of the turner in an informative fashion."—*Scotsman.*
"Mr. Hasluck's book will be a boon to amateurs."—*Architect.*

Mechanic's Workshop Companion.

THE OPERATIVE MECHANIC'S WORKSHOP COM-PANION, and THE SCIENTIFIC GENTLEMAN'S PRAC-TICAL ASSISTANT. By W. TEMPLETON. 12th Edit., with Mechanical Tables for Operative Smiths, Millwrights, Engineers, &c.; and an Extensive Table of Powers and Roots, 12mo, 5s. bound.
"Admirably adapted to the wants of a very large class. It has met with great success in the engineering workshop, as we can testify; and there are a great many men who, in a great measure, owe their rise in life to this little work."—*Building News.*

Engineer's and Machinist's Assistant.

THE ENGINEER'S, MILLWRIGHT'S, and MACHINIST'S PRACTICAL ASSISTANT; comprising a Collection of Useful Tables, Rules, and Data. By WM. TEMPLETON. 18mo, 2s. 6d.
"A more suitable present to an apprentice to any of the mechanical trades could not possibly be made."—*Building News.*

Superficial Measurement.

THE TRADESMAN'S GUIDE TO SUPERFICIAL MEA-SUREMENT. Tables calculated from 1 to 200 inches in length, by 1 to 108 inches in breadth. For the use of Architects, Engineers, Timber Merchants, Builders, &c. By J. HAWKINGS. Fcp. 3s. 6d. cl.

The High-Pressure Steam Engine.

THE HIGH-PRESSURE STEAM ENGINE; an Exposition of its Comparative Merits, and an Essay towards an Improved System of Construction, adapted especially to secure Safety and Economy. By Dr. ERNST ALBAN. Translated from the German, with Notes, by Dr. POLE, F.R.S. 8vo, 16s. 6d. cloth.

Steam Boilers.

A TREATISE ON STEAM BOILERS: their Strength, Con-struction, and Economical Working. By R. WILSON, C.E. Fifth Edition. 12mo, 6s. cloth.
"The best work on boilers which has come under our notice."—*Engineering.*
"The best treatise that has ever been published on steam boilers."—*Engineer.*

Power in Motion.

POWER IN MOTION: Horse Power, Toothed Wheel Gearing, Long and Short Driving Bands, Angular Forces, &c. By JAMES ARMOUR, C.E. With 73 Diagrams. 12mo, 3s., cloth.

Mechanics.

THE HANDBOOK OF MECHANICS. By DIONYSIUS LARDNER, D.C.L. New Edition, Edited and considerably En-larged, by BENJAMIN LOEWY, F.R.A.S., &c., post 8vo, 6s. cloth.
"Studiously popular .... The application of the various branches of physics to the industrial arts is carefully shown."—*Mining Journal.*

MATHEMATICS, TABLES, ETC.

Gregory's Practical Mathematics.

MATHEMATICS for PRACTICAL MEN ; being a Common-place Book of Pure and Mixed Mathematics. Designed chiefly for the Use of Civil Engineers, Architects, and Surveyors. Part I. PURE MATHEMATICS—comprising Arithmetic, Algebra, Geometry, Mensuration, Trigonometry, Conic Sections, Properties of Curves. Part II. MIXED MATHEMATICS—comprising Mechanics in general, Statics, Dynamics, Hydrostatics, Hydrodynamics, Pneumatics, Mechanical Agents, Strength of Materials. With an Appendix of copious Logarithmic and other Tables. By OLINTHUS GREGORY, LL.D., F.R.A.S. Enlarged by HENRY LAW, C.E. 4th Edition, revised by Prof. J. R. YOUNG. With 13 Plates. 8vo, 1l. 1s. cloth.
" The engineer or architect will here find ready to his hand, rules for solving nearly every mathematical difficulty that may arise in his practice. The rules are in all cases explained by means of examples clearly worked out."—Builder.

The Metric System.

A SERIES OF METRIC TABLES, in which the British Standard Measures and Weights are compared with those of the Metric System at present in use on the Continent. By C. H. DOWLING, C.E. 2nd Edit., revised and enlarged. 8vo, 10s. 6d. cl.
"Their accuracy has been certified by Prof. Airy, Astronomer-Royal."—Builder.

Inwood's Tables, greatly enlarged and improved.

TABLES FOR THE PURCHASING of ESTATES, Freehold, Copyhold, or Leasehold; Annuities, Advowsons, &c., and for the Renewing of Leases held under Cathedral Churches, Colleges, or other corporate bodies; for Terms of Years certain, and for Lives; also for Valuing Reversionary Estates, Deferred Annuities, Next Presentations, &c., together with Smart's Five Tables of Compound Interest, and an Extension of the same to Lower and Intermediate Rates. By WILLIAM INWOOD, Architect. The 21st edition, with considerable additions, and new and valuable Tables of Logarithms for the more Difficult Computations of the Interest of Money, Discount, Annuities, &c. By M. FÉDOR THOMAN. 12mo, 8s. cloth.
" Those interested in the purchase and sale of estates, and in the adjustment of compensation cases, as well as in transactions in annuities, life insurances, &c., will find the present edition of eminent service."—Engineering.

Geometry for the Architect, Engineer, &c.

PRACTICAL GEOMETRY, for the Architect, Engineer, and Mechanic. By E. W. TARN, M.A., Architect. Demy 8vo, 12s. 6d. cl.

Mathematical Instruments.

MATHEMATICAL INSTRUMENTS: Their Construction, Adjustment, Testing, and Use ; comprising Drawing, Measuring, Optical, Surveying, and Astronomical Instruments. By J. F. HEATHER, M.A. Enlarged Edition. 12mo, 5s. cloth.

Weights, Measures, Moneys, &c.

MEASURES, WEIGHTS, and MONEYS of all NATIONS, and an Analysis of the Christian, Hebrew, and Mahometan Calendars. Entirely New Edition, Revised and Enlarged. By W. S. B. WOOLHOUSE, F.R.A.S. 12mo, 2s. 6d. cloth boards.

Compound Interest and Annuities.

THEORY of COMPOUND INTEREST and ANNUITIES; with Tables of Logarithms for the more Difficult Computations of Interest, Discount, Annuities, &c., in all their Applications and Uses for Mercantile and State Purposes. By FEDOR THOMAN, of the Société Crédit Mobilier, Paris. 3rd Edit , 12mo, 4s. 6d. cl.
" A very powerful work, and the Author has a very remarkable command of his subject."—*Professor A. de Morgan.*

Iron and Metal Trades' Calculator.

THE IRON AND METAL TRADES' COMPANION : Being a Calculator containing a Series of Tables upon a new and comprehensive plan for expeditiously ascertaining the value of any goods bought or sold by weight, from 1s. per cwt. to 112s. per cwt., and from one farthing per lb. to 1s. per lb. Each Table extends from one lb. to 100 tons. By T. DOWNIE. 396 pp., 9s., leather.
" A most useful set of tables, and will supply a want, for nothing like them before existed."—*Building News.*

Iron and Steel.

'IRON AND STEEL': a Work for the Forge, Foundry, Factory, and Office. Containing Information for Ironmasters and their Stocktakers ; Managers of Bar, Rail, Plate, and Sheet Rolling Mills ; Iron and Metal Founders ; Iron Ship and Bridge Builders ; Mechanical, Mining, and Consulting Engineers; Architects, Builders, &c. By CHARLES HOARE, Author of ' The Slide Rule,' &c. Eighth Edition. With folding Scales of "Foreign Measures compared with the English Foot," and "fixed Scales of Squares, Cubes, and Roots, Areas, Decimal Equivalents, &c." Oblong, 32mo, 6s., leather, elastic-band.
" For comprehensiveness the book has not its equal."—*Iron.*

Comprehensive Weight Calculator.

THE WEIGHT CALCULATOR ; being a Series of Tables upon a New and Comprehensive Plan, exhibiting at one Reference the exact Value of any Weight from 1 lb. to 15 tons, at 300 Progressive Rates, from 1 Penny to 168 Shillings per cwt., and containing 186,000 Direct Answers, which, with their Combinations, consisting of a single addition (mostly to be performed at sight\), will afford an aggregate of 10,266,000 Answers ; the whole being calculated and designed to ensure Correctness and promote Despatch. By HENRY HARBEN, Accountant, Sheffield. New Edition. Royal 8vo, 1l. 5s., strongly half-bound.

Comprehensive Discount Guide.

THE DISCOUNT GUIDE : comprising several Series of Tables for the use of Merchants, Manufacturers, Ironmongers, and others, by which may be ascertained the exact profit arising from any mode of using Discounts, either in the Purchase or Sale of Goods, and the method of either Altering a Rate of Discount, or Advancing a Price, so as to produce, by one operation, a sum that will realise any required profit after allowing one or more Discounts : to which are added Tables of Profit or Advance from 1¼ to 90 per cent., Tables of Discount from 1¼ to 98¾ per cent., and Tables of Commission, &c., from ⅛ to 10 per cent. By HENRY HARBEN, Accountant. New Edition. Demy 8vo, 1l. 5s., half-bound.

SCIENCE AND ART.

The Construction of the Organ.

PRACTICAL ORGAN BUILDING. By W. E. DICKSON, M.A., Precentor of Ely Cathedral. Crown 8vo, 5s. cloth.

" In many respects the book is the best that has yet appeared on the subject. We cordially recommend it." —*English Mechanic.*

" Any practical amateur following the instructions here given might build an organ to his entire satisfaction."—*Leeds Mercury.*

Dentistry.

MECHANICAL DENTISTRY. A Practical Treatise on the Construction of the various kinds of Artificial Dentures. Comprising also Useful Formulæ, Tables, and Receipts for Gold l late, Clasps, Solders, etc., etc. By CHARLES HUNTER. With numerous Wood Engravings. Crown 8vo, 7s. 6d. cloth.

" The work is very practical."—*Monthly Review of Dental Surgery.*

" An authoritative treatise . . . . . We can strongly recommend Mr. Hunter's treatise to all students preparing for the profession of dentistry, as well as to every mechanical dentist."—*Dublin Journal of Medical Science.*   [*and Circular.*

" The best book on the subject with which we are acquainted."—*Medical Press*

Brewing.

A HANDBOOK FOR YOUNG BREWERS. By HERBERT EDWARDS WRIGHT, B.A. Crown 8vo, 3s. 6d. cloth.

" A thoroughly scientific treatise in popular language. It is evident that the author has mastered his subject in its scientific aspects."—*Morning Advertiser.*

" We would particularly recommend teachers of the art to place it in every pupil's hands, and we feel sure its perusal will be attended with advantage."—*Brewer.*

Gold and Gold-Working.

THE GOLDSMITH'S HANDBOOK : containing full instructions for the Alloying and Working of Gold. Including the Art of Alloying, Melting, Reducing, Colouring, Collecting and Refining. The processes of Manipulation, Recovery of Waste, Chemical and Physical Properties of Gold, with a new System of Mixing its Alloys ; Solders, Enamels, and other useful Rules and Recipes, &c. By GEORGE E. GEE, Goldsmith and Silversmith. Second Edition, considerably enlarged. 12mo, 3s. 6d. cloth boards.

" The best work yet printed on its subject for a reasonable price. ' —*Jeweller.*

" We consider that the trade owes not a little to Mr. Gee, who has in two volumes compressed almost the whole of its literature, and we doubt n t that many a young beginner will owe a part of his future success to a diligent study of the pages which are peculiarly well adapted to his use."—*Clerkenwell Press.*

" Essentially a practical manual, well adapted to the wants of amateurs and apprentices, containing trustworthy information that only a practical man can supply.'—*English Mechanic.*

Silver and Silver Working.

THE SILVERSMITH'S HANDBOOK, containing full Instructions for the Alloying and Working of Silver, including the different modes of refining and melting the metal, its solders, the preparation of imitation alloys, &c. By GEORGE E. GEE, Jeweller, &c. 12mo, 3s. 6d. cloth boards.

" The chief merit of the work is its practical character. The workers in the trade will specoily discover its merits when they sit down to study it."—*English Mechanic.*

" This work forms a valuable sequel to the author's *Practical Goldworker*, and supplies a want long felt in the silver trade."—*Silversmith's Trade Journal.*

Electric Lighting.

ELECTRIC LIGHT : Its Production and Use, embodying plain Directions for the Working of Galvanic Batteries, Electric Lamps, and Dynamo-Electric Machines. By J. W. URQUHART, C. E., Author of "Electroplating : a Practical Handbook." Edited by F. C. WEBB, M.I.C.E., M.S.T.E. With 94 Illustrations. Crown 8vo, 7s. 6d. cloth.

"It is the only work at present available, which gives a general but concise hist r of the means which have been adopted up to the present time in producing th electric light."—*Metropolitan.*

"An important addition to the literature of the electric light. Students of the subject should not fail to read it."—*Colliery Guardian.*

Electroplating, &c.

ELECTROPLATING : A Practical Handbook. By J. W. URQUHART, C.E. Crown 8vo, 5s. cloth.

"A large amount of thoroughly practical information."—*Telegraphic Journal.*

"An excellent practical manual."—*Engineering.*

"The information given appears to be based on direct personal knowledge. . . . Its science is sound, and the style is always clear."—*Athenæum.*

"Any ordinarily intelligent person may become an adept in electro-deposition with a very little science indeed, and this is the book to show him or her the way."—*Builder.*

"The volume is without a rival in its particular sphere."—*Design and Work.*

Electrotyping, &c.

ELECTROTYPING : a Practical Manual on the Reproduction and Multiplication of Printing Surfaces and Works of Art by the Electro-deposition of Metals. By J. W. URQUHART, C.E. Crown 8vo, 5s. cloth. [*Just published.*

"Will serve as a guide, not only to beginners in the art, but to those who still practise the old and imperfect methods of electrotyping."—*Iron.*

"The book throughout is entirely practical, is lucid and clear in style, and the minutest details are so stated that amateurs will find no difficulty whatever in following them out. We have no hesitation in recommending it as a reliable work."—*Paper and Printing Trades Journal.*

The Military Sciences.

AIDE-MÉMOIRE to the MILITARY SCIENCES. Framed from Contributions of Officers and others connected with the different Services. Originally edited by a Committee of the Corps of Royal Engineers. Second Edition, most carefully revised by an Officer of the Corps, with many additions ; containing nearly 350 Engravings and many hundred Woodcuts. 3 vols. royal 8vo, extra cloth boards, and lettered, 4l. 10s.

Field Fortification.

A TREATISE on FIELD FORTIFICATION, the ATTACK of FORTRESSES, MILITARY MINING, and RECONNOITRING. By Colonel I. S. MACAULAY, late Professor of Fortification in the R. M. A., Woolwich. Sixth Edition, crown 8vo, cloth, with separate Atlas of 12 Plates, 12s. complete.

Dye-Wares and Colours.

THE MANUAL of COLOURS and DYE-WARES : their Properties, Applications, Valuation, Impurities, and Sophistications. For the Use of Dyers, Printers, Drysalters, Brokers, &c. By J. W. SLATER. Post 8vo, 7s. 6d. cloth.

The Alkali Trade—Sulphuric Acid, &c.

A MANUAL OF THE ALKALI TRADE, including the Manufacture of Sulphuric Acid, Sulphate of Soda, and Bleaching Powder. By JOHN LOMAS, Alkali Manufacturer, Newcastle-upon-Tyne and London. With 232 Illustrations and Working Drawings, and containing 386 pages of text. Super-royal 8vo, 2*l* 12*s*. 6*d*. cloth.   [*Just published*.

This work provides (1) *a Complete Handbook for intending Alkali and Sulphuric Acid Manufacturers, and for those already in the field who desire to improve their plant, or to become practically acquainted with the latest processes and developments of the trade*; (2) *a Handy Volume which Manufacturers can put into the hands of their Managers and Foremen as a useful guide in their daily rounds of duty.*

SYNOPSIS OF CONTENTS.

Chap. I. Choice of Site and General Plan of Works—II. Sulphuric Acid—III. Recovery of the Nitrogen Compounds, and Treatment of Small Pyrites —IV. The Salt Cake Process—V. Legislation upon the Noxious Vapours Question—VI. The Hargreaves' and Jones' Processes—VII. The Balling Process—VIII. Lixiviation and Salting Down— IX. Carbonating or Finishing—X. Soda Crystals — XI. Refined Alkali — XII. Caustic Soda — XIII. Bi-carbonate of Soda — XIV. Bleaching Powder— XV. Utilisation of Tank Waste—XVI. General Remarks—Four Appendices, treating of Yields, Sulphuric Acid Calculations, Anemometers, and Foreign Legislation upon the Noxious Vapours Question.

"The author has given the fullest, most practical, and, to all concerned in the alkali trade, most valuable mass of information that, to our knowledge, has been published in any language."—*Engineer*.

"This book is written by a manufacturer for manufacturers. The working details of the most approved forms of apparatus are given, and these are accompanied by no less than 232 wood engravings, all of which may be used for the purposes of construction. Every step in the manufacture is very fully described in this manual, and each improvement explained. Everything which tends to introduce economy into the technical details of this trade receives the fullest attention. The book has been produced with great completeness."—*Athenæum*.

"The author is not one of those clever compilers who, on short notice, will 'read up' any conceivable subject, but a practical man in the best sense of the word. We find here not merely a sound and luminous explanation of the chemical principles of the trade, but a notice of numerous matters which have a most important bearing on the successful conduct of alkali works, but which are generally overlooked by even the most experienced technological authors. This most valuable book, which we trust will be generally appreciated, we must pronounce a credit alike to its author and to the enterprising firm who have undertaken its publication."—*Chemical Review*.

Chemical Analysis.

THE COMMERCIAL HANDBOOK of CHEMICAL ANALYSIS; or Practical Instructions for the determination of the Intrinsic or Commercial Value of Substances used in Manufactures, in Trades, and in the Arts. By A. NORMANDY, Author of "Practical Introduction to Rose's Chemistry," and Editor of Rose's "Treatise on Chemical Analysis." *New Edition.* Enlarged, and to a great extent re-written, by HENRY M. NOAD, Ph. D., F.R.S. With numerous Illustrations. Cr. 8vo, 12*s*. 6*d*. cloth.

"We recommend this book to the careful perusal of every one; it may be truly affirmed to be of universal interest, and we strongly recommend it to our readers as a guide, alike indispensable to the housewife as to the pharmaceutical practitioner."—*Medical Times*.

"Essential to the analysts appointed under the new Act. The most recent results are given, and the work is well edited and carefully written."—*Nature*.

Dr. Lardner's Museum of Science and Art.

THE MUSEUM OF SCIENCE AND ART. Edited by
DIONYSIUS LARDNER, D.C.L., formerly Professor of Natural Philosophy and Astronomy in University College, London. With upwards of 1200 Engravings on Wood. In 6 Double Volumes.
Price £1 1s., in a new and elegant cloth binding, or handsomely
bound in half morocco, 31s. 6d.

OPINIONS OF THE PRESS.

"This series besides affording popular but sound instruction on scientific subjects,
with which the humblest man in the country ought to be acquainted, also undertakes
that teaching of 'common things' which every well-wisher of his kind is anxious to
promote. Many thousand copies of this serviceable publication have been printed,
in the belief and hope that the desire for instruction and improvement widely pre-
vails ; and we have no fear that such enlightened faith will meet with disappoint-
ment."—*Times.*

"A cheap and interesting publication, alike informing and attractive. The papers
combine subjects of importance and great scientific knowledge, considerable induc-
tive powers, and a popular style of treatment."—*Spectator.*

"The 'Museum of Science and Art' is the most valuable contribution that has
ever been made to the Scientific Instruction of every class of society."—*Sir David
Brewster in the North British Review.*

"Whether we consider the liberality and beauty of the illustrations, the charm of
the writing, or the durable interest of the matter, we must express our belief that
there is hardly to be found among the new books, one that would be welcomed by
people of so many ages and classes as a valuable present."—*Examiner.*

. *Separate books formed from the above, suitable for Workmen's
Libraries, Science Classes, &c.*

COMMON THINGS EXPLAINED. Containing Air, Earth, Fire,
Water, Time, Man, the Eye, Locomotion, Colour, Clocks and
Watches, &c.   233 Illustrations, cloth gilt, 5s.

THE MICROSCOPE. Containing Optical Images, Magnifying
Glasses, Origin and Description of the Microscope, Microscopic
Objects, the Solar Microscope, Microscopic Drawing and Engrav-
ing, &c.   147 Illustrations, cloth gilt, 2s.

POPULAR GEOLOGY. Containing Earthquakes and Volcanoes,
the Crust of the Earth, etc. 201 Illustrations, cloth gilt, 2s. 6d.

POPULAR PHYSICS. Containing Magnitude and Minuteness, the
Atmosphere, Meteoric Stones, Popular Fallacies, Weather Prog-
nostics, the Thermometer, the Barometer, Sound, &c. 85 Illustrations, cloth gilt, 2s. 6d.

STEAM AND ITS USES. Including the Steam Engine, the Locomotive, and Steam Navigation. 89 Illustrations, cloth gilt, 2s.

POPULAR ASTRONOMY. Containing How to Observe the
Heavens. The Earth, Sun, Moon, Planets. Light, Comets,
Eclipses, Astronomical Influences, &c. 182 Illustrations, 4s. 6d.

THE BEE AND WHITE ANTS: Their Manners and Habits.
With Illustrations of Animal Instinct and Intelligence. 135 Illustrations, cloth gilt, 2s.

THE ELECTRIC TELEGRAPH POPULARISED. To render
intelligible to all who can Read, irrespective of any previous Scientific Acquirements, the various forms of Telegraphy in Actual
Operation. 100 Illustrations, cloth gilt, 1s. 6d.

Dr. Lardner's Handbooks of Natural Philosophy.

. *The following five volumes, though each is Complete in itself, and to be purchased separately, form A COMPLETE COURSE OF NATURAL PHILOSOPHY, and are intended for the general reader who desires to attain accurate knowledge of the various departments of Physical Science, without pursuing them according to the more profound methods of mathematical investigation. The style is studiously popular. It has been the author's aim to supply Manuals such as are required by the Student, the Engineer, the Artisan, and the superior classes in Schools.*

THE HANDBOOK OF MECHANICS. Enlarged and almost rewritten by BENJAMIN LOEWY, F.R.A.S. With 378 Illustrations. Post 8vo, 6s. cloth.

"The perspicuity of the original has been retained, and chapters which had become obsolete, have been replaced by others of more modern character. The explanations throughout are studiously popular, and care has been taken to show the application of the various branches of physics to the industrial arts, and to the practical business of life."—*Mining Journal.*

THE HANDBOOK of HYDROSTATICS and PNEUMATICS. New Edition, Revised and Enlarged by BENJAMIN LOEWY, F.R.A.S. With 236 Illustrations. Post 8vo, 5s. cloth.

"For those ' who desire to attain an accurate knowledge of physical science without the profound methods of mathematical investigation,' this work is not merely intended, but well adapted."—*Chemical News.*

THE HANDBOOK OF HEAT. Edited and almost entirely Rewritten by BENJAMIN LOEWY, F.R.A.S., etc. 117 Illustrations. Post 8vo, 6s. cloth.

"The style is always clear and precise, and conveys instruction without leaving any cloudiness or lurking doubts behind."—*Engineering.*

THE HANDBOOK OF OPTICS. New Edition. Edited by T. OLVER HARDING, B.A. 298 Illustrations. Post 8vo, 5s. cloth.

"Written by one of the ablest English scientific writers, beautifully and elaborately illustrated."—*Mechanics' Magazine.*

THE HANDBOOK OF ELECTRICITY, MAGNETISM, and ACOUSTICS. New Edition. Edited by GEO. CAREY FOSTER, B.A., F.C.S. With 400 Illustrations. Post 8vo, 5s. cloth.

"The book could not have been entrusted to any one better calculated to preserve the terse and lucid style of Lardner, while correcting his errors and bringing up his work to the present state of scientific knowledge."—*Popular Science Review.*

Dr. Lardner's Handbook of Astronomy.

THE HANDBOOK OF ASTRONOMY. Forming a Companion to the "Handbooks of Natural Philosophy." By DIONYSIUS LARDNER, D.C.L., formerly Professor of Natural Philosophy and Astronomy in University College, London. Fourth Edition. Revised and Edited by EDWIN DUNKIN, F.R.S., Royal Observatory, Greenwich. With 38 Plates and upwards of 100 Woodcuts. In 1 vol., small 8vo, 550 pages, 9s. 6d., cloth.

"Probably no other book contains the same amount of information in so compendious and well-arranged a form—certainly none at the price at which this is offered to the public."—*Athenæum.*

"We can do no other than pronounce this work a most valuable manual of astronomy, and we strongly recommend it to all who wish to acquire a general—but at the same time correct—acquaintance with this sublime science."—*Quarterly Journal of Science.*

Dr. Lardner's Handbook of Animal Physics.

THE HANDBOOK OF ANIMAL PHYSICS. By DR. LARDNER. With 520 Illustrations. New edition, small 8vo, cloth, 732 pages, 7s. 6d.

"We have no hesitation in cordially recommending it."—*Educational Times.*

Dr. Lardner's School Handbooks.

NATURAL PHILOSOPHY FOR SCHOOLS. By Dr. Lardner. 328 Illustrations. Sixth Edition. 1 vol. 3s. 6d. cloth.
"Conveys, in clear and precise terms, general notions of all the principal divisions of Physical Science."—*British Quarterly Review.*

ANIMAL PHYSIOLOGY FOR SCHOOLS. By Dr. Lardner. With 190 Illustrations. Second Edition. 1 vol. 3s. 6d. cloth.
"Clearly written, well arranged, and excellently illustrated."—*Gardeners' Chronicle.*

Dr. Lardner's Electric Telegraph.

THE ELECTRIC TELEGRAPH. By Dr. Lardner. New Edition. Revised and Re-written, by E. B. Bright, F.R.A.S. 140 Illustrations. Small 8vo, 2s. 6d. cloth.
"One of the most readable books extant on the Electric Telegraph."—*Eng. Mechanic.*

Electricity.

A MANUAL of ELECTRICITY; including Galvanism, Magnetism, Diamagnetism, Electro-Dynamics, Magneto-Electricity, and the Electric Telegraph. By Henry M. Noad, Ph.D., F.C.S. Fourth Edition, with 500 Woodcuts. 8vo, 1l. 4s. cloth.
"The accounts given of electricity and galvanism are not only complete in a scientific sense, but, which is a rarer thing, are popular and interesting."—*Lancet.*

Text-Book of Electricity.

THE STUDENT'S TEXT-BOOK OF ELECTRICITY. By Henry M. Noad, Ph.D., F.R.S., F.C.S. New Edition, carefully Revised. With an Introduction and Additional Chapters by W. H. Preece, M.I.C.E., Vice-President of the Society of Telegraph Engineers, &c. With 470 Illustrations. Crown 8vo, 12s. 6d. cloth.
"A reflex of the existing state of Electrical Science adapted for students."—W. H. Preece, Esq., vide "Introduction."
"We can recommend Dr. Noad's book for clear style, great range of subject, a good index, and a plethora of woodcuts. Such collections as the present are indispensable."—*Athenæum.*
"An admirable text-book for every student—beginner or advanced—of electricity."—*Engineering.*
"Recommended to students as one of the best text-books on the subject that they can have. Mr. Preece appears to have introduced all the newest inventions in the shape of telegraphic, telephonic, and electric-lighting apparatus."—*English Mechanic.*
"The work contains everything that the student can require."—*Academy.*
"One of the best and most useful compendiums of any branch of science in our literature."—*Iron.*
"Under the editorial hand of Mr. Preece the late Dr. Noad's text-book of electricity has grown into an admirable handbook."—*Westminster Review.*

Carriage Building, &c.

COACH BUILDING: a Practical Treatise, Historical and Descriptive, containing full information of the various Trades and Processes involved, with Hints on the proper Keeping of Carriages, &c. With 57 Illustrations. By James W. Burgess. 12mo, 3s. cloth boards.   [*Just published.*

Geology and Genesis.

THE TWIN RECORDS OF CREATION; or, Geology and Genesis, their Perfect Harmony and Wonderful Concord. By George W. Victor Le Vaux. Fcap. 8vo, 5s. cloth.
"A valuable contribution to the evidences of revelation, and disposes very conclusively of the arguments of those who would set God's Works against God's Word. No real difficulty is shirked, and no sophistry is left unexposed."—*The Rock.*

Science and Scripture.

SCIENCE ELUCIDATIVE OF SCRIPTURE, AND NOT ANTAGONISTIC TO IT; being a Series of Essays on—1. Alleged Discrepancies; 2. The Theory of the Geologists and Figure of the Earth; 3. The Mosaic Cosmogony; 4. Miracles in general—Views of Hume and Powell; 5. The Miracle of Joshua—Views of Dr. Colenso: The Supernaturally Impossible; 6. The Age of the Fixed Stars, &c. By Prof. J. R. YOUNG. Fcap. 5s. cl.

Geology.

A CLASS-BOOK OF GEOLOGY: Consisting of "Physical Geology," which sets forth the Leading Principles of the Science; and "Historical Geology," which treats of the Mineral and Organic Conditions of the Earth at each successive epoch, especial reference being made to the British Series of Rocks. By RALPH TATE. With more than 250 Illustrations. Fcap. 8vo, 5s. cloth.

Practical Philosophy.

A SYNOPSIS OF PRACTICAL PHILOSOPHY. By Rev. JOHN CARR, M.A., late Fellow of Trin. Coll., Camb. 18mo, 5s. cl.

Mollusca.

A MANUAL OF THE MOLLUSCA; being a Treatise on Recent and Fossil Shells. By Dr. S. P. WOODWARD, A.L.S. With Appendix by RALPH TATE, A.L.S., F.G.S. With numerous Plates and 300 Woodcuts. 3rd Edition. Cr. 8vo, 7s. 6d. cloth.

Clocks, Watches, and Bells.

RUDIMENTARY TREATISE on CLOCKS, and WATCHES, and BELLS. By Sir EDMUND BECKETT, Bart. (late E. B. Denison), LL.D., Q.C., F.R.A.S. Sixth edition, revised and enlarged. Limp cloth (No. 67, Weale's Series), 4s. 6d.; cloth bds. 5s. 6d.

"As a popular and practical treatise it is unapproached."—*English Mechanic.*
"The best work on the subject probably extant. The treatise on bells is undoubtedly the best in the language."—*Engineering.*
"The only modern treatise on clock-making."—*Horological Journal.*

Grammar of Colouring.

A GRAMMAR OF COLOURING, applied to Decorative Painting and the Arts. By GEORGE FIELD. New edition, enlarged. By ELLIS A. DAVIDSON. With new Coloured Diagrams and Engravings. 12mo, 3s. 6d. cloth.

"The book is a most useful *résumé* of the properties of pigments."—*Builder.*

Pictures and Painters.

THE PICTURE AMATEUR'S HANDBOOK AND DICTIONARY OF PAINTERS: A Guide for Visitors to Picture Galleries, and for Art-Students, including methods of Painting, Cleaning, Re-Lining, and Restoring, Principal Schools of Painting, Copyists and Imitators. By PHILIPPE DARYL, B.A. Cr. 8vo, 3s. 6d. cl.

Woods and Marbles (Imitation of).

SCHOOL OF PAINTING FOR THE IMITATION OF WOODS AND MARBLES, as Taught and Practised by A. R. and P. VAN DER BURG, Directors of the Rotterdam Painting Institution. Illustrated with 24 full-size Coloured Plates; also 12 Plain Plates, comprising 154 Figures. Folio, 2l. 12s. 6d. bound.

Delamotte's Works on Illumination & Alphabets.

A PRIMER OF THE ART OF ILLUMINATION; for the use of Beginners: with a Rudimentary Treatise on the Art, Practical Directions for its Exercise, and numerous Examples taken from Illuminated MSS., printed in Gold and Colours. By F. DELA-MOTTE. Small 4to, 9s. Elegantly bound, cloth antique.

" The examples of ancient MSS. recommended to the student, which, with much good sense, the author chooses from collections accessible to all, are selected with judgment and knowledge, as well as taste."—*Athenæum.*

ORNAMENTAL ALPHABETS, ANCIENT and MEDIÆVAL; from the Eighth Century, with Numerals; including Gothic, Church-Text, German, Italian, Arabesque, Initials, Monograms, Crosses, &c. Collected and engraved by F. DELAMOTTE, and printed in Colours. New and Cheaper Edition. Royal 8vo, oblong, 2s. 6d. ornamental boards.

" For those who insert enamelled sentences round gilded chalices, who blazon shop legends over shop-doors, who letter church walls with pithy sentences from the Decalogue, this book will be useful."—*Athenæum.*

EXAMPLES OF MODERN ALPHABETS, PLAIN and ORNA-MENTAL; including German, Old English, Saxon, Italic, Perspective, Greek, Hebrew, Court Hand, Engrossing, Tuscan, Riband, Gothic, Rustic, and Arabesque, &c., &c. Collected and engraved by F. DELAMOTTE, and printed in Colours. New and Cheaper Edition. Royal 8vo, oblong, 2s. 6d. ornamental boards.

" There is comprised in it every possible shape into which the letters of the alphabet and numerals can be formed."—*Standard.*

MEDIÆVAL ALPHABETS AND INITIALS FOR ILLUMI-NATORS. By F. DELAMOTTE. Containing 21 Plates, and Illuminated Title, printed in Gold and Colours. With an Introduction by J. WILLIS BROOKS. Small 4to, 6s. cloth gilt.

THE EMBROIDERER'S BOOK OF DESIGN; containing Initials, Emblems, Cyphers, Monograms, Ornamental Borders, Ecclesiastical Devices, Mediæval and Modern Alphabets, and National Emblems. Collected and engraved by F. DELAMOTTE, and printed in Colours. Oblong royal 8vo, 1s. 6d. in ornamental boards.

Wood-Carving.

INSTRUCTIONS in WOOD-CARVING, for Amateurs; with Hints on Design. By A LADY. In emblematic wrapper, handsomely printed, with Ten large Plates, 2s. 6d.

" The handicraft of the wood-carver, so well as a book can impart it, may be learnt from 'A Lady's' publication."—*Athenæum.*

Popular Work on Painting.

PAINTING POPULARLY EXPLAINED; with Historical Sketches of the Progress of the Art. By THOMAS JOHN GULLICK, Painter, and JOHN TIMBS, F.S.A. Fourth Edition, revised and enlarged. With Frontispiece and Vignette. In small 8vo, 6s. cloth.

** *This Work has been adopted as a Prize-book in the Schools of Art at South Kensington.*

" Contains a large amount of original matter, agreeably conveyed."—*Builder.*

" Much may be learned, even by those who fancy they do not require to be taught, from the careful perusal of this unpretending but comprehensive treatise."—*Art Journal.*

AGRICULTURE, GARDENING, ETC.

Youatt and Burn's Complete Grazier.

THE COMPLETE GRAZIER, and FARMER'S and CATTLE-
BREEDER'S ASSISTANT. A Compendium of Husbandry.
By WILLIAM YOUATT, ESQ., V.S. 12th Edition, very considerably enlarged, and brought up to the present requirements of
agricultural practice. By ROBERT SCOTT BURN. One large 8vo.
volume, 860 pp. with 244 Illustrations. 1*l*, 1*s*. half-bound.

"The standard and text-book, with the farmer and grazier."—*Farmer's Magazine.*
"A treatise which will remain a standard work on the subject as long as British
agriculture endures."—*Mark Lane Express.*

History, Structure, and Diseases of Sheep.

SHEEP; THE HISTORY, STRUCTURE, ECONOMY,
AND DISEASES OF. By W. C. SPOONER, M.R.V.C., &c.
Fourth Edition, with fine engravings, including specimens of New
and Improved Breeds. 366 pp., 4*s*. cloth.

Production of Meat.

MEAT PRODUCTION. A Manual for Producers, Distributors,
and Consumers of Butchers' Meat. Being a treatise on means of
increasing its Home Production. Also comprehensively treating
of the Breeding, Rearing, Fattening, and Slaughtering of Meat-
yielding Live Stock; Indications of the Quality; Means for Preserving, Curing, and Cooking of the Meat, etc. By JOHN EWART.
Numerous Illustrations. Cr. 8vo, 5*s*. cloth.

"A compact and handy volume on the meat question, which deserves serious and
thoughtful consideration at the present time."—*Meat and Provision Trades' Review.*

Donaldson and Burn's Suburban Farming.

SUBURBAN FARMING. A Treatise on the Laying Out and
Cultivation of Farms adapted to the produce of Milk, Butter and
Cheese, Eggs, Poultry, and Pigs. By the late Professor JOHN
DONALDSON. With considerable Additions, Illustrating the more
Modern Practice, by R. SCOTT BURN. With Illustrations. Second
Edition. 12mo, 4*s*. cloth boards.

Modern Farming.

OUTLINES OF MODERN FARMING. By R. SCOTT BURN.
Soils, Manures, and Crops—Farming and Farming Economy—
Cattle, Sheep, and Horses—Management of the Dairy, Pigs, and
Poultry—Utilisation of Town Sewage, Irrigation, &c. New Edition.
In 1 vol. 1250 pp., half-bound, profusely illustrated, 12*s*.

"There is sufficient stated within the limits of this treatise to prevent a farmer
from going far wrong in any of his operations."—*Observer.*

Amateur Farming.

THE LESSONS of MY FARM: a Book for Amateur Agricul-
turists, being an Introduction to Farm Practice, in the Culture of
Crops, the Feeding of Cattle, Management of the Dairy, Poultry,
Pigs, &c. By R. SCOTT BURN. With numerous Illus. Fcp. 6*s*. cl.

"A complete introduction to the whole round of farming practice."—*John Bull.*

The Management of Estates.

LANDED ESTATES MANAGEMENT: Treating of the Varieties of Lands, Methods of Farming, the Setting-out of Farms, Construction of Roads and Farm Buildings, of Waste or Unproductive Lands, Irrigation, Drainage, &c. By R. SCOTT BURN. Second Edition. 12mo, 3s. cloth.
"A complete and comprehensive outline of the duties appertaining to the management of landed estates."—*Journal of Forestry.*

The Management of Farms.

OUTLINES OF FARM MANAGEMENT, and the Organization of Farm Labour. Treating of the General Work of the Farm, Field, and Live Stock, Details of Contract Work, Specialties of Labour, Economical Management of the Farmhouse and Cottage, Domestic Animals, &c. By ROBERT SCOTT BURN. 12mo, 3s.

Management of Estates and Farms.

LANDED ESTATES AND FARM MANAGEMENT. By R. SCOTT BURN, Author of "Outlines of Modern Farming," Editor of "The Complete Grazier," &c. With Illustrations. Consisting of the above Two Works in One vol., 6s. half-bound.

English Agriculture.

THE FIELDS OF GREAT BRITAIN. A Text-book of Agriculture, adapted to the Syllabus of the Science and Art Department. For Elementary and Advanced Students. By HUGH CLEMENTS (Board of Trade). With an Introduction by H. KAINS-JACKSON. 18mo, 2s. 6d. cloth. [*Just published.*
"A clearly written description of the ordinary routine of English farm-life."—*Land.*
"A carefully written text-book of Agriculture."—*Athenæum.*
"A most comprehensive volume, giving a mass of information."—*Agricultural [Economist.*

Kitchen Gardening.

KITCHEN GARDENING MADE EASY. Showing how to prepare and lay out the ground, the best means of cultivating every known Vegetable and Herb, etc. By GEORGE M. F. GLENNY. 12mo, 2s. cloth boards.

Culture of Fruit Trees.

FRUIT TREES, the Scientific and Profitable Culture of. From the French of DU BREUIL, revised by GEO. GLENNY. 12mo, 4s.

Good Gardening.

A PLAIN GUIDE TO GOOD GARDENING; or, How to Grow Vegetables, Fruits, and Flowers. With Practical Notes on Soils, Manures, Seeds, Planting, Laying-out of Gardens and Grounds, &c. By S. WOOD. Third Edition. Cr. 8vo, 5s. cloth.
"A very good book, and one to be highly recommended as a practical guide. The practical directions are excellent."—*Athenæum.*

Gainful Gardening.

MULTUM-IN-PARVO GARDENING; or, How to make One Acre of Land produce £620 a year, by the Cultivation of Fruits and Vegetables ; also, How to Grow Flowers in Three Glass Houses, so as to realise £176 per annum clear Profit. By SAMUEL WOOD. 3rd Edition, revised. Cr. 8vo, 2s. cloth.
"We are bound to recommend it as not only suited to the case of the amateur and gentleman's gardener, but to the market grower."—*Gardener's Magazine.*

Gardening for Ladies.

THE LADIES' MULTUM-IN-PARVO FLOWER GARDEN, and Amateur's Complete Guide. By SAMUEL WOOD. Author of "Good Gardening," &c. With Illustrations. Crown 8vo, 3s. 6d. cloth. [*Just published.*

Bulb Culture.

THE BULB GARDEN, or, How to Cultivate Bulbous and Tuberous-rooted Flowering Plants to Perfection. A Manual adapted for both the Professional and Amateur Gardener. By SAMUEL WOOD, Author of "Good Gardening," etc. With Coloured Illustrations and Wood Engravings. Cr. 8vo, 3s. 6d. cloth.

Tree Planting.

THE TREE PLANTER AND PLANT PROPAGATOR: Being a Practical Manual on the Propagation of Forest Trees, Fruit Trees, Flowering Shrubs, Flowering Plants, Pot Herbs, &c. Numerous Illustrations. By SAMUEL WOOD. 12mo, 2s. 6d. cloth.

Tree Pruning.

THE TREE PRUNER: Being a Practical Manual on the Pruning of Fruit Trees. Including also their Training and Renovation, also treating of the Pruning of Shrubs, Climbers, and Flowering Plants. By SAMUEL WOOD. 12mo, 2s. 6d. cloth.

Tree Planting, Pruning, & Plant Propagation.

THE TREE PLANTER, PROPAGATOR, AND PRUNER. By SAMUEL WOOD, Author of "Good Gardening," &c. Consisting of the above Two Works in One Vol., 5s. half-bound.

Potato Culture.

POTATOES, HOW TO GROW AND SHOW THEM: A Practical Guide to the Cultivation and General Treatment of the Potato. By JAMES PINK. With Illustrations. Cr. 8vo, 2s. cl.

Hudson's Tables for Land Valuers.

THE LAND VALUER'S BEST ASSISTANT: being Tables, on a very much improved Plan, for Calculating the Value of Estates. With Tables for reducing Scotch, Irish, and Provincial Customary Acres to Statute Measure, &c. By R. HUDSON, C.E. New Edition, royal 32mo, leather, gilt edges, elastic band, 4s.

Ewart's Land Improver's Pocket-Book.

THE LAND IMPROVER'S POCKET-BOOK OF FORMULÆ, TABLES, and MEMORANDA, required in any Computation relating to the Permanent Improvement of Landed Property. By JOHN EWART, Land Surveyor and Agricultural Engineer. Royal 32mo, oblong, leather, gilt edges, with elastic band, 4s.

Complete Agricultural Surveyor's Pocket-Book.

THE LAND VALUER'S AND LAND IMPROVER'S COMPLETE POCKET-BOOK; consisting of the above two works bound together, leather, gilt edges, with strap, 7s. 6d.

"We consider Hudson's book to be the best ready-reckoner on matters relating to the valuation of land and crops we have ever seen, and its combination with Mr. Ewart's work greatly enhances the value and usefulness of the latter-mentioned .. It is most useful as a manual for reference."—*North of England Farmer.*

'A Complete Epitome of the Laws of this Country.'

EVERY MAN'S OWN LAWYER; a Handy-Book of the Principles of Law and Equity. By A BARRISTER. New Edition, much enlarged. Corrected to the end of last Session. With Notes and References to the Authorities. Crown 8vo, cloth, price, 6s. 8d. (saved at every consultation).

COMPRISING THE RIGHTS AND WRONGS OF INDIVIDUALS, MERCANTILE AND COMMERCIAL LAW, CRIMINAL LAW, PARISH LAW, COUNTY COURT LAW, GAME AND FISHERY LAWS, POOR MEN'S LAW, THE LAWS OF

BANKRUPTCY—BILLS OF EXCHANGE—CONTRACTS AND AGREEMENTS—COPYRIGHT—DOWER AND DIVORCE—ELECTIONS AND REGISTRATION—INSURANCE—LIBEL AND SLANDER—MORTGAGES—SETTLEMENTS—STOCK EXCHANGE PRACTICE—TRADE MARKS AND PATENTS—TRESPASS, NUISANCES, ETC.—TRANSFER OF LAND, ETC. — WARRANTY — WILLS AND AGREEMENTS, ETC.

Also Law for Landlord and Tenant—Master and Servant—Workmen and Apprentices—Heirs, Devisees, and Legatees — Husband and Wife — Executors and Trustees — Guardian and Ward — Married Women and Infants—Partners and Agents — Lender and Borrower — Debtor and Creditor — Purchaser and Vendor — Companies and Associations —Friendly Societies—Clergymen, Churchwardens—Medical Practitioners, &c. — Bankers — Farmers — Contractors—Stock and Share Brokers—Sportsmen and Gamekeepers—Farriers and Horse-Dealers—Auctioneers, House-Agents—Innkeepers, &c.— Pawnbrokers — Surveyors — Railways and Carriers, &c., &c.

" No Englishman ought to be without this book."—*Engineer.*
"What it professes to be—a complete epitome of the laws of this country, thoroughly intelligible to non-professional readers. The book is a handy one to have in readiness when some knotty point requires ready solution."—*Bell's Life.*
" A useful and concise epitome of the law."—*Law Magazine.*

Auctioneer's Assistant.

THE APPRAISER, AUCTIONEER, BROKER, HOUSE AND ESTATE AGENT, AND VALUER'S POCKET ASSISTANT, for the Valuation for Purchase, Sale, or Renewal of Leases, Annuities, and Reversions, and of property generally; with Prices for Inventories, &c. By JOHN WHEELER, Valuer, &c. Fourth Edition, enlarged, by C. NORRIS. Royal 32mo, cloth, 5s.
"A concise book of reference, containing a clearly-arranged list of prices for inventories, a practical guide to determine the value of furniture, &c."—*Standard.*

Auctioneering.

AUCTIONEERS: THEIR DUTIES AND LIABILITIES. By ROBERT SQUIBBS, Auctioneer. Demy 8vo, 10s. 6d. cloth.

House Property.

HANDBOOK OF HOUSE PROPERTY: a Popular and Practical Guide to the Purchase, Mortgage, Tenancy, and Compulsory Sale of Houses and Land; including the Law of Dilapidations and Fixtures, &c. By E. L. TARBUCK. 2nd Edit. 12mo, 3s. 6d. cloth.
"We are glad to be able to recommend it."—*Builder.*
"The advice is thoroughly practical."—*Law Journal.*

Metropolitan Rating.

METROPOLITAN RATING: a Summary of the Appeals heard before the Court of General Assessment Sessions at Westminster, in the years 1871-80 inclusive. Containing a large mass of very valuable information with respect to the Rating of Railways, Gas and Waterworks, Tramways, Wharves, Public Houses, &c. By EDWARD and A. L. RYDE. 8vo, 12s. 6d. [*Just published.*

Bradbury, Agnew, & Co., Printers, Whitefriars, London.

WEALE'S RUDIMENTARY SCIENTIFIC SERIES.

. The volumes of this Series are freely Illustrated with Woodcuts, or otherwise, where requisite. Throughout the following List it must be understood that the books are bound in limp cloth, unless otherwise stated; *but the volumes marked with a ‡ may also be had strongly bound in cloth boards for 6d. extra.*

N.B.—In ordering from this List it is recommended, as a means of facilitating business and obviating error, to quote the numbers affixed to the volumes, as well as the titles and prices.

No.   ARCHITECTURE, BUILDING, ETC.

16. *ARCHITECTURE—ORDERS*—The Orders and their Æsthetic Principles. By W. H. LEEDS. Illustrated. 1s. 6d.

17. *ARCHITECTURE—STYLES*—The History and Description of the Styles of Architecture of Various Countries, from the Earliest to the Present Period. By T. TALBOT BURY, F.R.I.B.A., &c. Illustrated. 2s.
. ORDERS AND STYLES OF ARCHITECTURE, *in One Vol.,* 3s. 6d.

18. *ARCHITECTURE—DESIGN*—The Principles of Design in Architecture, as deducible from Nature and exemplified in the Works of the Greek and Gothic Architects. By E. L. GARBETT, Architect. Illustrated. 2s.6d.
. *The three preceding Works, in One handsome Vol., half bound, entitled* "MODERN ARCHITECTURE," *price* 6s.

22. *THE ART OF BUILDING*, Rudiments of. General Principles of Construction, Materials used in Building, Strength and Use of Materials, Working Drawings, Specifications, and Estimates. By E. DOBSON, 2s.‡

23. *BRICKS AND TILES*, Rudimentary Treatise on the Manufacture of; containing an Outline of the Principles of Brickmaking. By EDW. DOBSON, M.R.I.B.A. With Additions by C. TOMLINSON, F.R.S. Illustrated, 3s.‡

25. *MASONRY AND STONECUTTING*, Rudimentary Treatise on; in which the Principles of Masonic Projection and their application to the Construction of Curved Wing-Walls, Domes, Oblique Bridges, and Roman and Gothic Vaulting, are concisely explained. By EDWARD DOBSON, M.R.I.B.A., &c. Illustrated with Plates and Diagrams. 2s. 6d.‡

44. *FOUNDATIONS AND CONCRETE WORKS*, a Rudimentary Treatise on; containing a Synopsis of the principal cases of Foundation Works, with the usual Modes of Treatment, and Practical Remarks on Footings, Planking, Sand, Concrete, Béton, Pile-driving, Caissons, and Cofferdams. By E. DOBSON, M.R.I.B.A., &c. Fourth Edition, revised by GEORGE DODD, C.E. Illustrated. 1s. 6d.

42. *COTTAGE BUILDING.* By C. BRUCE ALLEN, Architect. Ninth Edition, revised and enlarged. Numerous Illustrations. 1s. 6d.

45. *LIMES, CEMENTS, MORTARS, CONCRETES, MASTICS, PLASTERING,* &c. By G. R. BURNELL, C.E. Eleventh Edition. 1s. 6d.

57. *WARMING AND VENTILATION*, a Rudimentary Treatise on; being a concise Exposition of the General Principles of the Art of Warming and Ventilating Domestic and Public Buildings, Mines, Lighthouses, Ships, &c. By CHARLES TOMLINSON, F.R.S., &c. Illustrated. 3s.

83**. *CONSTRUCTION OF DOOR LOCKS.* Compiled from the Papers of A. C. HOBBS, Esq., of New York, and Edited by CHARLES TOMLINSON, F.R.S. To which is added, a Description of Fenby's Patent Locks, and a Note upon IRON SAFES by ROBERT MALLET, M.I.C.E. Illus. 2s. 6d.

111. *ARCHES, PIERS, BUTTRESSES, &c.*: Experimental Essays on the Principles of Construction in; made with a view to their being useful to the Practical Builder. By WILLIAM BLAND. Illustrated. 1s. 6d.

The ‡ indicates that these vols. may be had strongly bound at 6d. extra.

LONDON : CROSBY LOCKWOOD AND CO.,

Architecture, Building, etc., *continued.*

116. *THE ACOUSTICS OF PUBLIC BUILDINGS;* or, The Principles of the Science of Sound applied to the purposes of the Architect and Builder. By T. ROGER SMITH, M.R.I.B.A., Architect. Illustrated. 1s. 6d.

124. *CONSTRUCTION OF ROOFS,* Treatise on the, as regards Carpentry and Joinery. Deduced from the Works of ROBISON, PRICE, and TREDGOLD. Illustrated. 1s. 6d.

127. *ARCHITECTURAL MODELLING IN PAPER,* the Art of. By T. A. RICHARDSON, Architect. Illustrated. 1s. 6d.

128. *VITRUVIUS — THE ARCHITECTURE OF MARCUS VITRUVIUS POLLO.* In Ten Books. Translated from the Latin by JOSEPH GWILT, F.S.A., F.R.A.S. With 23 Plates. 5s.

130. *GRECIAN ARCHITECTURE,* An Inquiry into the Principles of Beauty in ; with an Historical View of the Rise and Progress of the Art in Greece. By the EARL OF ABERDEEN. 1s.
. *The two preceding Works in One handsome Vol., half bound, entitled "*ANCIENT ARCHITECTURE," *price* 6s.

16, 17, 18, 128, *and* 130, *in One Vol., entitled "*ANCIENT AND MODERN ARCHITECTURE," *half bound,* 12s.

132. *DWELLING-HOUSES,* a Rudimentary Treatise on the Erection of. Illustrated by a Perspective View, Plans, Elevations, and Sections of a pair of Semi-detached Villas, with the Specification, Quantities, and Estimates, and every requisite detail, in sequence, for their Construction and Finishing. By S. H. BROOKS, Architect. New Edition, with Plates. 2s. 6d.‡

156. *QUANTITIES AND MEASUREMENTS,* How to Calculate and Take them in Bricklayers', Masons', Plasterers', Plumbers', Painters', Paperhangers', Gilders', Smiths', Carpenters', and Joiners' Work. By A. C. BEATON, Architect and Surveyor. New and Enlarged Edition. Illus. 1s. 6d.

175. *LOCKWOOD & CO.'S BUILDER'S AND CONTRACTOR'S* PRICE BOOK, for 1881, containing the latest Prices of all kinds of Builders' Materials and Labour, and of all Trades connected with Building : Lists of the Members of the Metropolitan Board of Works, of Districts, District Officers, and District Surveyors, and the Metropolitan Bye-laws. Edited by FRANCIS T. W. MILLER, Architect and Surveyor. 3s. 6d. ; half bound, 4s.

182. *CARPENTRY AND JOINERY*—THE ELEMENTARY PRINCIPLES OF CARPENTRY. Chiefly composed from the Standard Work of THOMAS TREDGOLD, C.E. With Additions from the Works of the most Recent Authorities, and a TREATISE ON JOINERY by E. WYNDHAM TARN, M.A. Numerous Illustrations. 3s. 6d.‡

182*. *CARPENTRY AND JOINERY. ATLAS* of 35 Plates to accompany the foregoing book. With Descriptive Letterpress. 4to. 6s. cloth boards, 7s. 6d.

187. *HINTS TO YOUNG ARCHITECTS.* By GEORGE WIGHTWICK. New, Revised, and enlarged Edition. By G. HUSKISSON GUILLAUME, Architect. With numerous Woodcuts. 3s. 6d.‡

188. *HOUSE PAINTING, GRAINING, MARBLING, AND SIGN WRITING:* A Practical Manual of, containing full information on the Processes of House-Painting, the Formation of Letters and Practice of Sign-Writing, the Principles of Decorative Art, a Course of Elementary Drawing for House-Painters, Writers, &c., &c. With 9 Coloured Plates of Woods and Marbles, and nearly 150 Wood Engravings. By ELLIS A. DAVIDSON. Third Edition, carefully revised. 5s. cloth limp ; 6s. cloth boards.

189. *THE RUDIMENTS OF PRACTICAL BRICKLAYING.* In Six Sections : General Principles ; Arch Drawing, Cutting, and Setting ; Pointing ; Paving, Tiling, Materials ; Slating and Plastering ; Practical Geometry, Mensuration, &c. By ADAM HAMMOND. Illustrated. 1s. 6d.

191. *PLUMBING.* A Text-Book to the Practice of the Art or Craft of the Plumber. With Chapters upon House Drainage, embodying the latest Improvements. Second Edition, enlarged. Containing 300 Illustrations. By W. P. BUCHAN, Sanitary Engineer. 3s. 6d.‡

☞ *The ‡ indicates that these vols. may be had strongly bound at 6d. extra.*

4   WEALE'S RUDIMENTARY SERIES.

Architecture, Building, etc., *continued.*
192. *THE TIMBER IMPORTER'S, TIMBER MERCHANT'S,*
and BUILDER'S STANDARD GUIDE; comprising copious and valuable Memoranda for the Retailer and Builder. By RICHARD E. GRANDY.
Second Edition, Revised.   3s.‡
205. *THE ART OF LETTER PAINTING MADE EASY.* By
J. G. BADENOCH. Illustrated with 12 full-page Engravings of Examples. 1s.
206. *A BOOK ON BUILDING, Civil and Ecclesiastical,* including
CHURCH RESTORATION. With the Theory of Domes and the Great Pyramid,
&c. By Sir EDMUND BECKETT, Bart., LL.D., Q.C., F.R.A.S. Second Edition,
enlarged, 4s. 6d.‡

CIVIL ENGINEERING, ETC.

219. *CIVIL ENGINEERING.*   By HENRY LAW, M.Inst. C.E.
Including a Treatise on HYDRAULIC ENGINEERING by GEO. R. BURNELL,
M.Inst.C.E. Sixth Edition, revised, WITH LARGE ADDITIONS ON RECENT
PRACTICE IN CIVIL ENGINEERING, by D. KINNEAR CLARK, M.Inst. C.E.,
Author of " Tramways : Their Construction," &c. 6s. 6d., Cloth boards, 7s. 6d.
29. *THE DRAINAGE OF DISTRICTS AND LANDS.* By G.
DRYSDALE DEMPSEY, C.E.   [*New Edition in preparation.*
30. *THE DRAINAGE OF TOWNS AND BUILDINGS.* By
G. DRYSDALE DEMPSEY, C.E.   [*New Edition in preparation.*
31. *WELL-DIGGING, BORING, AND PUMP-WORK.* By JOHN
GEORGE SWINDELL, A.R.I.B.A. New Edition, by G. R. BURNELL, C.E. 1s. 6d.
35. *THE BLASTING AND QUARRYING OF STONE,* for
Building and other Purposes. With Remarks on the Blowing up of Bridges.
By Gen. Sir JOHN BURGOYNE, Bart., K.C.B. Illustrated. 1s. 6d.
62. *RAILWAY CONSTRUCTION,* Elementary and Practical Instructions on the Science of. By Sir M. STEPHENSON, C.E. New Edition,
by EDWARD NUGENT, C.E. With Statistics of the Capital, Dividends, and
Working of Railways in the United Kingdom. By E. D. CHATTAWAY. 4s.
80*. *EMBANKING LANDS FROM THE SEA,* the Practice of.
Treated as a Means of Profitable Employment for Capital. With Examples
and Particulars of actual Embankments, &c. By J. WIGGINS, F.G.S. 2s.
81. *WATER WORKS,* for the Supply of Cities and Towns. With
a Description of the Principal Geological Formations of England as influencing Supplies of Water ; and Details of Engines and Pumping Machinery
for raising Water. By SAMUEL HUGHES, F.G.S., C.E. New Edition. 4s.‡
117. *SUBTERRANEOUS SURVEYING,* an Elementary and Practical Treatise on. By THOMAS FENWICK. Also the Method of Conducting
Subterraneous Surveys without the Use of the Magnetic Needle, and other
Modern Improvements. By THOMAS BAKER, C.E. Illustrated. 2s. 6d.‡
118. *CIVIL ENGINEERING IN NORTH AMERICA,* a Sketch
of. By DAVID STEVENSON, F.R.S.E., &c. Plates and Diagrams. 3s.
197. *ROADS AND STREETS (THE CONSTRUCTION OF),*
in two Parts : I. THE ART OF CONSTRUCTING COMMON ROADS, by HENRY
LAW, C.E., revised and condensed by D. KINNEAR CLARK, C.E. ; II. RECENT
PRACTICE, including pavements of Stone, Wood, and Asphalte. Second
Edition, revised, by D. K. CLARK, M.I.C.E. 4s. 6d.‡
203. *SANITARY WORK IN THE SMALLER TOWNS AND IN*
VILLAGES. Comprising :—1. Some of the more Common Forms of
Nuisance and their Remedies ; 2. Drainage ; 3. Water Supply. A useful
book for Members of Local Boards and Rural Sanitary Authorities, Health
Officers, Engineers, Surveyors, &c. By CHARLES SLAGG, A.I.C.E. 2s. 6d.‡
212. *THE CONSTRUCTION OF GAS-WORKS,* and the Manu-
facture and Distribution of Coal Gas. Originally written by SAMUEL
HUGHES, C.E. Sixth Edition, re-written and much Enlarged by WILLIAM
RICHARDS, C.E. With 72 Illustrations. 4s. 6d.‡   [*Just published.*
213. *PIONEER ENGINEERING.* A Treatise on the Engineering
Operations connected with the Settlement of Waste Lands in New Countries. By EDWARD DOBSON, Assoc. Inst. C.E. 4s. 6d.‡

☞ *The ‡ indicates that these vols. may be had strongly bound at 6d. extra.*

LONDON : CROSBY LOCKWOOD AND CO.,

MECHANICAL ENGINEERING, ETC.

33. *CRANES*, the Construction of, and other Machinery for Raising Heavy Bodies for the Erection of Buildings, and for Hoisting Goods. By JOSEPH GLYNN, F.R.S., &c. Illustrated. 1s. 6d.

34. *THE STEAM ENGINE*, a Rudimentary Treatise on. By Dr. LARDNER. Illustrated. 1s. 6d.

59. *STEAM BOILERS*: their Construction and Management. By R. ARMSTRONG, C.E. Illustrated. 1s. 6d.

67. *CLOCKS, WATCHES, AND BELLS*, a Rudimentary Treatise on. By Sir EDMUND BECKETT (late EDMUND BECKETT DENISON), LL.D., Q.C. A New, Revised, and considerably Enlarged Edition (the 6th), with very numerous Illustrations. 4s. 6d. cloth limp; 5s. 6d. cloth boards, gilt.

82. *THE POWER OF WATER*, as applied to drive Flour Mills, and to give motion to Turbines and other Hydrostatic Engines. By JOSEPH GLYNN, F.R.S., &c. New Edition, Illustrated. 2s.‡

98. *PRACTICAL MECHANISM*, the Elements of; and Machine Tools. By T. BAKER, C.E. With Remarks on Tools and Machinery, by J. NASMYTH, C.E. Plates. 2s. 6d.‡

114. *MACHINERY*, Elementary Principles of, in its Construction and Working. By C. D. ABEL, C.E. 1s. 6d.

139. *THE STEAM ENGINE*, a Treatise on the Mathematical Theory of, with Rules and Examples for Practical Men. By T. BAKER, C.E. 1s. 6d.

162. *THE BRASS FOUNDER'S MANUAL*; Instructions for Modelling, Pattern-Making, Moulding, Turning, Filing, Burnishing, Bronzing, &c. With copious Receipts, &c. By WALTER GRAHAM. 2s.‡

164. *MODERN WORKSHOP PRACTICE*, as applied to Marine, Land, and Locomotive Engines, Floating Docks, Dredging Machines, Bridges, Cranes, Ship-building, &c., &c. By J. G. WINTON. Illustrated. 3s.‡

165. *IRON AND HEAT*, exhibiting the Principles concerned in the Construction of Iron Beams, Pillars, and Bridge Girders, and the Action of Heat in the Smelting Furnace. By J. ARMOUR, C.E. 2s. 6d.‡

166. *POWER IN MOTION*: Horse-Power, Toothed-Wheel Gearing, Long and Short Driving Bands, and Angular Forces. By J. ARMOUR. 2s.6d.‡

167. *IRON BRIDGES, GIRDERS, ROOFS, AND OTHER WORKS*. By FRANCIS CAMPIN, C.E. 2s. 6d.‡

171. *THE WORKMAN'S MANUAL OF ENGINEERING DRAWING*. By JOHN MAXTON, Engineer. Fourth Edition. Illustrated with 7 Plates and nearly 350 Woodcuts. 3s. 6d.‡

190. *STEAM AND THE STEAM ENGINE*, Stationary and Portable. Being an extension of Mr. John Sewell's "Treatise on Steam." By D. K. CLARK, M.I.C.E. Second Edition, revised. 3s. 6d.‡

200. *FUEL*, its Combustion and Economy. By C. W. WILLIAMS, A.I.C.E. With extensive additions on Recent Practice in the Combustion and Economy of Fuel—Coal, Coke, Wood, Peat, Petroleum, &c.—by D. K. CLARK, M.I.C.E. 2nd Edition. 3s. 6d.‡

202. *LOCOMOTIVE ENGINES*. By G. D. DEMPSEY, C.E.; with large additions treating of the Modern Locomotive, by D. KINNEAR CLARK, M.I.C.E. 3s.‡

211. *THE BOILERMAKER'S ASSISTANT* in Drawing, Templating, and Calculating Boiler and Tank Work. By JOHN COURTNEY, Practical Boiler Maker. Edited by D. K. CLARK, C.E. 100 Illustrations. 2s.

216. *MATERIALS AND CONSTRUCTION*; A Theoretical and Practical Treatise on the Strains, Designing, and Erection of Works of Construction. By FRANCIS CAMPIN, C.E. 3s.‡ [*Just published.*

217. *SEWING MACHINERY*, being a Practical Manual of the Sewing Machine; comprising its History and Details of its Construction, with full Technical Directions for the Adjusting of Sewing Machines. By J. W. URQUHART, C.E. 2s.‡ [*Just published.*

223. *MECHANICAL ENGINEERING*, A Practical Treatise on. Comprising Metallurgy, Moulding, Casting, Forging, Tools, Workshop Machinery, Mechanical Manipulation, Manufacture of the Steam Engine, &c. By FRANCIS CAMPIN, C.E. 2s. 6d.‡ - [*Just published.*

☞ *The ‡ indicates that these vols. may be had strongly bound at 6d. extra.*

SHIPBUILDING, NAVIGATION, MARINE ENGINEERING, ETC.

51. *NAVAL ARCHITECTURE*, the Rudiments of; or an Exposition of the Elementary Principles of the Science, and their Practical Application to Naval Construction. Compiled for the Use of Beginners. By JAMES PEAKE, School of Naval Architecture, H.M. Dockyard, Portsmouth. Fourth Edition, corrected, with Plates and Diagrams. 3s. 6d.‡

53*. *SHIPS FOR OCEAN AND RIVER SERVICE*, Elementary and Practical Principles of the Construction of. By HAKON A. SOMMERFELDT, Surveyor of the Royal Norwegian Navy. With an Appendix. 1s. 6d.

53**. *AN ATLAS OF ENGRAVINGS* to Illustrate the above. Twelve large folding plates. Royal 4to, cloth. 7s. 6d.

54. *MASTING, MAST-MAKING, AND RIGGING OF SHIPS*, Rudimentary Treatise on. Also Tables of Spars, Rigging, Blocks; Chain, Wire, and Hemp Ropes, &c., relative to every class of vessels. With an Appendix of Dimensions of Masts and Yards of the Royal Navy. By ROBERT KIPPING, N.A. Fourteenth Edition. Illustrated. 2s.‡

54*. *IRON SHIP-BUILDING*. With Practical Examples and Details for the Use of Ship Owners and Ship Builders. By JOHN GRANTHAM, Consulting Engineer and Naval Architect. 5th Edition, with Additions. 4s.

54**. *AN ATLAS OF FORTY PLATES* to Illustrate the above. Fifth Edition. Including the latest Examples, such as H.M. Steam Frigates "Warrior," "Hercules," "Bellerophon;" H.M. Troop Ship "Serapis," Iron Floating Dock, &c., &c. 4to, boards. 38s.

55. *THE SAILOR'S SEA BOOK*: a Rudimentary Treatise on Navigation. Part I. How to Keep the Log and Work it off. Part II. On Finding the Latitude and Longitude. By JAMES GREENWOOD, B.A. To which are added, the Deviation and Error of the Compass; Great Circle Sailing; the International (Commercial) Code of Signals; the Rule of the Road at Sea; Rocket and Mortar Apparatus for Saving Life; the Law of Storms; and a Brief Dictionary of Sea Terms. With numerous Woodcuts and Coloured Plates of Flags. New, thoroughly revised and much enlarged edition. By W. H. ROSSER. 2s. 6d.‡

80. *MARINE ENGINES, AND STEAM VESSELS*, a Treatise on. Together with Practical Remarks on the Screw and Propelling Power, as used in the Royal and Merchant Navy. By ROBERT MURRAY, C.E., Engineer-Surveyor to the Board of Trade. With a Glossary of Technical Terms, and their Equivalents in French, German, and Spanish. Seventh Edition, revised and enlarged. Illustrated. 3s.‡

83*bis*. *THE FORMS OF SHIPS AND BOATS*: Hints, Experimentally Derived, on some of the Principles regulating Ship-building. By W. BLAND. Seventh Edition, revised, with numerous Illustrations and Models. 1s. 6d.

99. *NAVIGATION AND NAUTICAL ASTRONOMY*, in Theory and Practice. With Attempts to facilitate the Finding of the Time and the Longitude at Sea. By J. R. YOUNG, formerly Professor of Mathematics in Belfast College. Illustrated. 2s. 6d.

100*. *TABLES* intended to facilitate the Operations of Navigation and Nautical Astronomy, as an Accompaniment to the above Book. By J. R. YOUNG. 1s. 6d.

106. *SHIPS' ANCHORS*, a Treatise on. By G. COTSELL, N.A.   1s. 6d.

149. *SAILS AND SAIL-MAKING*, an Elementary Treatise on. With Draughting, and the Centre of Effort of the Sails. Also, Weights and Sizes of Ropes; Masting, Rigging, and Sails of Steam Vessels, &c., &c. Eleventh Edition, enlarged, with an Appendix. By ROBERT KIPPING, N.A., Sailmaker, Quayside, Newcastle. Illustrated. 2s. 6d.‡

155. *THE ENGINEER'S GUIDE TO THE ROYAL AND MERCANTILE NAVIES*. By a PRACTICAL ENGINEER. Revised by D. F. M'CARTHY, late of the Ordnance Survey Office, Southampton. 3s.

55 & 204. *PRACTICAL NAVIGATION*. Consisting of The Sailor's Sea-Book. By JAMES GREENWOOD and W. H. ROSSER. Together with the requisite Mathematical and Nautical Tables for the Working of the Problems. By HENRY LAW, C.E., and J. R. YOUNG, formerly Professor of Mathematics in Belfast College. Illustrated with numerous Wood Engravings and Coloured Plates. 7s. Strongly half-bound in leather.

The ‡ indicates that these vols. may be had strongly bound at 6d. extra.

LONDON : CROSBY LOCKWOOD AND CO.,

PHYSICAL SCIENCE, NATURAL PHILO-SOPHY, ETC.

1. *CHEMISTRY*, for the Use of Beginners. By Professor GEORGE FOWNES, F.R.S. With an Appendix on the Application of Chemistry to Agriculture. 1s.

2. *NATURAL PHILOSOPHY*, Introduction to the Study of; for the Use of Beginners. By C. TOMLINSON, Lecturer on Natural Science in King's College School, London. Woodcuts. 1s. 6d.

4. *MINERALOGY*, Rudiments of; a concise View of the Properties of Minerals. By A. RAMSAY, Jun. Woodcuts and Steel Plates. 3s.‡

6. *MECHANICS*, Rudimentary Treatise on; being a concise Exposition of the General Principles of Mechanical Science, and their Applications. By CHARLES TOMLINSON. Illustrated. 1s. 6d.

7. *ELECTRICITY*; showing the General Principles of Electrical Science, and the purposes to which it has been applied. By Sir W. SNOW HARRIS, F.R.S., &c. With Additions by R. SABINE, C.E., F.S.A. 1s. 6d.

7*. *GALVANISM*, Rudimentary Treatise on, and the General Principles of Animal and Voltaic Electricity. By Sir W. SNOW HARRIS. New Edition, with considerable Additions by ROBERT SABINE, C.E., F.S.A. 1s. 6d.

8. *MAGNETISM*; being a concise Exposition of the General Principles of Magnetical Science, and the Purposes to which it has been applied. By Sir W. SNOW HARRIS. New Edition, revised and enlarged by H. M. NOAD, Ph.D., Vice-President of the Chemical Society, Author of "A Manual of Electricity," &c., &c. With 165 Woodcuts. 3s. 6d.‡

11. *THE ELECTRIC TELEGRAPH*; its History and Progress; with Descriptions of some of the Apparatus. By R. SABINE, C.E., F.S.A. 3s.

12. *PNEUMATICS*, for the Use of Beginners. By CHARLES TOMLINSON. Illustrated. 1s. 6d.

72. *MANUAL OF THE MOLLUSCA*; a Treatise on Recent and Fossil Shells. By Dr. S. P. WOODWARD, A.L.S. Fourth Edition. With Appendix by RALPH TATE, A.L.S., F.G.S. With numerous Plates and 300 Woodcuts. 6s. 6d. Cloth boards, 7s. 6d.

79**. *PHOTOGRAPHY*, Popular Treatise on; with a Description of the Stereoscope, &c. Translated from the French of D. VAN MONCKHOVEN, by W. H. THORNTHWAITE, Ph.D. Woodcuts. 1s. 6d.

96. *ASTRONOMY*. By the Rev. R. MAIN, M.A., F.R.S., &c. New Edition, with an Appendix on "Spectrum Analysis." Woodcuts. 1s. 6d.

97. *STATICS AND DYNAMICS*, the Principles and Practice of; embracing also a clear development of Hydrostatics, Hydrodynamics, and Central Forces. By T. BAKER, C.E. 1s. 6d.

138. *TELEGRAPH*, Handbook of the; a Manual of Telegraphy, Telegraph Clerks' Remembrancer, and Guide to Candidates for Employment in the Telegraph Service. By R. BOND. Fourth Edition, revised and enlarged: to which is appended, QUESTIONS on MAGNETISM, ELECTRICITY, and PRACTICAL TELEGRAPHY, for the Use of Students, by W. McGREGOR, First Assistant Supnt., Indian Gov. Telegraphs. 3s.‡

143. *EXPERIMENTAL ESSAYS*. By CHARLES TOMLINSON. I. On the Motions of Camphor on Water. II. On the Motion of Camphor towards the Light. III. History of the Modern Theory of Dew. Woodcuts. 1s.

173. *PHYSICAL GEOLOGY*, partly based on Major-General PORTLOCK's "Rudiments of Geology." By RALPH TATE, A.L.S., &c. Woodcuts. 2s.

174. *HISTORICAL GEOLOGY*, partly based on Major-General PORTLOCK's "Rudiments." By RALPH TATE, A.L.S., &c. Woodcuts. 2s. 6d.

173 & 174. *RUDIMENTARY TREATISE ON GEOLOGY*, Physical and Historical. Partly based on Major-General PORTLOCK's "Rudiments of Geology." By RALPH TATE, A.L.S., F.G.S., &c. In One Volume. 4s. 6d.‡

183 & 184. *ANIMAL PHYSICS*, Handbook of. By Dr. LARDNER, D.C.L., formerly Professor of Natural Philosophy and Astronomy in University College, Lond. With 520 Illustrations. In One Vol. 7s. 6d., cloth boards.

   ⁎ Sold also in Two Parts, as follows :—

183. ANIMAL PHYSICS. By Dr. LARDNER. Part I., Chapters I.—VII. 4s.
184. ANIMAL PHYSICS. By Dr. LARDNER. Part II., Chapters VIII.—XVIII. 3s.

☞ *The ‡ indicates that these vols. may be had strongly bound at 6d. extra.*

MINING, METALLURGY, ETC.

117. *SUBTERRANEOUS SURVEYING*, Elementary and Practical Treatise on, with and without the Magnetic Needle. By THOMAS FENWICK, Surveyor of Mines, and THOMAS BAKER, C.E. Illustrated. 2s. 6d.‡

133. *METALLURGY OF COPPER*; an Introduction to the Methods of Seeking, Mining, and Assaying Copper, and Manufacturing its Alloys. By ROBERT H. LAMBORN, Ph.D. Woodcuts. 2s. 6d.‡

134. *METALLURGY OF SILVER AND LEAD.* A Description of the Ores; their Assay and Treatment, and valuable Constituents. By Dr. R. H. LAMBORN. Woodcuts. 2s. 6d.‡

135. *ELECTRO-METALLURGY;* Practically Treated. By ALEXANDER WATT, F.R.S.S.A. 7th Edition, revised, with important additions, including the Electro-Deposition of Nickel, &c. Woodcuts. 3s.‡

172. *MINING TOOLS*, Manual of. For the Use of Mine Managers, Agents, Students, &c. By WILLIAM MORGANS. 2s. 6d.‡

172*. *MINING TOOLS, ATLAS* of Engravings to Illustrate the above, containing 235 Illustrations, drawn to Scale. 4to. 4s. 6d.; cloth boards, 6s.

176. *METALLURGY OF IRON.* Containing History of Iron Manufacture, Methods of Assay, and Analyses of Iron Ores, Processes of Manufacture of Iron and Steel, &c. By H. BAUERMAN, F.G.S. 4th Edition. 4s. 6d.‡

180. *COAL AND COAL MINING*, A Rudimentary Treatise on. By WARINGTON W. SMYTH, M.A., F.R.S. Fifth Edition, revised and enlarged. With numerous Illustrations. 3s. 6d.‡ [*Just published.*

195. *THE MINERAL SURVEYOR AND VALUER'S COMPLETE GUIDE*, with new Traverse Tables, and Descriptions of Improved Instruments; also the Correct Principles of Laying out and Valuing Mineral Properties. By WILLIAM LINTERN, Mining and Civil Engineer. 3s. 6d.‡

214. *SLATE AND SLATE QUARRYING*, Scientific, Practical, and Commercial. By D. C. DAVIES, F.G.S., Mining Engineer, &c. With numerous Illustrations and Folding Plates. 3s.‡

215. *THE GOLDSMITH'S HANDBOOK*, containing full Instructions for the Alloying and Working of Gold, including the Art of Alloying, Melting, Reducing, Colouring, Collecting, and Refining; Chemical and Physical Properties of Gold; with a New System of Mixing its Alloys; Solders, Enamels, &c. By GEORGE E. GEE, Goldsmith and Silversmith. Second Edition, considerably enlarged. 3s.‡ [*Just published.*
THE SILVERSMITH'S HANDBOOK, containing full Instructions for the Alloying and Working of Silver. By GEORGE E. GEE. 3s.‡

220. *MAGNETIC SURVEYING, AND ANGULAR SURVEYING*, with Records of the Peculiarities of Needle Disturbances. Compiled from the Results of carefully made Experiments. By WILLIAM LINTERN, Mining and Civil Engineer and Surveyor. 2s. [*Just published.*

FINE ARTS.

20. *PERSPECTIVE FOR BEGINNERS.* Adapted to Young †Students and Amateurs in Architecture, Painting, &c. By GEORGE PYNE. 2s.

40 & 41. *GLASS STAINING*; or, The Art of Painting on Glass. From the German of Dr. GESSERT. With an Appendix on THE ART OF ENAMELLING, &c.; together with THE ART OF PAINTING ON GLASS. From the German of EMANUEL OTTO FROMBERG. In One Volume. 2s. 6d.

69. *MUSIC*, A Rudimentary and Practical Treatise on. With numerous Examples. By CHARLES CHILD SPENCER. 2s. 6d.

71. *PIANOFORTE*, The Art of Playing the. With numerous Exercises & Lessons. From the Best Masters, by CHARLES CHILD SPENCER. 1s. 6d.

181. *PAINTING POPULARLY EXPLAINED*, including Fresco, Oil, Mosaic, Water Colour, Water-Glass, Tempera, Encaustic, Miniature, Painting on Ivory, Vellum, Pottery, Enamel, Glass. &c. With Historical Sketches of the Progress of the Art by THOMAS JOHN GULLICK, assisted by JOHN TIMBS, F.S.A. Fourth Edition, revised and enlarged. 5s.‡

186. *A GRAMMAR OF COLOURING*, applied to Decorative Painting and the Arts. By GEORGE FIELD. New Edition, enlarged and adapted to the Use of the Ornamental Painter and Designer. By ELLIS A. DAVIDSON. With two new Coloured Diagrams, &c. 3s.‡

☞ *The ‡ indicates that these vols. may be had strongly bound at 6d. extra.*

LONDON : CROSBY LOCKWOOD AND CO.,

AGRICULTURE, GARDENING, ETC.

29. THE DRAINAGE OF DISTRICTS AND LANDS. By G. DRYSDALE DEMPSEY, C.E. [New Edition in preparation.

66. CLAY LANDS & LOAMY SOILS. By Prof. DONALDSON. 1s.

131. MILLER'S, MERCHANT'S, AND FARMER'S' READY RECKONER, for ascertaining at sight the value of any quantity of Corn, from One Bushel to One Hundred Quarters, at any given price, from £1 to £5 per Qr. With approximate values of Millstones, Millwork, &c. 1s.

140. SOILS, MANURES, AND CROPS. (Vol. 1. OUTLINES OF MODERN FARMING.) By R. SCOTT BURN. Woodcuts. 2s.

141. FARMING & FARMING ECONOMY, Notes, Historical and Practical, on. (Vol. 2. OUTLINES OF MODERN FARMING.) By R. SCOTT BURN. 3s.

142. STOCK; CATTLE, SHEEP, AND HORSES. (Vol. 3. OUTLINES OF MODERN FARMING.) By R. SCOTT BURN. Woodcuts. 2s. 6d.

145. DAIRY, PIGS, AND POULTRY, Management of the. By R. SCOTT BURN. With Notes on the Diseases of Stock. (Vol. 4. OUTLINES OF MODERN FARMING.) Woodcuts. 2s.

146. UTILIZATION OF SEWAGE, IRRIGATION, AND RECLAMATION OF WASTE LAND. (Vol. 5. OUTLINES OF MODERN FARMING.) By R. SCOTT BURN. Woodcuts. 2s. 6d.

** Nos. 140-1-2-5-6, in One Vol., handsomely half-bound, entitled "OUTLINES OF MODERN FARMING." By ROBERT SCOTT BURN. Price 12s.

177. FRUIT TREES, The Scientific and Profitable Culture of. From the French of DU BREUIL. Revised by GEO. GLENNY. 187 Woodcuts. 3s. 6d.‡

198. SHEEP; THE HISTORY, STRUCTURE, ECONOMY, AND DISEASES OF. By W. C. SPOONER, M.R.V.C., &c. Fourth Edition, considerably enlarged; with numerous fine engravings, including some specimens of New and Improved Breeds. 366 pp. 3s. 6d.‡

201. KITCHEN GARDENING MADE EASY. Showing how to prepare and lay out the ground, the best means of cultivating every known Vegetable and Herb, with cultural directions for the management of them all the year round. By GEORGE M.F.GLENNY, Author of "Floriculture,"&c. 1s.6d.‡

207. OUTLINES OF FARM MANAGEMENT, and the Organization of Farm Labour: Treating of the General Work of the Farm; Field and Live Stock; Details of Contract Work; Specialities of Labour; Economical Management of the Farmhouse and Cottage, and their Domestic Animals. By ROBERT SCOTT BURN. 2s. 6d.‡ [Just published.

208. OUTLINES OF LANDED ESTATES MANAGEMENT: Treating of the Varieties of Lands, Methods of Farming, Farm Buildings, Irrigation, Drainage, &c. By R. SCOTT BURN. 2s. 6d.‡

** Nos. 207 & 208 in One Vol., handsomely half-bound, entitled "OUTLINES OF LANDED ESTATES AND FARM MANAGEMENT." By R. SCOTT BURN. Price 6s.

209. THE TREE PLANTER AND PLANT PROPAGATOR: Being a Practical Manual on the Propagation of Forest Trees, Fruit Trees, Flowering Shrubs, Flowering Plants, Pot-Herbs, &c.; with numerous Illustrations of Grafting, Layering, Budding, Cuttings, &c., Useful Implements, Houses, Pits, &c. By SAMUEL WOOD. 2s.‡ [Just published.

210. THE TREE PRUNER: Being a Practical Manual on the Pruning of Fruit Trees, including also their Training and Renovation; also treating of the Pruning of Shrubs, Climbers and Flowering Plants. By SAMUEL WOOD. 2s.‡ [Just published.

** Nos. 209 & 210 in One Vol., handsomely half-bound, entitled "THE TREE PLANTER, PROPAGATOR AND PRUNER." By SAMUEL WOOD. Price 5s.

219. THE HAY AND STRAW MEASURER: Being New Tables for the Use of Auctioneers, Valuers, Farmers, Hay and Straw Dealers, &c., forming a complete Calculator and Ready-Reckoner, especially adapted to persons connected with Agriculture. Third Edition. By JOHN STEELE. 2s.

222. SUBURBAN FARMING. The Laying-out and Cultivation of Farms, adapted to the Produce of Milk, Butter, and Cheese, Eggs, Poultry, and Pigs. By the late Prof. JOHN DONALDSON. With Additions by R. SCOTT BURN. Second Edition. 3s. 6d.‡ [Just published.

☞ The ‡ indicates that these vols. may be had strongly bound at 6d. extra.

ARITHMETIC, GEOMETRY, MATHEMATICS, ETC.

32. *MATHEMATICAL INSTRUMENTS*, a Treatise on; in which their Construction and the Methods of Testing, Adjusting, and Using them are concisely Explained. By J. F. HEATHER, M.A., of the Royal Military Academy, Woolwich. Original Edition, in 1 vol., Illustrated. 1s. 6d.

. *In ordering the above, be careful to say, "Original Edition" (No. 32), to distinguish it from the Enlarged Edition in 3 vols. (Nos. 168-9-70.)*

60. *LAND AND ENGINEERING SURVEYING*, a Treatise on; with all the Modern Improvements. Arranged for the Use of Schools and Private Students; also for Practical Land Surveyors and Engineers. By T. BAKER, C.E. New Edition, revised by EDWARD NUGENT, C.E. Illustrated with Plates and Diagrams. 2s.‡

61*. *READY RECKONER FOR THE ADMEASUREMENT OF LAND.* By ABRAHAM ARMAN, Schoolmaster, Thurleigh, Beds. To which is added a Table, showing the Price of Work, from 2s. 6d. to £1 per acre, and Tables for the Valuation of Land, from 1s. to £1,000 per acre, and from one pole to two thousand acres in extent, &c., &c. 1s. 6d.

76. *DESCRIPTIVE GEOMETRY*, an Elementary Treatise on; with a Theory of Shadows and of Perspective, extracted from the French of G. MONGE. To which is added, a description of the Principles and Practice of Isometrical Projection; the whole being intended as an introduction to the Application of Descriptive Geometry to various branches of the Arts. By J. F. HEATHER, M.A. Illustrated with 14 Plates. 2s.

178. *PRACTICAL PLANE GEOMETRY*: giving the Simplest Modes of Constructing Figures contained in one Plane and Geometrical Construction of the Ground. By J. F. HEATHER, M.A. With 215 Woodcuts. 2s.

179. *PROJECTION*: Orthographic, Topographic, and Perspective: giving the various Modes of Delineating Solid Forms by Constructions on a Single Plane Surface. By J. F. HEATHER, M.A. [*In preparation.*]

. *The above three volumes will form a* COMPLETE ELEMENTARY COURSE OF MATHEMATICAL DRAWING.

83. *COMMERCIAL BOOK-KEEPING.* With Commercial Phrases and Forms in English, French, Italian, and German. By JAMES HADDON, M.A., Arithmetical Master of King's College School, London. 1s. 6d.

84. *ARITHMETIC*, a Rudimentary Treatise on: with full Explanations of its Theoretical Principles, and numerous Examples for Practice. For the Use of Schools and for Self-Instruction. By J. R. YOUNG, late Professor of Mathematics in Belfast College. New Edition, with Index. 1s. 6d.

84*. A KEY to the above, containing Solutions in full to the Exercises, together with Comments, Explanations, and Improved Processes, for the Use of Teachers and Unassisted Learners. By J. R. YOUNG. 1s. 6d.

85. *EQUATIONAL ARITHMETIC*, applied to Questions of Interest,
85*. Annuities, Life Assurance, and General Commerce; with various Tables by which all Calculations may be greatly facilitated. By W. HIPSLEY. 2s.

86. *ALGEBRA*, the Elements of. By JAMES HADDON, M.A., Second Mathematical Master of King's College School. With Appendix, containing miscellaneous Investigations, and a Collection of Problems in various parts of Algebra. 2s.

86*. A KEY AND COMPANION to the above Book, forming an extensive repository of Solved Examples and Problems in Illustration of the various Expedients necessary in Algebraical Operations. Especially adapted for Self-Instruction. By J. R. YOUNG. 1s. 6d.

88. *EUCLID*, THE ELEMENTS OF: with many additional Propositions
89. and Explanatory Notes: to which is prefixed, an Introductory Essay on Logic. By HENRY LAW, C.E. 2s. 6d.‡

. *Sold also separately, viz. :— **

88. EUCLID, The First Three Books. By HENRY LAW, C.E. 1s. 6d.
89. EUCLID, Books 4, 5, 6, 11, 12. By HENRY LAW, C.E. 1s. 6d.

☞ *The ‡ indicates that these vols. may be had strongly bound at 6d. extra.*

LONDON : CROSBY LOCKWOOD AND CO.,

Arithmetic, Geometry, Mathematics, etc., *continued.*

90. *ANALYTICAL GEOMETRY AND CONIC SECTIONS,* a Rudimentary Treatise on. By JAMES HANN, late Mathematical Master of King's College School, London. A New Edition, re-written and enlarged by J. R. YOUNG, formerly Professor of Mathematics at Belfast College. 2s.‡

91. *PLANE TRIGONOMETRY,* the Elements of. By JAMES HANN, formerly Mathematical Master of King's College, London. 1s. 6d.

92. *SPHERICAL TRIGONOMETRY,* the Elements of. By JAMES HANN. Revised by CHARLES H. DOWLING, C.E. 1s.
  •.• *Or with "The Elements of Plane Trigonometry," in One Volume,* 2s. 6d.

93. *MENSURATION AND MEASURING,* for Students and Practical Use. With the Mensuration and Levelling of Land for the Purposes of Modern Engineering. By T. BAKER, C.E. New Edition, with Corrections and Additions by E. NUGENT, C.E. Illustrated. 1s. 6d.

102. *INTEGRAL CALCULUS,* Rudimentary Treatise on the. By HOMERSHAM COX, B.A. Illustrated. 1s.

103. *INTEGRAL CALCULUS,* Examples on the. By JAMES HANN, late of King's College, London. Illustrated. 1s.

101. *DIFFERENTIAL CALCULUS,* Elements of the. By W. S. B. WOOLHOUSE, F.R.A.S., &c. 1s. 6d.

105. *MNEMONICAL LESSONS.* — GEOMETRY, ALGEBRA, AND TRIGONOMETRY, in Easy Mnemonical Lessons. By the Rev. THOMAS PENYNGTON KIRKMAN, M.A. 1s. 6d.

136. *ARITHMETIC,* Rudimentary, for the Use of Schools and Self-Instruction. By JAMES HADDON, M.A. Revised by ABRAHAM ARMAN. 1s. 6d.

137. A KEY TO HADDON'S RUDIMENTARY ARITHMETIC. By A. ARMAN. 1s. 6d.

168. *DRAWING AND MEASURING INSTRUMENTS.* Including—I. Instruments employed in Geometrical and Mechanical Drawing, and in the Construction, Copying, and Measurement of Maps and Plans. II. Instruments used for the purposes of Accurate Measurement, and for Arithmetical Computations. By J. F. HEATHER, M.A., late of the Royal Military Academy, Woolwich, Author of "Descriptive Geometry," &c., &c. Illustrated. 1s. 6d.

169. *OPTICAL INSTRUMENTS.* Including (more especially) Telescopes, Microscopes, and Apparatus for producing copies of Maps and Plans by Photography. By J. F. HEATHER, M.A. Illustrated. 1s. 6d.

170. *SURVEYING AND ASTRONOMICAL INSTRUMENTS.* Including—I. Instruments Used for Determining the Geometrical Features of a portion of Ground. II. Instruments Employed in Astronomical Observations. By J. F. HEATHER, M.A. Illustrated. 1s. 6d.
  •.• *The above three volumes form an enlargement of the Author's original work, "Mathematical Instruments: their Construction, Adjustment, Testing, and Use," the Thirteenth Edition of which is on sale, price* 1s. 6d. (See No. 32 in the Series.)

168.⎫ *MATHEMATICAL INSTRUMENTS.* By J. F. HEATHER,
169.⎬ M.A. Enlarged Edition, for the most part entirely re-written. The 3 Parts as
170.⎭ above, in One thick Volume. With numerous Illustrations. 4s. 6d.‡

158. *THE SLIDE RULE, AND HOW TO USE IT;* containing full, easy, and simple Instructions to perform all Business Calculations with unexampled rapidity and accuracy. By CHARLES HOARE, C.E. With a Slide Rule in tuck of cover. 2s. 6d.‡

185. *THE COMPLETE MEASURER;* setting forth the Measurement of Boards, Glass, &c., &c.; Unequal-sided, Square-sided, Octagonal-sided, Round Timber and Stone, and Standing Timber. With a Table showing the solidity of hewn or eight-sided timber, or of any octagonal-sided column. Compiled for Timber-growers, Merchants, and Surveyors, Stonemasons, Architects, and others. By RICHARD HORTON. Third Edition, with valuable additions. 4s.; strongly bound in leather, 5s.

196. *THEORY OF COMPOUND INTEREST AND ANNUITIES;* with Tables of Logarithms for the more Difficult Computations of Interest, Discount, Annuities, &c. By FÉDOR THOMAN. 4s.‡

☞ *The ‡ indicates that these vols. may be had strongly bound at 6d. extra.*

Arithmetic, Geometry, Mathematics, etc., *continued.*

199. *INTUITIVE CALCULATIONS;* or, Easy and Compendious Methods of Performing the various Arithmetical Operations required in Commercial and Business Transactions; together with Full Explanations of Decimals and Duodecimals, several Useful Tables, &c. By DANIEL O'GORMAN. Twenty-fifth Edition, corrected and enlarged by J. R. YOUNG, formerly Professor of Mathematics in Belfast College. 3s.‡

204. *MATHEMATICAL TABLES,* for Trigonometrical, Astronomical, and Nautical Calculations; to which is prefixed a Treatise on Logarithms. By HENRY LAW, C.E. Together with a Series of Tables for Navigation and Nautical Astronomy. By J. R. YOUNG, formerly Professor of Mathematics in Belfast College. New Edition. 3s. 6d.‡

221. *MEASURES, WEIGHTS, AND MONEYS OF ALL NA-TIONS,* and an Analysis of the Christian, Hebrew, and Mahometan Calendars. By W. S. B. WOOLHOUSE, F.R.A.S., F.S.S. Sixth Edition, carefully revised and enlarged. 2s.‡   [*Just published.*

MISCELLANEOUS VOLUMES.

36. *A DICTIONARY OF TERMS used in ARCHITECTURE, BUILDING, ENGINEERING, MINING, METALLURGY, ARCHÆ-OLOGY, the FINE ARTS, &c.* By JOHN WEALE. Fifth Edition. Revised by ROBERT HUNT, F.R.S., Keeper of Mining Records. Numerous Illustrations. 5s. cloth limp; 6s. cloth boards.

50. *THE LAW OF CONTRACTS FOR WORKS AND SER-VICES.* By DAVID GIBBONS. Third Edition, enlarged. 3s.‡

112. *MANUAL OF DOMESTIC MEDICINE.* By R. GOODING, B.A., M.D. Intended as a Family Guide in all Cases of Accident and Emergency. 2s.‡

112*. *MANAGEMENT OF HEALTH.* A Manual of Home and Personal Hygiene. By the Rev. JAMES BAIRD, B.A. 1s.

150. *LOGIC,* Pure and Applied. By S. H. EMMENS. 1s. 6d.

152. *PRACTICAL HINTS FOR INVESTING MONEY.* With an Explanation of the Mode of Transacting Business on the Stock Exchange. By FRANCIS PLAYFORD, Sworn Broker. 1s. 6d.

153. *SELECTIONS FROM LOCKE'S ESSAYS ON THE HUMAN UNDERSTANDING.* With Notes by S. H. EMMENS. 2s.

154. *GENERAL HINTS TO EMIGRANTS.* Containing Notices of the various Fields for Emigration. With Hints on Preparation for Emigrating, Outfits, &c., &c. With Directions and Recipes useful to the Emigrant. With a Map of the World. 2s.

157. *THE EMIGRANT'S GUIDE TO NATAL.* By ROBERT JAMES MANN, F.R.A.S., F.M.S. Second Edition, carefully corrected to the present Date. Map. 2s.

193. *HANDBOOK OF FIELD FORTIFICATION,* intended for the Guidance of Officers Preparing for Promotion, and especially adapted to the requirements of Beginners. By Major W. W. KNOLLYS, F.R.G.S., 93rd Sutherland Highlanders, &c. With 163 Woodcuts. 3s.‡

194. *THE HOUSE MANAGER:* Being a Guide to Housekeeping, Practical Cookery, Pickling and Preserving, Household Work, Dairy Management, the Table and Dessert, Cellarage of Wines, Home-brewing and Wine-making, the Boudoir and Dressing-room, Travelling, Stable Economy, Gardening Operations, &c. By AN OLD HOUSEKEEPER. 3s. 6d.‡

194. *HOUSE BOOK (The).* Comprising :—I. THE HOUSE MANAGER. 112. By an OLD HOUSEKEEPER. II. DOMESTIC MEDICINE. By RALPH GOODING, & M.D. III. MANAGEMENT OF HEALTH. By JAMES BAIRD. In One Vol., 112*. strongly half-bound. 6s.

224. *COACH BUILDING;* A Practical Treatise, Historical and Descriptive, containing full information of the various Trades and Processes involved, with Hints on the proper Keeping of Carriages, &c. With 57 Illustrations. By JAMES W. BURGESS. 2s. 6d.‡   [*Just published.*

The ‡ indicates that these vols. may be had strongly bound at 6d. extra.

EDUCATIONAL AND CLASSICAL SERIES.

HISTORY.

1. **England, Outlines of the History of;** more especially with reference to the Origin and Progress of the English Constitution. By WILLIAM DOUGLAS HAMILTON, F.S.A., of Her Majesty's Public Record Office. 4th Edition, revised. 5s.; cloth boards, 6s.

5. **Greece, Outlines of the History of;** in connection with the Rise of the Arts and Civilization in Europe. By W. DOUGLAS HAMILTON, of University College, London, and EDWARD LEVIEN, M.A., of Balliol College, Oxford. 2s. 6d.; cloth boards, 3s. 6d.

7. **Rome, Outlines of the History of:** from the Earliest Period to the Christian Era and the Commencement of the Decline of the Empire. By EDWARD LEVIEN, of Balliol College, Oxford. Map, 2s. 6d.; cl. bds. 3s. 6d.

9. **Chronology of History, Art, Literature, and Progress,** from the Creation of the World to the Conclusion of the Franco-German War. The Continuation by W. D. HAMILTON, F.S.A. 3s.; cloth boards, 3s. 6d.

50. **Dates and Events in English History,** for the use of Candidates in Public and Private Examinations. By the Rev. E. RAND. 1s.

ENGLISH LANGUAGE AND MISCELLANEOUS.

11. **Grammar of the English Tongue,** Spoken and Written. With an Introduction to the Study of Comparative Philology. By HYDE CLARKE, D.C.L. Fourth Edition. 1s. 6d.

11*. **Philology:** Handbook of the Comparative Philology of English, Anglo-Saxon, Frisian, Flemish or Dutch, Low or Platt Dutch, High Dutch or German, Danish, Swedish, Icelandic, Latin, Italian, French, Spanish, and Portuguese Tongues. By HYDE CLARKE, D.C.L. 1s.

12. **Dictionary of the English Language,** as Spoken and Written. Containing above 100,000 Words. By HYDE CLARKE, D.C.L. 3s. 6d.; cloth boards, 4s. 6d.; complete with the GRAMMAR, cloth bds., 5s. 6d.

48. **Composition and Punctuation,** familiarly Explained for those who have neglected the Study of Grammar. By JUSTIN BRENAN. 17th Edition. 1s. 6d.

49. **Derivative Spelling-Book:** Giving the Origin of Every Word from the Greek, Latin, Saxon, German, Teutonic, Dutch, French, Spanish, and other Languages; with their present Acceptation and Pronunciation. By J. ROWBOTHAM, F.R.A.S. Improved Edition. 1s. 6d.

51. **The Art of Extempore Speaking:** Hints for the Pulpit, the Senate, and the Bar. By M. BAUTAIN, Vicar-General and Professor at the Sorbonne. Translated from the French. 7th Edition, carefully corrected. 2s.6d.

52. **Mining and Quarrying,** with the Sciences connected therewith. First Book of, for Schools. By J. H. COLLINS, F.G.S., Lecturer to the Miners' Association of Cornwall and Devon. 1s.

53. **Places and Facts in Political and Physical Geography,** for Candidates in Examinations. By the Rev. EDGAR RAND, B.A. 1s.

54. **Analytical Chemistry,** Qualitative and Quantitative, a Course of. To which is prefixed, a Brief Treatise upon Modern Chemical Nomenclature and Notation. By WM. W. PINK and GEORGE E. WEBSTER. 2s.

THE SCHOOL MANAGERS' SERIES OF READING BOOKS,

Adapted to the Requirements of the New Code. Edited by the Rev. A. R. GRANT, Rector of Hitcham, and Honorary Canon of Ely; formerly H.M. Inspector of Schools.

INTRODUCTORY PRIMER, 3d.

	s. d.		s. d.
FIRST STANDARD	0 6	FOURTH STANDARD	1 2
SECOND ,,	0 10	FIFTH ,,	1 6
THIRD ,,	1 0	SIXTH ,,	1 6

LESSONS FROM THE BIBLE. Part I. Old Testament. 1s.
LESSONS FROM THE BIBLE. Part II. New Testament, to which is added THE GEOGRAPHY OF THE BIBLE, for very young Children. By Rev. C. THORNTON FORSTER. 1s. 2d. ** Or the Two Parts in One Volume. 2s.

FRENCH.

24. **French Grammar.** With Complete and Concise Rules on the Genders of French Nouns. By G. L. STRAUSS, Ph.D. 1s. 6d.
25. **French-English Dictionary.** Comprising a large number of New Terms used in Engineering, Mining, &c. By ALFRED ELWES. 1s. 6d.
26. **English French Dictionary.** By ALFRED ELWES. 2s.
25,26. **French Dictionary** (as above). Complete, in One Vol., 3s.; cloth boards, 3s. 6d. *.* Or with the GRAMMAR, cloth boards, 4s. 6d.
47. **French and English Phrase Book :** containing Introductory Lessons, with Translations, several Vocabularies of Words, a Collection of suitable Phrases, and Easy Familiar Dialogues. 1s. 6d.

GERMAN.

39. **German Grammar.** Adapted for English Students, from Heyse's Theoretical and Practical Grammar, by Dr. G. L. STRAUSS. 1s.
40. **German Reader:** A Series of Extracts, carefully culled from the most approved Authors of Germany; with Notes, Philological and Explanatory. By G. L. STRAUSS, Ph.D. 1s.
41-43. **German Triglot Dictionary.** By NICHOLAS ESTERHAZY S. A. HAMILTON. In Three Parts. Part I. German-French-English. Part II. English-German-French. Part III. French-German-English. 3s., or cloth boards, 4s.
41-43 **German Triglot Dictionary** (as above), together with German & 39. Grammar (No. 39), in One Volume, cloth boards, 5s.

ITALIAN.

27. **Italian Grammar,** arranged in Twenty Lessons, with a Course of Exercises. By ALFRED ELWES. 1s. 6d.
28. **Italian Triglot Dictionary,** wherein the Genders of all the Italian and French Nouns are carefully noted down. By ALFRED ELWES. Vol. 1. Italian-English-French. 2s. 6d.
30. **Italian Triglot Dictionary.** By A. ELWES. Vol. 2. English-French-Italian. 2s. 6d.
32. **Italian Triglot Dictionary.** By ALFRED ELWES. Vol. 3. French-Italian-English. 2s. 6d.
28,30, **Italian Triglot Dictionary** (as above). In One Vol., 7s. 6d. 32. Cloth boards.

SPANISH AND PORTUGUESE.

34. **Spanish Grammar,** in a Simple and Practical Form. With a Course of Exercises. By ALFRED ELWES. 1s. 6d.
35. **Spanish-English and English-Spanish Dictionary.** Including a large number of Technical Terms used in Mining, Engineering, &c., with the proper Accents and the Gender of every Noun. By ALFRED ELWES. 4s.; cloth boards, 5s. *.* Or with the GRAMMAR, cloth boards, 6s.
55. **Portuguese Grammar,** in a Simple and Practical Form. With a Course of Exercises. By ALFRED ELWES. 1s. 6d.
56. **Portuguese-English and English-Portuguese Dictionary,** with the Genders of each Noun. By ALFRED ELWES.
[In preparation.

HEBREW.

46*. **Hebrew Grammar.** By Dr. BRESSLAU. 1s. 6d.
44. **Hebrew and English Dictionary,** Biblical and Rabbinical; containing the Hebrew and Chaldee Roots of the Old Testament Post-Rabbinical Writings. By Dr. BRESSLAU. 6s. *.* Or with the GRAMMAR, 7s.
46. **English and Hebrew Dictionary.** By Dr. BRESSLAU. 3s.
44,46. **Hebrew Dictionary** (as above), in Two Vols., complete, with 46*. the GRAMMAR, cloth boards, 12s.

LONDON : CROSBY LOCKWOOD AND CO.,

LATIN.

19. **Latin Grammar.** Containing the Inflections and Elementary Principles of Translation and Construction. By the Rev. THOMAS GOODWIN, M.A., Head Master of the Greenwich Proprietary School. 1s.

20. **Latin-English Dictionary.** By the Rev. THOMAS GOODWIN, M.A. 2s.

22. **English-Latin Dictionary;** together with an Appendix of French and Italian Words which have their origin from the Latin. By the Rev. THOMAS GOODWIN, M.A. 1s. 6d.

20,22. **Latin Dictionary** (as above). Complete in One Vol., 3s. 6d.; cloth boards, 4s. 6d. *.* Or with the GRAMMAR, cloth boards, 5s. 6d.

LATIN CLASSICS. With Explanatory Notes in English.

1. **Latin Delectus.** Containing Extracts from Classical Authors, with Genealogical Vocabularies and Explanatory Notes, by H. YOUNG. 1s. 6d.

2. **Cæsaris Commentarii de Bello Gallico.** Notes, and a Geographical Register for the Use of Schools, by H. YOUNG. 2s.

3. **Cornelius Nepos.** With Notes. By H. YOUNG. 1s.

4. **Virgilii Maronis Bucolica et Georgica.** With Notes on the Bucolics by W. RUSHTON, M.A., and on the Georgics by H. YOUNG. 1s. 6d.

5. **Virgilii Maronis Æneis.** With Notes, Critical and Explanatory, by H. YOUNG. New Edition, revised and improved. With copious Additional Notes by Rev. T. H. L. LEARY, D.C.L., formerly Scholar of Brasenose College, Oxford. 3s.

5*. ——— Part 1. Books i.—vi., 1s. 6 l.
5** ——— Part 2. Books vii.—xii., 2s.

6. **Horace;** Odes, Epode, and Carmen Sæculare. Notes by H. YOUNG. 1s. 6d.

7. **Horace;** Satires, Epistles, and Ars Poetica. Notes by W. BROWNRIGG SMITH, M.A., F.R.G.S. 1s. 6d.

8. **Sallustii Crispi Catalina et Bellum Jugurthinum.** Notes, Critical and Explanatory, by W. M. DONNE, B.A., Trin. Coll., Cam. 1s. 6d.

9. **Terentii Andria et Heautontimorumenos.** With Notes, Critical and Explanatory, by the Rev. JAMES DAVIES, M.A. 1s. 6d.

10. **Terentii Adelphi, Hecyra, Phormio.** Edited, with Notes, Critical and Explanatory, by the Rev. JAMES DAVIES, M.A. 2s.

11. **Terentii Eunuchus, Comœdia.** Notes, by Rev. J. DAVIES, M.A. 1s. 6d.

12. **Ciceronis Oratio pro Sexto Roscio Amerino.** Edited, with an Introduction, Analysis, and Notes, Explanatory and Critical, by the Rev. JAMES DAVIES, M.A. 1s.

13. **Ciceronis Orationes in Catilinam, Verrem, et pro Archia.** With Introduction, Analysis, and Notes, Explanatory and Critical, by Rev. T. H. L. LEARY, D.C.L. formerly Scholar of Brasenose College, Oxford. 1s. 6d.

14. **Ciceronis Cato Major, Lælius, Brutus, sive de Senectute, de Amicitia, de Claris Oratoribus Dialogi.** With Notes by W. BROWNRIGG SMITH, M.A., F.R.G.S. 2s.

16. **Livy; History of Rome.** Notes by H. YOUNG and W. B. SMITH, M.A. Part 1. Books i., ii., 1s. 6d.

16*. ——— Part 2. Books iii., iv., v., 1s. 6d.
17. ——— Part 3. Books xxi., xxii., 1s. 6d.

19. **Latin Verse Selections,** from Catullus, Tibullus, Propertius, and Ovid. Notes by W. B. DONNE, M.A., Trinity College, Cambridge. 2s.

20. **Latin Prose Selections,** from Varro, Columella, Vitruvius, Seneca, Quintilian, Florus, Velleius Paterculus, Valerius Maximus Suetonius, Apuleius, &c. Notes by W. B. DONNE, M.A. 2s.

21. **Juvenalis Satiræ.** With Prolegomena and Notes by T. H. S. ESCOTT, B.A., Lecturer on Logic at King's College, London. 2s.

GREEK.

14. **Greek Grammar,** in accordance with the Principles and Philological Researches of the most eminent Scholars of our own day. By HANS CLAUDE HAMILTON. 1s. 6d.

15,17. **Greek Lexicon.** Containing all the Words in General Use, with their Significations, Inflections, and Doubtful Quantities. By HENRY R. HAMILTON. Vol. 1. Greek-English, 2s. 6d.; Vol. 2. English-Greek, 2s. Or the Two Vols. in One, 4s. 6d.: cloth boards, 5s.

14,15. **Greek Lexicon** (as above). Complete, with the GRAMMAR, in 17. One Vol., cloth boards, 6s.

GREEK CLASSICS. With Explanatory Notes in English.

1. **Greek Delectus.** Containing Extracts from Classical Authors, with Genealogical Vocabularies and Explanatory Notes, by H. YOUNG. New Edition, with an improved and enlarged Supplementary Vocabulary, by JOHN HUTCHISON, M.A., of the High School, Glasgow. 1s. 6d.

2, 3. **Xenophon's Anabasis;** or, The Retreat of the Ten Thousand. Notes and a Geographical Register, by H. YOUNG. Part 1. Books i. to iii., 1s. Part 2. Books iv. to vii., 1s.

4. **Lucian's Select Dialogues.** The Text carefully revised, with Grammatical and Explanatory Notes, by H. YOUNG. 1s. 6d.

5-12. **Homer, The Works of.** According to the Text of BAEUMLEIN. With Notes, Critical and Explanatory, drawn from the best and latest Authorities, with Preliminary Observations and Appendices, by T. H. L. LEARY, M.A., D.C.L.

THE ILIAD:	Part 1. Books i. to vi., 1s. 6d.	Part 3. Books xiii. to xviii., 1s. 6d.
	Part 2. Books vii. to xii., 1s. 6d.	Part 4. Books xix. to xxiv., 1s. 6d.
THE ODYSSEY:	Part 1. Books i. to vi., 1s. 6d	Part 3. Books xiii. to xviii., 1s. 6d.
	Part 2. Books vii. to xii., 1s. 6d.	Part 4. Books xix. to xxiv., and Hymns, 2s.

13. **Plato's Dialogues:** The Apology of Socrates, the Crito, and the Phædo. From the Text of C. F. HERMANN. Edited with Notes, Critical and Explanatory, by the Rev. JAMES DAVIES, M.A. 2s.

14-17. **Herodotus, The History of,** chiefly after the Text of GAISFORD. With Preliminary Observations and Appendices, and Notes, Critical and Explanatory, by T. H. L. LEARY, M.A., D.C.L.
    Part 1. Books i., ii. (The Clio and Euterpe), 2s.
    Part 2. Books iii., iv. (The Thalia and Melpomene), 2s.
    Part 3. Books v.-vii. (The Terpsichore, Erato, and Polymnia), 2s.
    Part 4. Books viii., ix. (The Urania and Calliope) and Index, 1s. 6d.

18. **Sophocles:** Œdipus Tyrannus. Notes by H. YOUNG. 1s.

20. **Sophocles:** Antigone. From the Text of DINDORF. Notes, Critical and Explanatory, by the Rev. JOHN MILNER, B.A. 2s.

23. **Euripides:** Hecuba and Medea. Chiefly from the Text of DINDORF. With Notes, Critical and Explanatory, by W. BROWNRIGG SMITH, M.A., F.R.G.S. 1s. 6d.

26. **Euripides:** Alcestis. Chiefly from the Text of DINDORF. With Notes, Critical and Explanatory, by JOHN MILNER, B.A. 1s. 6d.

30. **Æschylus:** Prometheus Vinctus: The Prometheus Bound. From the Text of DINDORF. Edited, with English Notes, Critical and Explanatory, by the Rev. JAMES DAVIES, M.A. 1s.

32. **Æschylus:** Septem Contra Thebes: The Seven against Thebes. From the Text of DINDORF. Edited, with English Notes, Critical and Explanatory, by the Rev. JAMES DAVIES, M.A. 1s.

40. **Aristophanes:** Acharnians. Chiefly from the Text of C. H. WEISE. With Notes, by C. S. T. TOWNSHEND, M.A. 1s. 6d.

41. **Thucydides:** History of the Peloponnesian War. Notes by H. YOUNG. Book 1. 1s.

42. **Xenophon's Panegyric on Agesilaus.** Notes and Introduction by Lt. F. W. JEWITT. 1s. 6d.

43. **Demosthenes.** The Oration on the Crown and the Philippics. With English Notes. By Rev. T. H. L. LEARY, D.C.L., formerly Scholar of Brasenose College, Oxford. 1s. 6d.

CROSBY LOCKWOOD AND CO., 7, STATIONERS' HALL COURT, E.C.

Trieste

Trieste Publishing has a massive catalogue of classic book titles. Our aim is to provide readers with the highest quality reproductions of fiction and non-fiction literature that has stood the test of time. The many thousands of books in our collection have been sourced from libraries and private collections around the world.

The titles that Trieste Publishing has chosen to be part of the collection have been scanned to simulate the original. Our readers see the books the same way that their first readers did decades or a hundred or more years ago. Books from that period are often spoiled by imperfections that did not exist in the original. Imperfections could be in the form of blurred text, photographs, or missing pages. It is highly unlikely that this would occur with one of our books. Our extensive quality control ensures that the readers of Trieste Publishing's books will be delighted with their purchase. Our staff has thoroughly reviewed every page of all the books in the collection, repairing, or if necessary, rejecting titles that are not of the highest quality. This process ensures that the reader of one of Trieste Publishing's titles receives a volume that faithfully reproduces the original, and to the maximum degree possible, gives them the experience of owning the original work.

We pride ourselves on not only creating a pathway to an extensive reservoir of books of the finest quality, but also providing value to every one of our readers. Generally, Trieste books are purchased singly - on demand, however they may also be purchased in bulk. Readers interested in bulk purchases are invited to contact us directly to enquire about our tailored bulk rates. Email: customerservice@triestepublishing.com

You May Also Like

Mounting and Framing Pictures

Paul N. Hasluck

ISBN: 9780649030040
Paperback: 172 pages
Dimensions: 6.14 x 0.37 x 9.21 inches
Language: eng

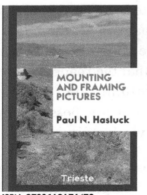

Mounting and Framing Pictures

Paul N. Hasluck

ISBN: 9780649474172
Paperback: 174 pages
Dimensions: 6.14 x 0.37 x 9.21 inches
Language: eng

You May Also Like

Smiths' Work

Paul N. Hasluck

ISBN: 9780649468423
Paperback: 172 pages
Dimensions: 6.14 x 0.37 x 9.21 inches
Language: eng

Rustic Carpentry; With Numerous Engravings and Diagrams

Paul N. Hasluck

ISBN: 9780649458714
Paperback: 170 pages
Dimensions: 6.14 x 0.36 x 9.21 inches
Language: eng

www.triestepublishing.com

You May Also Like

ISBN: 9780649333158
Paperback: 84 pages
Dimensions: 6.14 x 0.17 x 9.21 inches
Language: eng

Report of the Department of Farms and Markets, pp. 5-71

Various

ISBN: 9780649324132
Paperback: 78 pages
Dimensions: 6.14 x 0.16 x 9.21 inches
Language: eng

Catalogue of the Episcopal Theological School in Cambridge Massachusetts, 1891-1892

Various

You May Also Like

Three Hundred Tested Recipes

Various

ISBN: 9780649352142
Paperback: 88 pages
Dimensions: 6.14 x 0.18 x 9.21 inches
Language: eng

A Basket of Fragments

Anonymous

ISBN: 9780649419418
Paperback: 108 pages
Dimensions: 6.14 x 0.22 x 9.21 inches
Language: eng

Find more of our titles on our website. We have a selection of thousands of titles that will interest you. Please visit

www.triestepublishing.com

Lightning Source UK Ltd.
Milton Keynes UK
UKHW02f1044300118
317064UK00006B/495/P